MW01518066

# A STONE FOR THE FOX

## KINMOND SMITH

This Encore Press edition © 2023

This is a work of fiction. Other than the occasional use of actual names and places, the incidents and other characters portrayed in this book are wholly fictional.

All rights reserved. No part of this publication may be reproduced, distributed, or transmitted in any form or by any means, including photocopying, recording, or other electronic or mechanical methods, without the prior written permission of the author, except in the case of brief quotations embodied in critical reviews and certain other non-commercial uses permitted by copyright law. For permission requests, write to the publisher, addressed "Attention: Permissions Coordinator," at the address below. Contact also available via website.

Copyright © 2023 Kinmond Smith

Encore Press Inc,
278 St. Clarens Ave.
Toronto, ON
M6H 3W3
Canada
www.encore-press.com

Ordering Information:
Quantity sales. Special discounts are available on quantity purchases by corporations, associations, and others. For details, contact the publisher at the address above.

Published in Canada

ISBN: 978-1-989728-17-8
Electronic edition ISBN: 978-1-989728-09-3

This book is dedicated to Tanya Kirouac.
This book would not have been written were it not for her love and support.
And because we've always believed in each other -
even after we stopped being us...


And my deepest thanks to my dear friend and editor Wendy Morley.
This book would not have been published if she hadn't re-appeared from the
mists of our youth, to reconnect as old friends once again.

# A STONE FOR THE FOX

KINMOND SMITH

# Prologue

*A*widening shaft of light broke the gloom as the elevator doors shuddered open on their greased tracks. The man stepped off and began walking through the underground garage, up the gradual slope of the ramp. He passed row after row of vehicles, many covered by fitted tarpaulins with tires peeking out from beneath like heavy-lidded black eyes, most sporting an even film of dust. It was an older person's building and their cars didn't get out much. His footfalls echoed around him. Pressing the button on the remote once to de-arm, he heard the driver's door unlock itself with a clunk. The pillar beside the car was grimy with trapped exhaust residue so the man was careful to edge around it. He cranked the engine over, giving it a minute to warm up, and punched the button to turn the radio on, but there was no reception deep in the garage. He glanced over his shoulder at the legal boxes sitting on the back seat and resisted the temptation to flip through them while he waited. When the engine settled into a lower rhythm, he dropped it into drive and headed for the exit.

Corner after corner the wheels provided their low rhythmic drumming on the seamed concrete until he found the exit. The front of the car tripped the reflected beam and the aluminum garage doors lumbered up, the sections of the door squealing in unified protest. The headlights hit the steep ramp and picked up the herringbone pattern in the concrete that helped to drain the winter melt. When he had enough clearance under the door he edged forward, careful not to scrape the low front spoiler on the steep ramp. As the car reached the top of the ramp, his headlights swept across the tailgate of a pickup parked in the nightshade of a huge weeping willow. He signaled and turned left down the apartment building's driveway. When he reached the street he signaled again and looked for any traffic. At three in the morning, there was none, even on Yonge Street. As *soon as he turned, the pickup truck started its engine, swung out of the parking space, drove out and fell in behind.*

*The two vehicles crested the hill at the old city limits and continued south. The man in the car shook his head a little sadly. The area had changed so much in the last two decades. The old movie theatre, Hall's Dairy Bar, St. Germain convenience store, Teddy's Texaco; they had all been replaced by upscale women's clothing stores, expensive florists and more-expensive restaurants. It wasn't so much a neighbourhood anymore but rather a complete retail experience.*

*The rear view mirror telescoped headlight beams across the car's interior as the pickup truck, complete with a fog light array above the cab, blasted by him in the right-hand lane. The truck hammered through the amber light at Lawrence and roared on as the man slowed the car and stopped at the intersection.*

*When the light changed, he continued down Yonge, past the library where he'd worked as a teenager shelving returned books three nights a week. The apartments on his right loomed over the grassy depressions on the other side of the street that led to the larger park system.*

*As he reached the next intersection he saw another vehicle coming from the south cresting the steep hill above Muir Park, its headlights picking up the glint of the still wet pavement. No, he thought, it must be a truck, the headlights were set up too far apart to be … suddenly the front of the approaching vehicle lit up like the sun, the light filling his vision and creating painful, repeating spots even behind his eyelids. The truck swerved into his lane when it was halfway down the hill. He could hear the roar of the truck's exhaust as it accelerated toward him. He looked quickly at the right lane, trying to clear the spots from his eyes and saw parked cars. No chance there. The truck began to veer madly across the width of the roadway. He wrenched the wheel to the left, into the northbound lanes, trying to find a way past the blinding lights. And as the truck flashed past, he felt the bush bar on the front of the truck make contact with the back of his car.*

*The car spun completely around as it slid across the two northbound lanes and slammed into the curb sideways. The front driver's-side tire exploded and the car dove its nose into the pavement. The rear of the car, its momentum intact, lifted off the ground and bounced over the edge of the curb. The centrifugal force of the spin pressed him into his seat, his hands locked on the steering wheel in terror. The rear end smashed into the low stone wall and planters at the inside edge of the sidewalk, wiping out the* old stacked stones and shearing off the rear axle. The back window of the car imploded, showering the interior, and he felt the back of his neck peppered by the safety glass as it rushed past him and collected on the dashboard like a crystalline snowdrift. The momentum almost spent, the car did a nose-stand before it finally tipped over the stone wall and bounced once before dropping sideways onto the iron fence of the rose garden thirty feet below. The thinner, decorative ironwork collapsed under the car's weight while the sturdier iron pilings of the fence punctured the doors and fenders and held the car on its side like some horrid showroom exhibition of the undercarriage. The piling that came through the driver's door caught him just under the rib cage. It punched through his side, shattered three ribs and then decimated his left lung and a kidney before exiting the small of his back. With a minor-key tinkling of glass and a bass note of rending metal, everything became silent and still.

He dangled sideways in his seat belt and coughed up a fine spray of blood, which floated momentarily in front of his eyes like dust motes in a sunny room before falling away out of the smashed window beside him. Waves of unreality washed over him… stream of consciousness… howcouldthishappen… wasthiswhatwascoming… dontbelonghere. Systems that were supposed to keep him alive began to shut down. He closed his eyes and gritted his teeth as a geyser of pain erupted within him. He wept, not so much at the pain, which was beyond infinite and therefore incomprehensible, but rather at the monumental unfairness of it. He sobbed suddenly and knew immediately that he shouldn't have because something inside him tore, sending waves of cyclic pain through his battered body.

When the crisis was over he tried to stop crying. He'd always thought that when he died, someday, it would go easy. Be old. Have lived. Not now for chrissake! He looked through the spider-web of the windshield and saw the rose bushes caught in the glare of the remaining headlight. He wanted to smile; he could feel his mind fighting between his view and his agony. His breath hitched at the sadness of it and he passed out from the exquisite pain that moving his chest had suddenly engendered.

When he awoke again, he became aware of the acrid smell of gasoline burning his nostrils. Without thinking, he craned his neck looking for the leak and anything might spark it. The sudden movement flooded his senses with pain and he sobbed once more as the darkness swallowed him just before the bullet hit the gas tank and the car exploded.

Sitting in the idling truck on the winding street above the park, the driver watched *as the trees surrounding the wreck became spattered with orange firelight like paint from a careless brush. He lowered the AWC G2 sniper rifle, pulling the scope off from above the breach and disassembling the stock and barrel. It was perfect for using while sitting in a vehicle due to its compact length. And its MOA accuracy made it ideal for medium distances. The driver cherished it, as fewer than 100 G2's had been manufactured. And even if the car fire yielded what was left of the NATO round, the rarity of the weapon would not allow any bullet rifling to be matched. He took exceptional care of the weapon and it had served him well tonight, as always. When the component parts were back in their case, the driver put the truck in gear as the faraway sirens began to sound closer.*

# Chapter 1

Time may be linear but our memories of time are not. Fragments become jumbled and moments become distilled and spun together, making a patchwork of intersecting moments that occurred decades apart. I was being drawn back to a place and a past. A place and a past I had left, in fact, to try and escape.

Whenever I look back on my childhood, it is always hazy and unfocused. Occasionally I have abrupt remembrances like a light momentarily cutting through mist. Suddenly recalling a phrase somebody said, or the rough outlines of a singular moment. I'm sure the memories are real. But we live in a world now where almost nothing seems like ours anymore. When I think of easy, casual memories like throwing a football back and forth in front of the house on Sundays with my father, I sometimes wonder if it really happened or was something I saw on a television after-school special.

I have always envied those who can remember their childhood with clarity, who are full of colourful anecdotes of their early years, who retain a knowledge of who and what they were. I remember very little of the boy I used to be; only very brief snatches in time. And when I recall a photograph of myself when I was small, I feel strangely detached, as if I had sprung upon this world full in the bloom of my years. I sometimes felt like I had slept for almost four decades and found myself suddenly thrust into a life I neither owned nor asked for.

There are only a few strong childhood memories that have stayed and left any kind of lasting impression and almost all were tied to Chris in some way. Now that he was dead, I felt as if I had been robbed of the one touchstone to my childhood that I could always count on to take me back.

Heading northeast from Monroe took me up to the always-depressing Detroit/
Windsor corridor and closer to home. When it comes to crossing the 49$^{th}$, the
border posts are poorly organized, sullenly staffed and uniformly ugly. From the
bridge at Alexandria Bay, which nicely mars the surrounding islands; to the
congested tourism of Niagara Falls; to the grotesque industry around the Ambassa-
dor Bridge at Windsor; disasters all. I reached inside my leather jacket and shut off
the music. I pulled up and stopped at the booth and pushed my visor up.

The woman inside the Customs booth looked tired and annoyed.

"Citizenship?" she asked.

"Canadian," and I handed over my passport since gone are the days when a
birth certificate or driver's license would do the trick. And my ten-year passport
was about to expire.

"How long have you been in the United States?"

"Nine-and-a-half years."

She regarded me further askance. "Do you have anything to declare?" I shook
my head again.

"Are you carrying any firearms or explosives?" She surveyed all the possible
hiding places on the bike.

I couldn't help but smirk. "No, nothing to declare. No firearms or explosives," I
said, handing over the bike's Florida registration from the bag strapped to the top
of the gas tank.

I fished into the tank bag again bringing out the confirmation from the rental
agency and handed it to her. She glanced at it and said, "Thank you, Mr. Birnam.
Have a nice stay," and gave me back the paper.

After I cleared the customs area, I started looking for the signs to pick up the
Trans Canada, which would take me up through the southwest end of the province and back home. Reaching inside my leather jacket, with one hand on the
throttle, I fiddled with the volume until I could hear over the wind rush and roar
of exhaust pipes. I had wanted to finish the trip by looping back across upstate
New York and the New Hampshire and Maine wilderness, figuring I could pick
up something to do for the winter in New England ski country. But the call had
changed everything and now I was heading back to the city as fast as I could.

Ten years is a long time to spend on the road but having a motorcycle made it bearable. The freedom and exhilaration are always there on a bike, though in shorter supply when the weather didn't cooperate. The closest I had come to the same feeling was on the boat back in Florida. I'm not one of those danger junkies who hurl themselves off bridges with bungee cords tied to their ankles. But there is something almost primordial about knowing that every decision you make is important, like every course correction at sea.

When you're in a car it's just not the same. Being squeezed into some lead rocket and rushing to wherever you were trying to get to is fun in the same way my recent dinner was food. In a car there is no sense of being a part of your surroundings, of being in and of the moment. Every car I passed contained grim, white-knuckled creatures hunched over the wheel; their tension only increased by screaming moppets in the back seat and a harried partner beside them. And every time I moved beyond one, the moppets would point and laugh and wave, fascinated by the bright maroon bike whizzing past. The poor soul behind the wheel would watch with a baleful hatred of the ease, or perhaps a wistful longing for the freedom.

As I crossed the Windsor city limits, the pinpoint red light on the instrument panel from the radar detector mounted under the cowling started flashing, so I jammed it down a gear and took my speed down to a hundred and ten. A black Mazda rocketed by me in the passing lane and twenty seconds later, a cruiser pulled out from behind a bridge abutment and took off in pursuit.

After passing the cop and his latest customer at the side of the road, I wound the bike back up and settled in. I roared on past the re-purposed tobacco fields of Tillsonburg and the multitude of highway-side industry flashing past, occasionally broken by the open pastureland of dairy farms. After a couple of hours I could feel the city, and my old life, getting closer. My shoulders bunched at the thought. The farmland diminished, the traffic increased and the night sky began to brighten with reflected light. As I wound off the highway the lights of the downtown core appeared, casting their malevolent silhouettes against the dark, like hulking carrion eaters. I truly was home again, and still not ready to face what was coming.

The last thing I wanted to do right then was deal with either my family or Chris' so I headed into Parkdale and soon I was sitting in a local café nursing a beer. The neighbourhood was still in the throes of the reclamation pains it had been feeling since I had left.

At the turn of the previous century, Parkdale had been a lovely and monied part of the city. It boasted a magnificent, elevated view of the lake, with the Romanesque Sunnyside Bathing Pavilion and the Palais Royale below. The area was settled in the late eighteen-hundreds and expansive Victorian homes had sprung up. But in the nineteen-sixties and early seventies the disenfranchised had taken over the area. Now the gracious homes that lined the north side of King Street were flophouses and low-income apartments. A few blocks north, Queen Street became nothing but dollar stores, taverns, cheap textile outlets and lazy greengrocers who spilled their wares onto the sidewalk like recalcitrant children leaving their toys littered on the driveway.

Then, in the early eighties, yuppies rediscovered the area and began buying up the now relatively inexpensive century homes. And as they restored the grand old houses, a very quiet war broke out. The new immigrant families who lived in the high-rise apartment buildings that ran north from the lake were now cheek to jowl with waspy couples who stayed locked up in their restored masterpieces, only venturing out into the neighbourhood to scour the second-hand shops for antique bric-a-brac or to meet friends at the newest bistro. You couldn't blame either side. But it left Parkdale with a cultural and social disparity. Whenever I had gone there, I could feel a palpable weariness from everybody on the street, one group trying their best to create something out of not enough and the other upset that the local store would not stock their preferred health drink. Decades later the disparity hadn't gotten any better.

Roncesvalles Avenue ran north to form the central conduit for Little Poland, lined with butchers, grocers, credit unions and cafés. In university, I had found the dark little place I was looking for near the top of the street. I had grown to love it in university because on the first Monday of every month, a bunch of fledgling writers would gather to try out new stories and ideas on each other. Now it was a hipster joint with dozens of craft brews and everyone had a beard. Except Keiko, who still owned the place. The glasses in the drying rack behind the bar were clinking together from the vibrations of the fridge's compressor. I hadn't minded the noise in the past, but I was still chilled from the ride and tonight it was rattling my teeth.

The small café tables at the front looked out on the street through windows covered in condensation. Beyond that was the bar, which gave way to ten or twelve booths upholstered in worn wine-red vinyl that stretched to the back on either side of the room. An old, tired carpet runner with an indistinguishable pattern ran down the centre and the booths were dimly lit by hanging lampshade-covered bulbs. To my knowledge the place was always dim because I had never been there when it wasn't. Keiko moved over to me when I drained the pilsener glass and put it down on the moisture-blistered coaster.

"You want 'nother drink? Something eat?" Her lined face was impassive, as if set in stone. God knew I wanted one, but I was trying to be a little more reasonable in my drinking practices.

"No, thank you Keiko," I said smiling.

She looked at me a moment, a growing look of recognition on her face.

"I know you," she muttered, shaking her head. "You been here before? Yes ... not for years now. I remember you," and she shook an admonishing finger at me for being so long away.

She left and then returned with a small plate of salami, Gouda cheese and crackers, and tried once more to ply me with alcohol. I wasn't sure if the unsolicited food was because she remembered me, or whether she took pity on all such haggard-looking individuals who happened across her doorstep. I smiled and shook my head. She had an unlit cigarette stuck to her lower lip. I had never figured out exactly how she did that, but it was a skill I admired nonetheless.

My gaze followed her as she wove her way through the tables, shuffling her feet on the dirty carpet runner. The darkened booths contained couples very intent on each other. I wondered what the chances were they had met only minutes earlier by swiping a certain way. Or maybe I was just being disconsolate. Or maybe I was just lonely.

There is a curious malaise that seems to have infected so many of us. It strikes me that the burgeoning of the self-interested has taken us to the point where we are all just appraisers. That we regard each other as little more than interestingly packaged meat. In the course of trying to find what we ascribe to true love, we tear off little strips from one another under the guise of need and sharing. And we seem to be blind to the fact that as we work away at others, we ourselves are being shorn away. Like speculators we move in, make use of what we want at that moment; and after the pretty varnish is yellowed and cracked, after the gloss is gone from the coat, whatever is left over is discarded. Love, need, caring, and sharing. It feels like somewhere along the way, we lost something. There are a lot of lessons we have to re-learn. And one of them is that finesse is no substitute for feeling.

I didn't want to be there anymore. I didn't want to be home anymore, if indeed I was home. My mind was suddenly churning with anger and frustration and the prospect of heading to the unknown apartment where I would be staying was not an appealing one. I dropped a US twenty down on the bar, collected my helmet and my keys, and moved out into the warm, late summer night.

I had left the rain behind in Detroit, but I knew it would follow me here. Making my way down towards the lake I popped my visor up at the corner. A heavy gust of warm wind came fluting around, threatening to knock me over and I had a look out at the lake. Sure enough there were thunderheads rolling in from the American side obscuring the few stars that could be seen beyond the incandescent glow of the city. I hung a right and, because there wasn't much traffic out, I wound the bike up into the power band and kept it there, listening to the high-rpm whine of the engine. Downshifting and counter-balancing my weight, I swung the bike in a low left turn. I crossed Lakeshore Boulevard, turning left again and pulled the bike up next to the Bathing Pavilion at the beach as another gust of wind hit, whipping circles of dust and refuse off the semi-circular stairs in front of the grand structure. There was a white stretch limousine parked against the curb with its four-ways on. In the twenties and thirties, the Pavilion had been a popular place to come; just down the beach, couples could dance to small orchestras at the Palais Royale. But as time passed, progress had rolled forward, the lake had become less swimmable, the Palais had lost its pier, and both structures had fallen into disuse and finally disrepair. The Palais had eventually been taken over by a Polish social committee, and the Pavilion, though refurbished by the city, was merely used to serve as shower and change facility for the ugly swimming pool some municipal politician had tacked onto its side.

Twenty-foot-high wrought iron gates prevented pedestrian traffic from accessing the upper level but tonight the lock was off the gates and on the upper level I found a wedding party in elegant dress, talking nervously and excitedly about the approaching storm. As I reached the top of the stairs they glanced over at me, but since I wasn't dressed in my rented best, they dismissed me. I moved beyond them and found an open portico to myself. Inside the breakwater the water was flat calm, but a mile offshore, white caps were breaking. An impending-rain smell suffused the air and made it feel heavy. The first flash of lightning came and I unconsciously fell into the pattern of childhood, one thousand, two thousand, three thousand, four- ... a rumble of thunder. As we all watched, the white caps rolled over the breakwater and the rain pockmarked its way up the beach and broke over our heads. The group down from me jumped away from their portico, yelling and laughing and holding wet tuxedo shirts and chiffon blouses away from their skin. I was wearing my rain gear, so I didn't much care that I was suddenly drenched. The wind came with the rain and howled through the cavernous interior.

There was a blinding flash, which reflected off the white walls of the Pavilion, and then a huge crash of thunder reverberated through the empty hall. The group at the end decided they had had enough and after more laughter, began to run down the stairs to their limo. I was left alone with the storm as it raged over my head. The thunder was cacophonous, echoing and amplifying in the long hallway. I remembered reading once that the average storm cell lasts for only eleven minutes. We only have the appearance of long storms because as one cell dwindles, another rises to take its place. After forty minutes of revolving storm cells, the ferocity of the storm slipping from hissing diminuendo to pounding crescendo and back again, the rain eventually dissipated as the storm moved slowly northeast through the city.

I stayed and watched the restless lake slowly calm itself, feeling very old. Even though I had grown up in this city, it didn't feel like mine anymore. Too big, too detached, too cold. I turned and trudged down the hall towards the stairs, my jacket and pants leaving a line of drip marks leading back to the rain-soaked portico like crumbs in uncertain woods.

Riding north into High Park, moving up Lord Colbourne Drive, which wound through the center of the forest, I tried to avoid the traffic that would be building on the major thoroughfares. The traction wasn't that bad, but I knew the other drivers would move along at a snail's pace as if they were on an oil slick. I'd never figured out exactly why the residents of this city, despite the fact they drove in every conceivable kind of weather in any given year, never actually learned how to drive.

After forty minutes of dodging, I managed to get back uptown to where I was staying. The rental service had followed my instructions to find something central and cheap. This building fronted on Yonge with a franchise pizza place at street level and the apartments above. I parked in the back and locked the steering column. After unbolting my saddlebags, I climbed the three flights of wrought-iron fire escape stairs. When I got to the third floor, I found the back door locked and the key I had been sent didn't turn the bolt; it must have only worked the front door. I didn't feel like going all the way back down and around to the front. Beside the metal door was a paned window that somebody had left open a crack. I got my fingers in as far as I could, then tugged at the edge, the over-painted hinges resisting. When it was open enough, I slipped my helmet over my arm, lifted my saddlebags in ahead of me, and boosted myself through the window and dropped down into the hallway.

I walked down the hall towards the apartment while the old wooden floor creaked and groaned beneath me. The doors to the other apartments were worn and the dark brown paint had chipped from most of them. Each one had a brand-new deadbolt lock set above the door handles, a bailing can for a boat already underwater. At the top of each door was a pane of frosted glass about four feet square. The harsh light of TV screens worked its way out of some of the stippled panes, but that was the only sign of life in the corridor. Otherwise, the place appeared deserted. At the door to number 11, I fumbled in my breast pocket for the key again. The sparks from the streetcars down below played light splashes up against the side of the building in a futile attempt to compete with the passing lightning.

I opened the door, shook the beaded water off my jacket and pants and walked into the small living room. It might have been nice once, but too many tenants and not enough caring had left it disheveled. The off-white plaster walls were spider-webbed by cracks that ran from floor to ceiling, like an aged crone whose foundation makeup had finally given up. An oak plate rail, which ran around the living and dining rooms, had entire sections broken off. The old urethane was peeling from the pieces still attached. Heavily scratched hardwood floors had buckled from water damage and showed patched areas with boards of varying widths and colours. In the kitchen I found the basic utensils and an old set of pots and pans with dulled black, Bakelite handles. The cupboard had salt and pepper shakers, a container with sugar, another with instant coffee and a box of teabags.

The fridge was clean and empty. I closed the cupboards and went back to the living room.

I pulled off the wet gear and the leather underneath and dropped onto the couch. An old television sat on a cart with wheels against the wall, a ring bolt through the back and a chain locking it to another ring bolt set in the floor. Charming. When I snapped the television on, the original Catch-22 was playing. It was the scene in the hospital where Alan Arkin is lying in his cot after talking to Anthony Perkins' well-meaning chaplain about why he's desperate to leave the army. Two improbably built nurses come in talking about something or other and giggling. They stand over some poor sod in a body cast, take the full catheter bottle and the empty IV. bottle, switch them, and then exit still giggling. When Alan Arkin screamed into the camera, I mouthed it along with him.

# Chapter 2

I stumbled out of sleep with the sheet plastered to my chest and my back plastered to the mattress of the pull-out couch. Inky tendrils of a bad dream fell away from memory as dirty sunlight filtered through the lead-paned windows. My joints felt as if they were full of sand, and there was an unlovely taste in my mouth. I reached over the coffee table to where my cigarettes had fallen on the floor. My phone told me it was 7 a.m. Pushing back the sheet, I got up and wandered into the kitchen and pulled a pot out of the cupboard. I turned the cold water tap and filled it and put it under heat on the stove and then wandered to the back of the kitchen onto the sun porch at the back of the apartment. I snapped a cigarette lit by striking a match against the doorjamb and leaned a forearm on one of the windows that overlooked the back parking area. I could see the bike below, the gas tank and seat still misted by evening rain and morning dew.

After the water boiled I made a three-bag brew in another pot and once it had steeped, poured myself a cup and took it back to the sun porch. The wooden floor creaked underfoot and, given the gaps between the window frames and the jambs that held them in place, I was grateful that I had rented the place in summer. Once my second cup of tea and third cigarette were behind me, I felt I could face the day. I had promised myself to visit Chris' family as soon as I got back. I went and grabbed the phone and dialed the number from memory. But his mother didn't answer; Nick his older brother did and told me the news.

She had evidently been troubled for years with forgetfulness, which was now turning towards dementia. The strain of her youngest's death had taken its toll. I asked where she was and he said they had moved her to a purpose-built place downtown. Indecision tugged at me like a sore tooth and I knew I'd have to make the effort but the whole idea of going to the hospital felt like an atonement, which, I suppose, it was.

Once I had showered and dressed, I went down to the corner to get some flowers from a street vendor. The rain-soaked pavement was steaming with the warmth of the new day. We wrangled over the price, and finally I haggled him down to seven bucks for some carnations and roses. While he wrapped them, I watched the men and women around me scurry into their tall steel, glass, and stressed-concrete towers. The outside facade of the facility in which Mrs. Allinson now spent her time was cold and characterless with broad concrete steps leading from the sidewalk to sliding doors. The reception area was filled with people bustling about, pushing cleaning trolleys, reading medical charts, much to-ing and fro-ing. The desk told me where I could find Chris' mother. My riding boots rang loudly off the tile floor as I wandered in the direction I had been given. Broadly painted stripes ran along the corridor walls, colour-coded for the different sections of the wing. I followed the appropriate stripe until I came to the area I had been directed to. The carpet changed colour to a deep rose and there was a heavily padded railing at waist level that ran along every wall. As I read the names posted beside each door I passed an elderly woman in the hallway staring intently and cooing at a fire alarm lever on the wall. Mrs. Allinson's room was empty, except for the institutional furniture and the overwhelming smell of antiseptic. When I turned around, the fire alarm lady was staring at me and I realized who it was.

"This is my room!" she declared.

"Mrs. Allinson? It's me, Jonathan. Jonathan Birnam."

"Jonathan?" She looked querulously at me. Then she dropped her gaze and for a full minute stared at the helmet in my hand until she realized what it was. When she looked back at me it was more the woman I remembered from my youth.

"How are you, Jonathan?" She smiled up at me and squeezed my free hand in hers. "Well! Aren't you all grown up!" she reached up and patted my chest with a bony hand. "Take me for a walk!" she commanded. And with that she wheeled around and set off down the corridor expecting me to follow.

When I caught up with her, she smiled up at me and said, "Before anything else, we must go to the principal's office."

I couldn't dredge up the name from memory.

"Um, why don't we go to his office later?" I was firmly in non-sequitur land, but I thought it best to try and keep up.

"Oh! Why would we want to go to his office?" she said, surprised.

Down the hall, a shrunken old man was making his way towards us. His tousled hair stood nearly straight up and he was badly overdue for a shave. He fixed us with a stare as we drew level until he nodded to himself and moved on past, as if he was looking into our heads rather than at them.

"See that man?" she whispered. "He thinks he owns this hotel. He walks around here like the ghost of Banquo."

We sat down in a sitting area at the end of the corridor and while I waited for more signs of cognition, she stared out the window at the slowly drying streets and the pedestrians carrying their raincoats.

I remembered how vibrant and alive she had been as my high school English teacher two years running. And after class I would be over at their house nearly every afternoon. Her parents were first-generation Italian immigrants and she had always made these traditional anise-flavoured cookies in a waffle iron. Maybe her own family didn't like them, or maybe they had just tired of them but she had been overjoyed to learn how much I liked them. As I got older and stopped going over after school because of team practices or other commitments, I always imagined that some closet was slowly filling up with waffle cookies because I was no longer coming around. Mrs. Allinson had possessed seemingly endless stores of energy back then. This woman before me was like a strange caricature of the person I had known. Sitting in a chair, twisting the clothes of her lap into slow knots and then smoothing them out again, over and over.

I opened my mouth to say something positive but said instead, "I have to go now Mrs. Allinson."

"Oh. Am I going with you?"

"No."

"Oh, I see." She sighed resignedly. "I guess I'm being incarcerated then."

She turned away from me then. I reached over and put the flowers in her lap. She didn't notice them and they slid off her lap, unimpeded. She merely stared out the window. And I left her there.

I sat down on the steps in front of the building and brought myself under control, shivering despite the warmth of the late-morning sun.

We are born in a state of totalities. Total innocence, purity, goodness, happiness, and love. It was hard to think of the elderly residents as having once been the cherished objects of new parent's affection. But then maybe they were luckier than the rest of us. Their needs cared for, their surroundings predictable, their pace unhurried, and their thoughts unsullied.

I glanced up the boulevarded lanes and saw the buildings of my old University in the distance. Once my four years were completed and my final exams finally behind me, I had gone to a graduation party at a professor's house on campus. It had begun as most parties do, with everybody congregating in the kitchen rather than the living room. As the rooms filled and the evening lengthened, the gathering became progressively louder. I moved out onto the balcony despite the chill of the night, and stared out at the substantial garden. Looking down, I noticed there was someone sitting by themselves on the edge of the garden's fountain.

I went downstairs and out to join whoever it was while the party played on behind me. It was a girl, a fellow graduate from the department. I'd never met her, but she offered me to sit and together we shared silence. Finally, with a sigh, she asked me what I was looking forward to now that we had finished and were on the cusp of true adulthood. I waited for her to continue because though it seemed a standard question to ask at the time, there was an edge to her voice that I couldn't identify. She said she wasn't sure what she wanted to do now that eighteen years of education had come to end. I smiled ruefully and waited for her to tell me what she wanted out of life, because I couldn't think of anything to say. But she was silent as well. After a time she asked me again what I wanted. I turned around and looked back at the celebration that I didn't feel a part of. I shifted my gaze to her and said one word. Ignorance.

Since then I've thought about that one word. And, of course, there have certainly been times when I have achieved that particular goal, but since that evening, after much deliberation, I have come to the less-than-surprising conclusion that peace of mind is an absurdly hard thing to come by. Maybe the happiness and innocence that we knew as children is only achievable at one extreme or the other. That we can only find that unconditional love, that wonderful innocence, that elemental truth, through extraordinary self-knowledge or total ignorance. Like the pedestrians I had regarded that morning, for instance. They didn't strike me as the kind of people who possessed self-knowledge to any greater degree than I did. I could only assume that after a day of trying to keep up with the guy down the hall, they went home in the status symbol vehicle of the year to tackle the problem of keeping up with the Whatevers across the street. Perhaps it was a matter of settling not for what they wanted, but what they could take.

I have long known that I am fundamentally incapable of existing in such a social and professional milieu. But I still don't know why I rail against conformity and opportunism, why I don't trade my bike in for a compact car or worse, an SUV. Probably because the only available evidence shows that to do so would also mean a receding hairline, an ever-spreading rear-end and an increasingly hapless existence. I felt that even now, my time for picket fences had already passed. And if I am indeed being overly nasty toward my fellows, I am possessed of the inescapable conclusion that such a life would be stultifying.

The truth of the matter, of course, was that I didn't have the answers that I pretended to. And my moribund philosophizing was probably great for cappuccino talk but otherwise was getting me absolutely nowhere. I spent the rest of the afternoon driving all over the city wondering if Mrs. Allinson still dreamt about her old life, the mortal thoughts of her now dead son, bodies under sheets and fleeting innocence.

That night I took another drive to the lake, but this time to the east, to Cherry Beach, near the docklands. The large gravel parking lot was dotted with cars wherein couples with no other available means of privacy enjoyed one another. Several wits had left spray-paint mementos on the beach buildings. Along with the usual valentine hearts and phone numbers was the claim that one Jojo was willing and able to perform a feat that sounded perhaps embarrassing, and certainly painful. One caught my eye that read, "O rubs the sperm of the Prime Minister into her toast she thinks, the need to love the word." I had no idea what it meant. As long as it meant something to the artist.

I set the bike on its sidestand, wandered on foot down to the bay and sat down in the cold, wet sand. The beach was littered with the detritus of illegal campfires. The sand stretched and meandered for a couple of miles until it was broken by the bulk of the filtration plant at Ashbridge's Bay. I could see the red warning lights on the plant's smokestack pulsing rhythmically to warn planes going to and from the Island airport. Floating docks stretching from the lifeguard's shack into the bay creaked and strained with the gentle movement of the water and the shallows, which had been warmed by the day's sun, were now misted over as the water cooled in the chill of the night. The siren at the Port Authority sounded its sporadic and lonely call, and a single tanker passing the spit across the small bay sent back a solitary reply.

The centre of me felt icy and still. Maybe my sister was right and I should be a little more responsible. I hadn't exactly run away when I had left ten years earlier, but I hadn't exactly *not* run away either. My city had changed and I didn't like it much anymore. I wasn't sure whether I liked myself anymore either. And now my oldest friend was gone.

From the outset, ours had not been a usual friendship. On the day we met in kindergarten, we took an instant dislike to each other. We fought tooth and nail at recess for years. When I was eleven years old, my family moved into a bigger house about seven blocks north, which put us in a different school district. The following September I skulked into junior high and there he was with his new best friends. Their families had moved that summer as well, although at the time I was convinced they had just wanted to follow me so the abuse could continue.

That was the year everything changed. It was the year that I achieved a truce that became friendship with Chris and the rest of them. It was the year Mack and I became great friends. And it was the year I met Tara.

That was the year when things began to change for me. And within a decade more, I'd screwed it up.

# Chapter 3

They say the apple never falls far from the tree. In the case of my sister, the apple bounced back up and reattached. So much so that she and her family had assumed possession of our old house. As I wound through the streets of my childhood I kept expecting to see the same kids playing street hockey, or snapping yo-yos, or riding their bikes. Now, of course, it was new families with new kids. But it was the same houses that my friends and I had lived in, the same trees we had played in, the same back yards we had run through.

I parked the motorcycle in the shade of the chestnut tree that overhung the driveway and set the side-stand. Pulling off my helmet I took a deep breath. The air here always smelled different, though it was probably an illusion. It was as if I had left the city and arrived in the country — only a half-hour drive from downtown but somehow the air tasted cleaner and purer here.

I looked across the street and thought about the old Scottish gentleman. God, what was his name ... who had always repaired my bike whenever I blew a tire? We'd pull the tire and then ease out the damaged inner tube, making sure not to tear it on the steel rim. He'd shown me the trick of inflating the inner tube and then putting it underwater to find the leak. After we'd find the problem, he'd have me sand the rubber a little so the cemented patch would have something to hold to. Then after the bike was fixed he'd make me do some minor chore for him, put a stepladder away, haul the trash to the curb, whatever, as a thank you. Damn, what the hell was his name? MacDonald? MacKenzie?

I heard the front door open and turned to see my sister and her husband Jeff standing in the doorway. Katherine's face was scrubbed free of make-up and her brown hair was pulled tight into a ponytail. Jeff's broad, friendly face was cracked into a grin as he stood with his hand on Katherine's shoulder. He had been the best friend of Nick, Chris' older brother, and had met Katherine because of Chris and me. They had married right out of university. I smiled and walked over and gave a tentative hug to Katherine, then Jeff pumped my hand in his iron grip.

"Hey buddy, welcome home. How's the trip?"

He was eyeing the new bike with the same combination of curiosity and longing that he always reserved for them. One night, just before I had left, we sat around with too many beers and he'd told me he'd always wanted a bike but Katherine would freak on him if he bought one. He had given up complete hope when they had their second child, I think because Katherine had made it clear she was not going to risk being a single mother whether he wanted to make her one or not.

"A sweet time. Some beautiful country out there, but it's good to be back."

"So you comin' in or what?"

I looked across the street again, still thinking about the old neighbour. "Yeah," I said.

"Well, come inside then," said Katherine curtly.

The three of us headed into the house and through to the kitchen. The furniture was still the same old pieces and in the same places I remembered from childhood. Heavy, gold, patterned drapes still hung over the bay window in the living room, framed by the tall brass floor lamps on either side that looked out onto the street like sentries. In the living room was the gold striped felt wallpaper my father and I had hung twenty-five years earlier. I could hear their kids playing in the recreation room in the basement, just as Katherine and I had. Somewhere down there, I assumed, were the ten or twelve boxes of books, music, clothes and accumulated bits of my life that I had felt worth keeping and had asked them to store for me while I was gone. We sat down at the long Formica counter that looked out on the backyard littered with toys. There was a new swing set and a sandbox off to one side, and a tire hanging from a rope in the big maple in the back corner. Jeff took two beers out of the fridge, handed one to me and mixed two shandies with the other for himself and Katherine.

"So, obviously you missed the funeral," Katherine said reproachfully. "What took you so long to call?"

"Well, hello again to you too." I checked my tone and continued. "I was on the road non-stop for a week and when I got to Chicago, I called to check in. I feel worse than you could know."

"Well you missed the funeral. We had to represent the family."

"Kat," I said, using the name I'd called her as kids, "I came as soon as I could."

"Have you talked to Chris' family yet?" Jeff asked.

"Yeah, sort of… I spoke to Nick on the phone yesterday. I went to see Mrs. Allinson yesterday as well…", my voice drifted off.

Jeff nodded. "Chris' death was hard on her. Since the diagnosis she's been going downhill fast. Nick saw her last week and she didn't know who he was at first. He's really worried about her. The way the accident happened and all … "

"Jeff," It was Katherine's warning tone, inherited from our mother.

"Jon's got a right to hear. They were friends for a long time," he countered.

"That's not the point."

I waved my hand in the air. "What are you two talking about?"

"After the funeral, some of your old schoolmates were talking about it and …" Jeff started.

"Which ones?"

He turned to Katherine with his eyebrows raised and began counting on his fingers. "Um, Ron, Mack, Paul, Jason, Tara."

"Tara?" I felt my throat get drier.

"Yes," said Katherine. "She came back for her mother's service a little while ago and I think she ended up getting a better job than she had out west. So she stayed. You should call her and say hello."

"Tara's mother is gone as well? Jesus."

"Well, what did you expect?" said Katherine. "You've been gone a long time Jonathan. A very long time."

Jeff broke in, trying to be peacemaker.

"Anyway," he said using more syllables than the word needed, paused and looked at Katherine to slow her down. "Yeah, Tara was there too. Whole bunch a' them."

I hadn't counted on seeing Tara when I got back. In fact, I had been hoping that she was still away so I wouldn't have to deal with her.

"Well, it'd be great to see her again, but I don't know where she's staying, so I probably won't get the chance to."

Jeff ran a thoughtful hand over his stubbly cheek and smirked, "Well, actually, we know. Her mother died. Uh ..." he looked at Katherine for confirmation, "last March, I think. Left her the house by the ravine. She opened the house again in May and she's living there now. In fact, she left a phone number in case you came back."

He reached up to the fridge and lifted one of the kids' colourful finger paintings — yellow trees and blue stick people with pink and red flowers. Underneath it, stuck there with a wooden ladybug fridge magnet, was a piece of paper with her name and phone number in her familiar handwriting. I felt my breath shorten a little.

"She was disappointed not to see you at the funeral," said Katherine. "Tara wanted you to call her if and when you arrived."

I cursed myself silently for asking the question. "Did, uh, her husband go with her? To the funeral?"

They shrugged in unison. "I didn't see anyone with her," said Jeff. "At least, nobody besides your old friends."

Katherine smiled at me for the first time since I'd arrived and said in a hanging-over-the-fence voice, "The last I heard, she came back because her marriage wasn't working out too well." She raised an eyebrow and gave me a short nod of the head that said yes that was exactly what had happened.

"Well, if I get a chance I will. So everybody was there, huh? Everybody from the old neighbourhood?"

"Yes, the whole gang came out. It was good to see them all together again," she said.

I smiled and looked out the kitchen window at the backyard where I had spent so much of my childhood. The deck where I'd fixed my skateboard time and time again. The garden where I'd stubbed toes, built and wrecked snow forts, trampled flowerbeds. A place I had run to when I wanted to be alone. To lie in dewy grass and look at the stars. The place where I'd asked Tara to marry me one day when we were still in high school. The place where she told me she was moving to the west coast and getting married to somebody else after university.

Jeff broke my reverie. "Where are you staying now?" he asked.

"I called a rental agency after I got your letter. I signed an agreement for a week at a time in an apartment down at Yonge and St. Clair. I'm covered."

"Well," Katherine said, "you should stay here while you're home."

"No. It's okay," and saw the immediate relief on her face. "It's already arranged. There's probably a penalty if I pull out. So, thanks, but I'll hang there for the time being."

Jeff jumped in. "No problem. We understand. Just let us know if we can do anything, and come for dinner once in a while. We missed you, buddy."

"I know, I just want to take some time and get things figured out. I've got a fair bit of money left so I'll take a little break, touch base with everybody. Figure out what my next move is." I shrugged. "Just stuff."

I had already figured out my next couple of moves, but hearing that Tara was back had confused the issue a little. Now, suddenly, what I wanted to do was little outside of seeing her again. But if I knew what was good for me, if I had any sense left at all, I'd stay away from the dangerous places in my heart that had taken a long time to scar over. If, if, if. A long time ago somebody once said to me that the "I don't knows" would hurt you, but the "ifs" would break your back. Nobody but a masochist knowingly looks for hurt. And there was a little voice way down deep saying wouldn't it be great to see her again? Why didn't her marriage work out? Wonder what she looks like now? Maybe she could use a friend. Yeah. And every kind thought is the hope of the world. Right?

# Chapter 4

The next morning I was up early knowing it was time to catch up with old friends. And it was too late to catch up with the one I'd come back for. So I had to find out where everybody else was these days. I pulled out my cell and looked up the number of the funeral home that Katherine had mentioned. The service had been several weeks or so back, but with a little persistence and some gentle prodding I found the person who had taken care of the actual arrangements. I made an appointment to see the director, and at one o'clock that afternoon, I pulled off the road into the parking lot of the funeral home.

It was built in the usual neo-classical style common to upscale funeral homes. A backlit sign in the parking lot reminded me it was never too late to pre-plan my own funeral. Four white Doric columns flanked the heavy oak door with tall spruce plantings lining the edges of the front entrance and stone steps. I opened the door and as soon as it closed behind me, all sounds of traffic outside were silenced. The front hall was paneled in light oak. There was wall-to-wall pink carpeting with rose and lily motifs running around the edges. A small reception desk to the right barely contained a large, middle-aged woman who smiled at me as I walked in. She was dressed in a tan camel's hair skirt and jacket with a white blouse and a cameo brooch pinned to the left lapel. Her hair was pulled back into a bun so tight it flattened the wrinkles in her face and made her eyes look comically open. The carpeted hallway beyond her led to doors with brass name plates affixed beside them, no doubt the chapels and viewing rooms.

"Hello," she said, her gigantic eyes brightening. "How can we help you?"

"Good afternoon, I have an appointment with Mr. Keller."

"Your name?"

I told her and she confirmed me in her date book, and then asked me to wait next door in the lobby waiting room. She picked up the phone and buzzed the intercom while I walked over to the waiting area. It was comfortably appointed in dark red leather chairs, a blue-striped couch underneath the window that overlooked the street and magazines artfully arranged on a low coffee table in the middle of the room. Everything seemed carefully designed for quiet reflection. Sitting there flipping through pages and not reading, I was struck by the oppressive quiet of the place. The people who moved back and forth between the various rooms never smiled or spoke above a whisper as I waited. I would have enjoyed a copy of *Embalmer's Monthly* but no such luck. Years before, when we were still in university, Mack's father had died and the when the gang turned up to pay their respects, none of us really knew how to act. It was the first time somebody in our group had experienced that kind of loss, so we all did what we thought we were supposed to do. We were nervous and apologetic until Mack couldn't take it anymore and told us to cut it the hell out. We spent the rest of the evening joking and generally pissing off the assembled adults. It wasn't just that we were just trying to keep him buoyed up, but that we were also celebrating life, in the midst of loss, with laughter and spirit.

When Keller, the director, did turn up, he was exactly as I had pictured him when I spoke with him on the phone. Late fifties, he was a tall, obsequious man with a balding pate, a pinched little face, and a solicitous whisper for a voice. He was, however, wearing impeccable patent leather shoes and an expensive charcoal-coloured European-cut suit with a fine pinstripe. Business was good.

I stuck my hand out. "Mr. Keller, we spoke on the phone. My name is Birnam."

"Ahh, yes," he whispered dramatically, giving me a firm, dry handshake. "Do come into my office."

Once inside the inner sanctum, he motioned me to a chair facing a massive polished oak desk. The walls were paneled in a darker wood than the reception area to match his over-sized desk, while painting after painting of past directors looked down from the walls with earnest, patronizing faces and folded hands on the same desk the present director now sat behind.

"Now, what service can I offer you, young man." It was a roundabout way to say

'What do you want?' but I supposed careful phrasing and supercilious compassion were what paid his tailor and his cobbler.

"Well," I began. "You handled the arrangements for Christopher Allinson's funeral a short time ago. Chris was a close friend and I only just got back and missed the funeral. I wondered if the guest register had been picked up yet by his family."

He smiled at me with raised eyebrows and said, "I'm not at all sure that it is still here." He pressed a button on the intercom on his desk. "Mr. Patterson, could you please check to see if the Allinson family took the guest register on the evening of ..." he glanced back through a date book to confirm," the fifteenth." He lifted his finger off the intercom and turned back to me. "We usually have the families take the register after the service."

"I understand that. I just wanted to add my name if it's still here. I feel terrible that I missed the ceremony."

He nodded his head in ultimate understanding and opened his hands in a supplicating gesture that showed he cared deeply for my troubles. There was a light rap on the door and a tall man with stooped shoulders shuffled into the office bearing a leather-bound volume with debossed gold lettering on the front.

"You seem to be in luck," he said. "It seems the family has not yet collected the register." He took the volume from his assistant and passed it to me. "Perhaps you'd like some time alone to record your thoughts." I nodded thanks and he stood and backed out of the office. After he left I could hear him being less than generous and hotly demanding to know what the register was still doing there and wondering what the assistant had to say for himself.

I slowly flipped through the pages looking at all the names. Some were familiar to me; others had just the faint echo of memory to them and others I didn't recognize at all. Old family friends, relatives, neighbours, and finally on the last page were the names and addresses of everybody from the old days. I added my name to the bottom of the list and then pulled a small pad of paper and a pen out of my jacket pocket. As I stood to make my notes on his desk, I saw the top of a small photocopier behind his chair on a low mahogany table underneath the window. I moved toward the door and listened to make sure the reprimand was still going on. It was. I opened the top of the copier, flipped the book upside down, and positioned it. A moment later, I had a complete list of everybody who had attended the service together with the addresses and phone numbers. I placed the book on his desk, folded the copied pages into my jacket pocket, and walked out.

Once outside I cranked up the bike and headed back to the apartment to go through the list and start making calls. I parked in the back as I had the previous nights and climbed the fire stairs to the third floor. Back inside, I pushed aside the detritus on the kitchen table and sat down to go through the list. I marked the names of everybody I'd been close to throughout school — the people who would remember Chris the same way I did.

I made a list on a pad of paper with the names and addresses and numbers provided until I had a list of seven names. The last name on the list was Tara's. And thanks to Katherine and Jeff, I already knew a little more about her than I wanted to.

The name on the top of the list was Mack's. It had been a long time. I hoped it wasn't too long. I went into the living room with the list, dropped onto the sofa and called the number I had copied from the master list. My watch said it was just after two. He'd probably be at whatever he worked at, but I could always leave him a message. After the phone rang a couple of times, there was a faint sound of transfer on the line and then a woman's voice answered. "Breakers"

"Hi, I'm looking for Mack." I asked uncertainly. She said to wait a minute and I heard the phone put down on something hard. Whoever she was yelled Mack's name and ten seconds later the phone was picked up again.

"Yeah, this' Mack, what can I do for ya?"

"Hey," I said simply. There was silence as he thought about the voice. Then the old familiar voice and attitude came hammering through the receiver.

"Jesus Christ! Jon, you sonofabitch! No it can't ... is that you? Jon, are you, you back? Ten goddamned years gone and you just call me up outatheblue! I'm gonna cut you off at the stones! Goddamn you, man. I oughta come down there, wherever you are and kick your ass up amongst your shoulder blades! Goddamn you." Then the voice dissolved in laughter, unable to keep up the tirade.

"Ah mate, always the witty and urbane conversationalist. How are you man!"

"SSDD my friend!" he said through his laughter. "Goddamn, it's good to know you're still in the land of the living. What the hell you been doing all this time? Where've you been man?"

"Oh hell, I don't know, this and that, whatever's going. You know…"

"No I don't goddamn know, so you're gonna tell… over beers… now."

"You got it," I said laughing, "where and when?"

"You remember The Breakers? Down in the Beach?"

"Sure… it's still around?

"Damn right! It's still here, where it's always been. So git yer ass down here. Half an hour."

"Didn't you work there or something when I left? You were managing the place on weekends weren't you?

"Yeah, that was then. C'mon and move your ass. Half an hour." And he cut the call off.

Smiling, I clicked the phone off and went to get my keys. He had dogged it all through school, coasted, and beat every single one of us on tests, exams, even the SAT's. It wasn't that he didn't care, because underneath his nonsense and swaggering, you could see he was proud that he did well. But for some reason, school just didn't do it for him. By the time he got to college, he needed a real change, a challenge, something to harness his energy and mind constructively. As usual, Mack coasted and eventually finished with a grade point average that shamed the rest of us.

After graduation, he had bummed around, even after the university offered him a free ride for graduate school with the promise of an associate professorship when he was finished. He passed on their offer and started working at jobs that were way below his capacity. Menial jobs, like shipping and receiving at a construction company or working as a bike courier, jobs that left the rest of us shaking our heads at lost promise. Just before I had left, he'd gotten a job as a bartender and weekend manager at the place in the Beach. I had no idea what he was up to now, but damned if I wasn't looking forward to finding out.

Half an hour later, sitting in The Breakers, Mack was beaming at me and clapping me on the shoulder. He hadn't changed much. Tall and gangly with an angular, open face, he still wore his blond hair cropped short and his beard and mustache were neatly trimmed. He was wearing the standard uniform of the bar manager: chinos, casual blue dress shirt and top-siders. It always amused me that people who lived in the Beach always dressed for sailing, at least sailing according to Ralph Lauren.

I shrugged off my leather jacket and hung it on a hook underneath the lip of the bar. At Mack's suggestion, the bartender took my helmet behind the bar. In the mid-afternoon, the place was maybe a third full, the lunch crowd beginning to peter out. The oak bar took up half of the front area with a dozen stools lined up in front of it. Two televisions were mounted on tilted platforms at either end. They were both tuned to replay sports channels — one had a hockey game, the other football. Just past the bar area were a couple of dartboards and beyond them, up a few steps, was a raised area surrounded by a low pony wall that made up the main dining room. One waitress worked the few tables that were occupied while two others scurried around checking stations and refilling condiment bottles. The few patrons who were at the bar and the tables that were near it were staring at the mercifully silent TVs. I asked for a pale ale and was pleased to see it delivered in a frosted pint glass. The bartender snapped a coaster down in front of me with a flourish and set the beer on top of it. When I tried to pay for it, she smiled and shook her head. Mack laughed and waved her away.

"On the house, old friend. Ten years away, the least I can do is pick up the tab," he said, grinning. "Besides which, I own the house."

"No kidding?"

"Yeah, no kidding," he looked around proudly. "After I'd been here a year or so, things were going well. Revenues were up, staff was happy, and the owner knew it was mostly my doing. I asked for a raise and he offered me equity instead. So after a couple of years I had about twenty points in the place and he wanted to get out anyway, so I got myself a loan… and now it's all mine, or will be in about ten more years."

"Well done mate, fat-ish and happy."

"Screw you," he said smiling. "Yup, found my place I guess. Now it's your turn."

"My turn for what, telling my story or finding my place?"

"Both."

I laughed, "What do you want to know?"

"Start somewhere man, ten years is a long time gone."

"Hell," I shrugged and took a sip of my beer. "You of all people should know how it was. I kicked around a little. You know I did my time in the reserves for the tuition, but after it was over, there was no way I was going into the service for good."

"Considering your incredible respect for authority? Wait." He held his hand up and stared at the ceiling. "No, nope. Sorry. Thought I was gonna be surprised there for a second."

I punched him lightly in the shoulder. "Yeah, well it served its purpose. So, anyway I graduated the academy and put in some years but that wasn't it either. So I bought the bike, made some loose plans and left."

"I remember the bike, sweet. Bright red, wasn't it? A ... uh ... Kawi, ZX-10, right? But this is all ancient history, my friend; I know all this already. Where the hell did you go?"

I shook my head, trying to sort out the timeline in my mind. "I started out west. I worked railroad for a while between Calgary and Golden doing track mainte-nance. Then I worked for a mountain tour company, taking people up into the high ground. I spent six months building a hunting cabin for somebody. After that I went to Vancouver. I was there for about a year, worked as a bartender in Gastown, then decided I'd head down to the States, see what happened," I realized I was getting uncomfortable talking about my recent past. In the telling it didn't sound very good. A reminder that my own failings made my judgments of others more than a little ironic.

"Yeah, and then..."

" Well, I, uh...I did anything and everything. Did some logging in Washington State. I worked restaurants on the Oregon coast. I went down to California and worked at a winery for a couple of seasons north of Sonoma. Sometimes I just moved with the weather, mostly I left when I got bored. I did construction; I tended bar at a place in New Orleans; I worked on a charter boat in the Keys for three years, whatever, you know? And when it was time to go, I went. I was working my way back this way when I heard about..."

"Aw, man," Mack shook his head in sad disgust. "Chris. That was godawful. You talked to anybody yet?"

"I phoned Nick the other day. I went to see Chris' mother. That was depressing. Jesus, what happened to her?"

"When Chris died it just… " he shook his head sadly. "I don't know all the details but… well there was just nothing any of us could do for her. We were all at the service, you shoulda… sorry."

I waved away his apologetic look. "It's fine. I know I should have been there. I called Katherine from the road a few days ago. I saw her and Jeff yesterday, they told me everybody was there, like old times."

"Yeah, it was good to have the group there. I still see Jeff and the guys every so often, usually for a couple of hockey games at the Hangar. I get free tickets from the beer reps. Sometimes we get together for a little poker, whatever." He paused looking at me over the top of his beer. "Seeing Tara was a bit of a surprise though…" The unasked question hung in the air between us, but I let it hang.

"Yeah? Katherine said she was back." I hoped my feigned indifference was enough to put him off. It wasn't.

"Yup, it sure was nice to see Tara again. Still looks great…"

"Hey, dog with a bone, drop it alright?" I said smiling. "When I feel like it."

"Sure, sure. When you feel like it." He glanced down. "Or part of you any-way…" He laughed and rolled his shoulder this time into another punch. Mack motioned to the bartender and circled the area around our empty glasses. She pulled two more and put them in front of us with fresh coasters.

"So listen," I said. "I hate to bring it all back again, but what happened with Chris? Katherine's letter said it was single car accident and he crashed into Muir Park."

"Yeah," he said flatly. "Nobody knows for sure. Chris was heading home from visiting his mother on a Sunday night. This is just before they were moving her. Well, really early Monday, I think the cops said around three. Roads were slippery. They think maybe a raccoon or a cat got in front of him. He swerved to avoid it, spun out and flipped the car into the park. Pure bad luck. Car was absolutely destroyed by the fire. They found him in the wreck."

"Wasn't there any investigation?"

"Like I said, nobody knows anything for sure. Cops I talked to said there was one set of skid marks, nobody else on the road to witness it. I got a couple of guys on the beat that are regulars here. Said he had been drinking, but Nick told me just a couple of glasses of wine with dinner. No witnesses, nothing. Some old lady in those apartments next to the park heard the crash and called. Sucks to say, but by the time they got there, he was a briquette. End of story."

End of Chris' story anyway. It wasn't fair, but since when was there an arbiter who made sure fairness was meted out accordingly. There were lots of lousy people flourishing out there and lots of good people not. And Chris had been one of the good ones.

"So what's your move?" Mack asked. "You got money? How long you gonna stay this time?"

"I'm flush for now. I had no expenses in Florida, I lived on a boat and ate a lot of fish," I said laughing. "I don't have to worry about working just yet. I've only signed a month's agreement for the apartment. Place is a disaster, but it's cheap."

"OK, but are you gonna look around? I mean, you puttin' down roots for a while or are you out of here again?"

"I don't know yet. I've been th inking about slowing down lately. Every time I think about staying somewhere for good, this is the only place that comes to mind. You know, I've been traveling all over the bloody place for a decade and as much as I don't feel like I know the city anymore, this is still the only place that makes any sense to me. I've been thinking about maybe a boat."

"A boat!? What d'ya mean a boat?" he reached over and tried to rap his knuckles on my forehead. "Canada, remember? Winter? White stuff comes falling out of the sky six months a year. Gets very cold. Lakes freeze. A boat…" he snorted.

"Yeah, a boat," I laughed. "I got bit by the bug in the Keys. Like I said, I used to work charter down there. I loved that job and I loved the water. So, you know, maybe a used forty-footer. Decent beam. Strong V-hull. Twin screws. A boat."

"This ain't Florida, and you're outta your mind. Nobody lives on a boat in this city. Not year round."

"Sure you can. Water mixers over the side to keep the ice away from the hull; wrap the bridge and topsides in plastic; heaters down below for the winter; nice sheltered tie-up. It'd be cozy."

"It'd be fuckin' freezing. But whatever…" he laughed. "You make your own rules, pal. You always did."

"All right, so we'll see. Listen, since I'm new here again, keep your ear to the ground for me. If you hear of something that comes up, you know, if some

Beacher wants to unload something, let me know. It's coming on to the end of the season so maybe there'll be some deals around."

"OK, OK. I hear anything, I'll let you know. In the meantime, what's your move?"

"I'm going to buy myself some fresh sets of clothes. Do a little thinking. Here…" I showed him the list I'd photocopied at the funeral home and explained how I got it.

"Sonofabitch," he said. "That was cute. Listen, the other guys and me are going to a Jays game Thursday night. Whyn't you come too? Surprise 'em. We'll go out after. Catch some beers."

"Definitely," I said. He stood, reaching over and fished around behind the bar for a moment and came up with an envelope. There was a brewery logo printed in the top corner. He opened it and handed me a ticket. It was for one of the exclusive boxes high above the diamond. Private food and drink service, personal bartender and hostess and your own balcony overlooking the action.

"Nice seats," I said. "Just how much beer flows through this place?"

Mack grinned at me. "Monday Night Football, Tuesday Dart League, Wednesday wings and live bands Saturday and Sunday in the bar. We do a hundred and fifty covers on average a night, through the dining room plus the bar trade. Old pal," he laughed. "You have no idea."

# Chapter 5

*I*t was a perfect day for playing summer hooky. Wednesday. Hump day. Bright August sunshine, and in the middle of the week, there'd be hardly anybody on the beach. Perfect. He reached back and patted the pannier affixed behind the seat of the mountain bike, feeling his towel and book under the soft nylon wall of the bike bag. He could ride to work and it was a perfect day for a cycle. Straddling the center bar, he moved forward on tiptoes with the small queue to buy a ticket for the Island. A school tour and some retirees were the only people sitting beyond the ticket kiosks in the waiting area. The children were craning their necks around looking for the Island ferry as it chugged slowly across the inner harbour. The ferry docks had three slips, each one pointing to a different portion of the three atolls that formed the island chain. He'd pass on the Centre Island ferry anyway. Better to head to Ward's Island. Less people. Nice little beach. Quietude. He came to the Island by himself every Wednesday in the summertime. The spoils of self-employment. And it was a good place to sit and forget.

When he and Laura came with the kids, they always went to Centreville — the little amusement park with its bumper cars, haunted house, antique cars that moved in tracks that the kids could pretend to drive, the log chute ride and the tiny petting zoo. They loved going as a family, but today was just for him. When he'd called Laura at her office to tell her he was skipping off for the day, she'd been crazy jealous as usual. Even if she'd been free, he would have wanted to go by himself. Quietude.

He got off his bike to buy his ticket from the girl in the kiosk, then wheeled between the kiosks. The large blue and white Centre Island ferry pulled slowly into its berth to his right, reversing its engines and rubbing its sides furiously against the monster tires, which sat on enormous iron pilings to cushion the landing of the ferries.

*The children jumped up excitedly when the steel loading ramp was lowered and clanged into place and the teachers did their best to contain their charges. A city ferry worker rolled the steel gate aside and the children piled into the belly of the ferry. He could hear them shouting and running up the stairs, and suddenly they appeared at the railings on the second level. Laughing and pointing at landmarks, jostling each other for position until the teachers caught up with them and herded them into seats. The last of the passengers boarded and the loading ramp was winched up into place. With a blast of the air horn, the propellers churned up the water and the ferry slid slowly out of its berth and headed across the harbour.*

*The ferry worker ambled over to the east gate and pushed it open for him. He nodded at the man and rolled his bike over the steel drop bridge and onto the ferry. Same design as the Centre Island one, it looked like a slightly miniaturized copy. The Islands formed a loose semi-circle and created a natural inner harbour for the city. The Island airport and Hanlan's Point at the west tip, then curving around a marina with a canal running through it to Centre Island with the amusement park, zoo and an elevated Promenade that ran out into the lake on the south side of the Islands. A bicycle path ran the entire southern perimeter of the Islands. They continued to curve eastward, past the RCYC to Ward's Island. There were about three hundred homes on Ward's, mostly inhabited by artist types who, it sometimes seemed, repaired their houses with whatever washed up on the beach. A few summer people had nicer, more cottage-y places, but true Islanders didn't go in for that kind of luxury. They couldn't afford it. He loved the bohemian feel of Ward's and often cycled up and down the cracked sidewalks that served as streets, marveling at the way some of houses seemed to stubbornly defy gravity and refuse to fall down.*

*He set the mountain bike on its kickstand and leaned his forearms on the pipe railing, staring down at the gray harbour water and thinking about the choices he had made. Laura and the kids were the best part of him. They brightened the dark corners. Especially the corners he had turned a blind eye to in order to make the best possible life for his family. And now that had told them he was out, he felt renewed. The murk of the old was behind him. A new life free and clear. Paid for by the old one to be sure. But no more. A fresh start. He grinned up at the sunshine. The ferry finally blew its horn and shifted slowly away from the mainland. After fifteen minutes of churning across the gray-green water, the ferry reached the dock at Ward's and crunched its* rubber fenders into the pilings that nosed it into position. He jumped on his bike and headed toward the beach on the far side of the island, beyond the funky houses.

When he got to the beach, he bounced the bike down into the sand and pedaled as far as he could. When the front wheel eventually dug in, he hopped off and pushed the bike the rest of the way to the water's edge. At the far end of the beach he saw a solitary fishermen, idly casting into the water, then reeling back in and casting again. He sat down in the sand and pulled off his tie and shirt and stowed them in the pannier on the bike. He pulled off his shoes and socks, put his wallet into one of the shoes and balled the socks down into the other, then wrapped it all up in his towel to make a pillow, rolled up his pants and lay down with his book. After an hour or so of reading he stuffed the book back into the pannier and rolled over onto his back. The high August sun beat down on him as he slowly fell asleep.

When he woke up, groggy from the heat, he had no idea how long he'd been out. He sat up to get his watch out of the pannier, but the bike was gone. He jumped up and rubbed the sleep out of his eyes, suddenly awake now, and scanned the beach. The fisherman was gone. He ran off the beach and looked up and down the concrete path. To his right, the sidewalk curved away out of sight, heading towards more Ward's Island homes. To his left the path became a wide, wooden boardwalk that followed the water's edge with a concrete retaining wall, deep tall thicket on the other land side. He started to jog along the path to his left, away from the houses. The Centre Island ferry ran more often than the others; maybe the prick who'd taken the bike would head that way. Or maybe he'd been out long enough that it didn't matter what goddamn ferry the bastard took. Every once in a while, the thicket to his right was broken by a dirt path, which formed T-junctions with the boardwalk. He glanced down the paths as he passed each one, hoping to catch a glimpse of his bike. The retaining wall to his left was a solid line stretching around and out of sight. He glanced over the wall, looking straight down and saw jagged boulders down at the water's edge fifteen feet below. After five minutes of running, he was too winded, so he stopped, his right hand massaging a cramp in his side.

At the mouth of the next dirt path, a flash of colour caught his eye. Bent over at the waist, trying to get his breath back, he reached down and picked up his book, lying in a tangle of grass. He looked down the path, closely defined by trees on either side. Beyond where the matted dirt and grass path came to an end was a clearing completely surrounded by thicket, the centre of which boasted a small gazebo. Dotted around the clearing were wooden *picnic tables and hibachi-style barbecues supported by single iron posts.*

*His bike was inside the gazebo, leaning against the brightly painted wooden railing. His breath caught in his throat as he willed the cramp in his side away. Kids! Some goddamn kids had taken the bike for a joyride and then ditched it. He ran to the gazebo as best he could, still massaging the stitch in his side, and checked the pannier. Everything was still inside, his watch, shirt and tie; the stupid little pricks hadn't taken anything.*

*He realized suddenly that he'd left his wallet and socks and shoes back at the beach. He bounced the bike down the stairs of the gazebo, jumped on and pedaled quickly across the clearing and up the dirt path leading back to the boardwalk and breakwater. He perceived a quick movement to his left in the trees. Suddenly he felt a blinding pain that radiated from the back of his head and stabbed him behind his eyes. He felt blood pouring down his forehead and from his nose. He lost control of his bike and veered off the dirt path, striking a maple tree dead centre.*

*The front wheel crumpled with the impact, the spokes bowing and snapping with the force, the inner tube exploding as it was stretched against the bending rim. He felt himself fly up and over the handlebars. He grabbed at the brake cables above the handlebars to stop himself but it was futile. His body glanced off the tree, leaving a bright smear of blood on the bark, and then landed in a pile of leaves, coming to rest face up.*

*The figure, which had melted back into the trees, emerged again from the thicket and walked up the remainder of the path to the boardwalk. He checked that the boardwalk was clear of people. Then he walked back down the path into the trees and stood over the body. The figure watched as the mouth opened and closed silently and the eyes slowly emptied until there was nothing left. Beside the body one of the metal and rubber brake pads had snapped off with the impact. The figure pocketed the little piece, then dragged the ruined bicycle out and up the path. At the edge of the breakwater he hoisted the bike onto his hip, then half turned and flung it out into the lake. The bike scissored into the water and sank out of sight. Then he took the folding fishing rod out from his jacket with a gloved hand and threw that over the wall as well. He rummaged in his pocket and pulled out the broken brake part. He hefted it in his hand to toss it after the bicycle. Then, grinning, he cocked his arm and spun the little piece as flat as he could onto the water's surface. The little shard skipped four times before it caught a wave the wrong way and sank with a tiny splash. Then he turned and walked back to the body lying in the woods.*

*As the water roiled, the stern cleared the giant rubber bumpers and the last evening ferry chugged across the harbour to the Ward's Island dock. On the flat deck, a small group of Island residents headed home after spending the evening having dinner and a movie downtown. The city worker manning the front ramp finished his cigarette and snapped it over the railing, following the orange ember as it trailed slowly down into the water. Light standards at the dock's edge made pools of muted yellow on the concrete slips. Some of the light spilled onto the styrofoam cups, shiny bits of plastic, old rope and algae that danced on the water, trapped by the U-shaped dock. As the ferry slowed and reversed its engines, the water that preceded the wide displacement hull washed between the slips and stirred up the flotsam. The man at the ramp looked down and then grabbed his radio and spoke rapid-fire to the bridge. Oh Christ reverse! Stop! Stop the ferry! There's something in the water! Contact the harbourmaster. Oh Christ, there's something in the water!*

# Chapter 6

I sat there on the idling motorcycle, the low throb of the aftermarket pipe burbling away. The playground was still there. That was good. High above the stands of trees, some of the older homes that had faced the park had been torn down and replaced with tall, soulless monster townhouses, devoid of patina or character. But the park was still there, untouched. That was good.

*"Welcome to the Machine."*

*"No way. Great tune, yeah. But no, no way."*

*"Fine then what?"*

*"I dunno man, what about the Fall of the House of Usher? Tales of Mystery and Imagination. Parsons Project."*

*"Unh-uhn. Floyd."*

*"Parsons."*

*"Floyd."*

*"Parsons."*

*The weekly argument. Girls, music, movies, books, it didn't matter. Every week we argued and debated anything and everything. Today it was best prog-rock British band of the 70's. We never agreed on music, but this was important stuff. More important than girls, almost more important than movies, definitely more important than school.*

*We were sitting in the tower of the playground in Sherwood Park like always. At one end was a fireman's pole where you could slide down a dozen feet into the sand below; at the other was a bunch of tires bolted together and hanging in an arc from the walkway down to the sand. In between were ramps and towers built from tar-soaked timbers. We were working on a couple of extra-large fries and Cokes from the place over on Mount Pleasant. Our bikes rested against each other at the base of the tire climb. Both of us were supposed to be home for dinner soon, but it was our weekly time — just him and me. Time to talk movies and music, TV and girls.*

*"Parsons, moron."*

*"Floyd, bastard boy."*

*"Chuck you, Farley."*

*"No, chuck you Farley."*

*I punched him in the shoulder, one knuckle out to give it a little hurt. He smacked me back and we fell apart laughing. Whenever one of us used that line, it always broke us up.*

Man, I missed him.

Memory is a sly and unfeeling mistress. She'll let you down most of the time, make you feel foolish when you grab for something just outside of your reach. Then sometimes she'll whisper something in your ear that puts a quiet smile on your face. She can make you feel perfect. She'll lift you up with an old, small victory — she can make your heart soar with the mere mention, just a small taste of something wonderful and personal.

But if she's feeling a little nasty, a little bitter — she'll slap you hard enough to make your eyes sting. Slam you down with something that you thought was buried. She'll drag it back just for you. Something she kept hidden for just the right occasion. When it's time, she'll dig it up and pull it from the cold earth. Wipe away the dirt from the empty eye sockets. Check the yellow teeth. Make sure the hands are still set in rictus hooks and send it capering and gibbering upon you. And if you don't like what she's got for you, then too damn bad.

Chuck you Farley.

It was Thursday afternoon and I'd been back now for three days. It was time to visit my friend. I'd spent the morning moving from place to place, from memory to memory. Being with Chris and my childhood the only way I knew how. The schoolyards; the hills of Hoggs Hollow where we'd played along the edge of the river; the baseball diamond at the end of Devere Gardens, the playground at Sherwood Park. Memory was doing what she would. Good and bad, whispering and capering.

I pulled my helmet back on and headed up the hill and back out to Sherwood

Avenue. I turned south and twenty minutes later I rolled into Mount Pleasant
Cemetery. It's not the oldest cemetery in the city, but it's certainly the grandest. It
stretches from Yonge Street in the west to Bayview Avenue in the east, Merton
Street to the north, Moore Avenue to the south and is bisected by Mount Pleasant
Road. I never knew which got named first, the graveyard or the road. But regardless, the old City of York had grown north from the lake, encircled Mount
Pleasant completely and now, of course, was a monster with tentacles stretching
farther than the founders could ever have dreamed. Once north of the city and
now smack in the middle of it, Mount Pleasant Cemetery often felt like the city
radiated outward from it, as if it was somehow the epicentre. A two-hundred-acre
green space filled with hundred-and-fifty-year-old weeping willows and maples, it
is the final home of some of Canada's famous: Glenn Gould, MacKenzie King,
Foster Hewitt, the victims of the Empress of Ireland and the Steamship Noronic.
Curving boulevards wind sinuously through the cemetery, passing monuments
that date back to the late nineteenth century. Souls taken by old age and childhood disease, by war and epidemic, by accident and murder. All of them resting
together now in a garden of marble and granite.

On the Yonge Street side, massive iron and stone gates opened onto a driveway
and the main house. I parked and went inside to find out where Chris was buried.
After getting directions and my bearings straight, I drove slowly into the cemetery,
keeping the bike in low second gear, one hand on the throttle, the other, elbow
crooked, resting on my thigh. I took it slow and easy down the boulevards. When
I reached the area I had been directed to I pulled in the clutch and knocked the
gear lever down into neutral, shut the motor off and rolled to a stop. Silence
descended as the pipe quieted and did its minor-key ticking while it cooled. Here
in the middle of the west part of the cemetery, there were no traffic sounds. Only
the quiet rustle and sway of the willows with birdsong and maple-dappled sunlight. I took my leather jacket off and draped it over the tank with my helmet
resting atop. I could feel the August sun on my shoulders and back through my tee
shirt. I could hear the high summer keening of a cicada somewhere close by.

The graveyard featured ornately carved grave markers as well as spartan ones.
Sonorous mausoleums of the rich mixed with the tiny flat markers of children.
Beatific angels atop smooth marbled headstones, their marble-veined wings spread in

imminent celestial flight. Rough-hewn stone crosses six feet tall with celtic patterns in their centres. A grouping of small spare markers attesting to an order of nuns.

His was a simple stone, dark granite with a curved top sitting on a low rectangular base with chiseled edges.

There was an inscription taken from a Frost poem:

> *We vainly wrestle with the blind belief*
> *That aught we cherish*
> *Can ever quite pass out of utter grief*
> *And wholly perish*

I remembered the title of a book I had read in high school, *Dark as the Grave Wherein my Friend is Laid.* The grass on this grave was still mending itself together; the cut lines in the sod still visible like healing scars. There were no flowers or adornments of any kind on the grave wherein my friend was laid. I hadn't brought any either. I had only brought my sadness and my guilt for not having come back sooner. And for not having talked to him for a long time.

I could feel my breathing getting harsher, my anger rising. In the middle of the nineteenth century graveyard a nineteenth century idiom occurred to me; that the urge for destruction is inherently a creative urge. I leaned on the top of the stone with my forehead on my arm and forced myself to be calm.

I hadn't been there. I wanted to tear the grave marker from the ground. I wanted to smash it to fragments and find some kind of absolution. If I destroyed the stone, maybe I could wipe away the shame; bring him back; make myself right again. The Victorians had it wrong; the urge for destruction isn't a creative one; it's a selfish one.

"Jesus, I'm sorry man," I mumbled. I had known him for almost twenty-five years. Grown up with him. Played baseball and football with him and the others. We'd been kids, and teenagers, and young adults. Then I'd left to seek my fortune, gone west young man, and hadn't called or written anybody from my old life in ten years. And now I was back. Amateur at everything, expert at nothing. Did I think I could pick up the old pieces? Did I want to? Did anybody else want me to? I had come back because my friend was dead. But what did I think I was going to accomplish by returning? I wasn't going to bring Chris back. So just what was I going to do?

I had been drifting rudderless for a decade. And I had the sense that when I left, that maybe some kind of elemental truth had been left behind as well. Maybe all that we imagine ourselves to be, all that we see of ourselves is mostly an understanding of how other people see us. That somehow the essence of ourselves is some kind of distillation of both who the people in our lives think we are and who we think ourselves to be.

I had left to find out what the world had to offer, and what I was capable of. And I had come back not much the wiser. But like the man said, conduct is founded on the hard rock or the wet marshes. I had missed one funeral. I had lost a good friend. Maybe it was time to make sure I didn't regret anything else before I lost another.

I headed back.

When I got back upstairs my cell buzzed in my pocket. I ignored it and went to grab a shower. When I got out of the shower with a towel around my waist, I padded into the kitchen and pulled a beer out of the fridge. Chill beer after a hot shower diluted some of the depressing thoughts to an acceptable level. I wandered into the living room and checked messages. My wet hair made small elliptical splotches on the phone screen. There was only one message and it was from Mack. After the message was finished, I got dressed, grabbed my helmet and keys and raced down to The Breakers in the warm summer evening.

# Chapter 7

We were sitting in the elevated dining area at The Breakers. The waitresses moved between the tables, serving people who had no idea what we were talking about, and probably wouldn't care if they did.

"How, man? How the hell did it happen?"

"I don't know. I got the call from Laura early this morning. They found him floating in the harbour last night. Guy working the ferry saw him."

I took a pull on my bourbon and waited until Mack looked up again. Beer was fine, but wasn't right under the circumstances. The circumstances called for something a little quicker acting.

"When are the others coming down?"

Mack looked immeasurably sad. "We're running out of friends."

"Mack, when are they coming?"

He looked at his wristwatch. "Shoulda been here by now."

We fell into individual silences. First Chris, now Paul. We weren't supposed to go this young. Die this young.

"Hey. Hey! When did it happen?"

"Yesterday, I already said!" he said too loudly, then paused and looked apologetic. "Sorry, man. He was supposed to pick up the kids after school. When he didn't show, the school called Laura at work. When he wasn't home by nine she called the cops. Couple hours later the cops called her. Had to ID the body. They found his stuff on the Island." Mack got up and went to the bar and refilled his glass then came back and sat down again.

"So what do you think?"

"Hell Jon, I'm not a goddamn cop, I don't know. She was too upset to give up any details. Just that he'd gone to the Island and … I don't know! She doesn't know anything …" His voice dwindled as he raised his eyes to the ceiling. I gave him some time and went to the bar and got another drink for myself. By the time I got back to the table his eyes were red-rimmed but he had it together again.

I heard the door open above the din and looked down beyond the bar. Two men walked in and it took me a second in the low light of the entrance to make out who they were. I saw them scanning the room, looking for Mack. I stood up from the table and held up my hand. They saw me but didn't register who I was at first — and then big smiles as they strode over together.

"Jonathan, man … Jonathan," Jason beamed. "Holy shit. Welcome back!"

We shook hands and clapped each other on the back, and then Ron and I did the same. Jason still looked as he always had, just a little heavier, a little less hair now. He was shorter than my six feet, with cropped red hair and the beginnings of a spare tire around his middle. His wide, friendly face was wearing an old familiar smile.

Ron had always been all elbows and knees, gangly and awkward, a stork. In high school he'd begun to fill out, made the squad with Mack and me and Chris and started putting on muscle. By the time we graduated high school, Ron was a very solid six foot four and a hell of a defensive tackle. He was probably somewhere in the 260 lb. range now, a bit flabby but you could see the remnants of the athlete he'd been in the way he carried himself, in the set of his shoulders. The waitress came by and took their drink order. She looked worriedly at Mack, who was staring at the tabletop. Their arrival allowed the conversation to shift tack.

"Jesus, it's good to see you two again," I said. "So how the hell are you guys. What's happening? You married? Single? You two finally come out of the closet and marry each other?" I laughed as Jason frisbee'd a beer coaster at me.

Jason flicked his hand back and forth indicating both of them. "Both married, I got one kid, he's got two," he said.

"Two?" I said, smiling at Ron. "A woman let you make love to her twice?"

Ron swatted one of his huge hands at my head. I ducked away still laughing.

"Screw you" he growled good-naturedly.

We talked about old times and new times, about where I'd been and the things

I'd done. Ron had started as a security guard for the burgeoning film industry and had moved up and done well. Jason had become an insurance broker in commercial transport.

The joking around was enough at least to break Mack out of his own morbid thoughts, and he smiled a little and joined in. But as the spaces between the laughter grew longer, our thoughts were turning back to Paul. There was a strained silence as everyone waited for someone else to break it.

"All right," I said. "So Paul was married too. Laura, right?" Everybody nodded. "Has anything been offered? Does she need any kind of help? The arrangements? Anything?"

"I told her I'd help with whatever she needed," said Mack. "She was too racked up when she called earlier. I'm going over to the house tomorrow. See what needs taking care of."

"I'll go with you," I said. "I know she doesn't know me, but I want to do what I can."

"Yeah, but lemme ask her first. I'm sure it'll be OK but I'll ask her tomorrow morning. Let you know."

"So where are you living now?" asked Ron. "You just visiting or back to stay?"

"I don't know yet. I'm thinking about hanging in for a bit. I'm kind of tired of traveling around. I made some money, done my traveling for now."

"Oh, shit I forgot," said Mack. "I heard about a boat last night, got the info here." He pulled a scrap of paper out of his shirt pocket. There was a phone number and a name in a scrawl. It wasn't the time to talk about the details, so I half-stood and shoved the piece of paper into the front pocket of my jeans.

"So what," Jason asked. "They don't have phones where you were?"

"Mea culpa," I said, holding up my hands, "I should have kept in touch. I thought about calling or writing, but ... I should have done my bit. You know after my parents were gone, I had no reason to stay, I mean, other than you guys. I had no career, still don't," I smiled at them self-consciously, knowing that whatever I said it wasn't going to help them understand. Hell, I didn't understand. "I just, I don't know, expected more from myself, from the way my life was going. I thought maybe I could shake things up by heading out."

"And did you?" asked Ron.

I was uncomfortable talking about myself this way. Despite the history I had with them. "I guess maybe I learned a few things, picked up a few talents along the way. I'm still not sure what to do just yet. And the time, she is passing. First I've got to find a real place to live," I patted my pocket with the scrap of paper in it. "Then who knows? I've got one or two ideas," Cheshire Cat smile in place I said, "I'm working on it."

"Well, whatever you do, glad you're good and stay in touch this time," Jason said.

"Hey, in my own defense, I got the list of everybody from Chris' service," I pulled the list from inside my jacket and showed it to them. "And I was gonna call."

The mention of Chris pulled the conversation down again. Mack broke the silence. "What do you guys think?"

"Think about what?" asked Jason.

"What are you talking about, Mack?" said Ron.

Mack was quiet again, lost. I remembered something that Katherine and Jeff had said the other day, so I picked up the thread.

"I don't know," I started. I shook my head. "I haven't been here for a long time. I don't know what's been going on. But I can't believe that we've lost two friends within three weeks. You know? I mean, you guys remember my sister? Yeah, of course you do. I saw her and Jeff a couple of days ago. Jeff said there was talk going around about Chris. About what happened."

"Yeah," said Jason. "None of us liked the idea of Chris losing control like that. Didn't make sense. He was better than that, a better driver than that. He wouldn't wipe himself out for a stray or whatever."

"So what does that mean?'

"It means what the hell are we talking about?" said Ron angrily. "Oh, what, Chris then Paul. Not happening." he said shaking his head.

"I know. It sounds ridiculous, but…"

"Jon, I'm not buying it. Who'd they ever hurt? It's bullshit."

"Listen, I know it sounds crazy. I know Chris was a good driver. Had that old beige Honda we all rode around in. Hell, he was our taxi service in high school. Even then he was good at it. So he wipes himself out into Muir Park because something runs in front of him? And then Paul drowns on the Island? Christ, I want to believe it's nothing but bad luck as much as anybody, but I'm having trouble with both of them being gone like that." I snapped my fingers. "Coincidence doesn't begin to cover it."

I felt like I was somehow betraying my old friends, especially Paul, who had still been alive that morning. He'd probably had breakfast with his family, kissed his wife goodbye. Went to work with an easy mind, made phone calls, shuffled papers, dealt with usual minutiae of every day. And a few hours later... None of us will know when the final leaving is upon us until it is too late. When the all the little machines and mechanisms that whir unseen and unimpeded inside all of us suddenly stop working, and all that is left is the awful white noise of final silence.

I wanted to know that it was just bad luck. Bad karma. I wanted a reason, an answer that I could grip. That I could understand. That I could wring the life out of. No gray areas, no unanswered questions, no wondering.

Jason was the first to speak. "You know, the cops talked to all of us when Chris went. Asked a ton of questions. Hell, we asked a ton of questions back. Same things, one answer. No other skid marks and no witnesses. They said he bled to death in the wreckage before anybody could get to him. And, there was evidently nothing left of the car after the fire."

"Well," I said, "the cops are looking at what happened yesterday. Maybe something'll come up that will make more sense. Something that explains what happened to Chris too."

"Look," said Jason. "Paul is ... shit, was, a lawyer with a big firm downtown. A lawyer for chrissake, straight arrow, successful guy. We used to kid him that a suit and tie would skip off every week and go hang out on the Island like a hippie. But that's who he was. So I don't know what happened yesterday any better than you do. But I don't want to think something crappy about him either."

"Neither do I," I said. "And I'm not thinking badly of him. But you all had your questions about the way Chris went; I just got back, so I'm allowed to have my questions too."

I could feel things were heating up between us. It was turning into me against the others again. Schoolyard nonsense long over. I tried to cool things off a little. I motioned the waitress over and ordered a round of drinks and paid for them when she returned.

"To Paul," I said, raising my glass.

Jason and Ron raised theirs and we clinked glasses. Mack sat sullenly for a moment longer, then sighed and lifted his to the rest.

"To Paul and Chris," he said quietly.

We all drank, quiet in our own thoughts.

*Saint Mary's had the best concrete anywhere. It was smooth and flawless with plenty of rolls and hills and even a decent pipe. It was like they'd designed it for boarding.*

*"C'mon," yelled Paul. He jumped on his board, the fibreglass flexing under his weight as he pushed hard with one leg to get up enough speed. Chris and I followed behind, trying to keep up with him. Paul was the best skateboarder of all of us. Mostly, we told ourselves, 'cause he had the best equipment. He had a brand-new rig his parents had bought him for his birthday from Rudy's Sport Shop. The coolest board with a flaming skull underneath, trick pad on the back, extra wide trucks, new urethane wheels and gorilla grip on top.*

*He launched himself into the pipe, sweeping from the top of one side, hanging motionless for a second, the twisting and zooming down to the middle and up the other side. At the far end of the pipe we'd set up a piece of plywood we'd found and raised it with some bricks. If you didn't have enough speed up when you got to it, the board would still be moving under the wood by the time you came down on other side. Or if you hit it too fast, the board would shoot out before you got to the end. Either way it hurt like a bitch.*

*Paul went roaring down the centre of the pipe, his hair flying behind him, bending his knees with his arms out beside him for balance. He didn't need the help though, he had perfect control. He always had.*

*Just as he got to the plywood, he bent lower and jumped straight up. His skateboard disappeared under the plywood as he soared over the top. He dropped down just as the scalloped fibreglass board appeared from under the wood. The board bent slightly when he landed on it. Paul had taught me to always land with your feet over the trucks just right. Otherwise, the board was liable to shimmy out from underneath you.*

*Chris flashed by me and did his jump. He almost didn't make it. He jumped too far forward and landed a few inches wrong on his board. He got it under control though and jumped off his board as he drew up beside Paul, snapping the tail of the board so that it stood on its end and he could grab it.*

*My turn came and I tried to make sure I did it right. I jumped up as I reached the platform. My old and scratched board disappeared from view. As I was coming down I saw the tip of it roll out from underneath the plywood. I landed just right, bending my knees to cushion the impact. As soon as I landed I tipped my weight back so the plastic pad screwed into the tail of the board scraped the concrete and slowed me down. I pulled up beside my friends, still doing a wheelie. They hollered and clapped as I skidded to a stop in front of them. Low fives and big grins. A three-G day. Glorious Goddamn Good Day.*

# Chapter 8

I am walking down a country road somewhere. There is no moon out, but my eyes have adjusted to the near darkness. The trees at the roadside rise high and branch out over the road cutting off the sky. It feels like I'm walking, or being drawn, down a natural tunnel. I don't know where I am, but I'm filled with a sense of purpose. Diffused light spills through the forest and illuminates shafts of mist, which cut the night.

I round a bend in the road and see a huge house about fifty yards on. The house is built from old weathered pine, stained gray with time. There is a series of Juliet balconies leading off French doors across the front of the second floor. The main body of the house is almost entirely dark. There is a screen door at the front of the house. It opens onto a corridor, which runs to the back. There is a single naked bulb hanging from a wire in the back room. Though it is the only light, it illuminates the corridor and sends a shaft of diffused yellow into the area I'm standing in. The mist swirls and eddies around my feet, then curls its way towards the house.

I can hear waves breaking somewhere, so I follow the sound away from the house and come upon a lake on the other side of a dune. I pick up some stones and chuck them into the water. The blackness of the lake is momentarily broken when the stones hit, sending up little white plumes, which disappear almost immediately. I feel rather than hear someone come up behind me. But when I turn to look there's no one there.

I stand and brush the sand off my pants. I stare at the lake for a moment more, then turn and climb the dune. The house rises in front of me as I clear the hill. It feels like the house is much closer than it was before, less than thirty feet away now, as if the house is somehow gravitating towards me.

Someone is pacing in the back room, the silhouette appearing momentarily in front of the light at the end of the corridor, and then moving out of sight again.

I move around the side of the house, trying to see inside the darkened rooms. I see the shapes of furniture, long fallen into disuse, covered in white sheets to protect them from time and dust.

When I round the back of the house, there is a large clearing surrounded by trees, which block out the night sky. In the centre of the clearing, there is a fire pit described by a circle of small stones. I walk towards the fire pit, but when I look there are only a few embers glowing weakly under a coating of ash.

I turn back to the house and...

I'm driving a car down a two-lane highway. It feels like cottage country, with the huge granite walls typical of Northern Ontario regularly rising up on both sides of the road. The guardrail on both sides is made up of four parallel wires tightly strung across two-foot high rough wooden posts. The road winds and twists, blind hills and turns. Then the road opens up. As I drive down a straight, flat piece of road I can see black lakes through the trees on either side. The road begins to curve to the left as it climbs another hill. As the headlights sweep across the shoulder, there is someone standing on the roadside. Chris, looks like Chris. He lifts his hand in greeting, his eyes following the approach of the car. I should stop and pick him up, but the car does not slow. The headlights illuminate his face and sweep by him. I look in the passenger side rear view mirror, the taillights bathing him in a horrid red glow. His features are distorted by the dim red light and heavy shadows play on his face, making his features appear sunken. It looks like his face is melting. I turn my attention back to the road as the headlights sweep across another figure standing on the shoulder, raised hand in hello...but then it's gone and in the passenger seat there's a silhouette turning...

I sat half upright in the bed, the tangled top sheet clutched in one rigid hand. My chest was covered in sweat and my heart was going like a trip-hammer. Weak morning sunlight illuminated the shabby bedroom. I reached over to the bedside table and fumbled out a cigarette, took a deep lung-full of smoke and let it rest there before exhaling slowly. My breath was still coming in little hitches. It was time to get out of this apartment.

# Chapter 9

She was a 47-foot Trojan from the early seventies. Built by Hatteras, she was one of the last wooden Trojans ever built. Good lines. I was familiar with her as I had crewed and then captained on a 65-foot Trojan in the Keys. She had a double plank mahogany hull on oak with a superstructure of fibreglass and a sizable fly bridge for sunny day cruising. The decks were teak but had not weathered especially well. No rot, but they needed to be stripped and sanded and resealed. The fibreglass foredeck was going to need some attention soon as well.

The sun bounced weakly off the heavily pitted brightwork railing that ran around the lower deck. The topside controls were in decent shape, protected by a white canvas canopy and though the fly bridge deck was scuffed and dirty, it would come up with a little effort. I turned the key and the panel came alive. I didn't turn the engines over; I wanted a look below decks before I did that. I hit the bilge switch and glanced over the side and aft. Dirty bilge water gouted out of the side and into the marina, but there wasn't a lot of it and it wasn't oily.

He was an oval-faced fellow, office white and office soft. His thinning hair was swept straight across in imitation of volume. Somewhere in his late forties, he was dressed in cream-coloured khakis and a white roll-neck knit sweater with deck shoes and no socks. Casual preppy marine. The only thing missing was a blue, peaked Greek captain's hat. It surprised me that someone who was around boats all the time wouldn't be a little more tanned and weathered. Brokering boats was obviously an avocation.

He told me that the elderly couple who owned her hadn't used her properly in six years. They evidently lived in a condo in the old Terminal Building at the foot of Bay about a block from the marina. Upscale shoppes and so-so restaurants on the first two floors; exclusive condos for six floors above that. The marina brought her out every year and floated her. Then the couple would come down from their nest for maybe two weekends a month and simply laze about. At the end of the season, the marina would lift her out and cradle her for the winter. The broker followed me as I inspected her from top to bottom, prattling on about the boat. It was obvious that even he was a little concerned about the shape she was in.

The fibreglass roof that was part and parcel of the superstructure covered half the aft deck. Four wicker wingback chairs surrounding a matching wicker table with a glass top sat on the teak deck. There was a sizable barbecue bolted to the rail with a large propane tank strapped to a stanchion below it.

The main salon was carpeted in medium pile gold carpet that showed some damage near the doors. A white and blue pull-out couch with two matching chairs, a blue jacquard wing chair and a low mahogany coffee table made up the main salon furnishings. The bulkheads on either side had sliding panels that held a few books and knick-knacks. There was also one of those small self-contained stereo units with a plugin for cell phone input. Beyond the salon the lower bridge panel had fared better than topside. I turned on the panel and the Ray/Jeff depth sounder came up. The VHF radio crackled a little with low static. I moved the gearshift levers and throttle controls back and forth a little, noting some slackness where there shouldn't have been any. I pointed it out to the broker, who sighed and smiled because he was making the same mental list that I was and it wasn't making him happy.

We went down a few stairs and moved through into the eating area and the galley. Hardly spacious, but it boasted a four-burner bottled-gas stove and a medium-sized fridge, and there was storage enough for cans and dry goods, pots, pans, crockery and glassware. There was a one-and-a-half sink to the right of the stove. I turned the faucets on and after a little sputtering the fresh water flowed out. I checked both hot and cold then, satisfied, shut them off. I went forward into the master stateroom, which was trimmed in mahogany accents with a huge clothes cupboard in the corner beside the bed. Finished in mahogany again and four posted — the mahogany posts were set seamlessly into the deck below and the bulkhead above. There was a matching desk on the port side with another

VHF and a now useless Loran set into the bulkhead. A small chart case was also set into the arrangement with a number of nautical charts rolled into tubes. The ensuite head was spacious and nicely appointed with a full-sized tub. The first guest stateroom was done in the same rich, dark wood as the master stateroom with a simpler, smaller bed and a freestanding armoire in the corner. Off to one side was a door that led to a three-piece ensuite head. The other stateroom was set up under the foredeck. I flipped open the bench seats and found all the gear to convert the benches into a triangular bed. There were two small sets of drawers set into the bulkhead on either side. Two hatchways, a small one for ventilation, and a larger one for emergencies were set in the ceiling and gave out onto the foredeck.

We made our way back to the main salon. I peeled back the edge of the carpeting and pulled open the trap door that led to the engine compartment and dropped down to have a look. There was a built-in 50-amp battery charger next to six fresh-looking batteries. Twin 440 Chryslers sat hulking, taking up almost the entire compartment. A 7.5 kW Onan generator squatted in the corner beside the heating/air-conditioning unit. The engines looked like they had been rebuilt. I pulled the sales sheet out of my back pocket, which assured me that they had been rebuilt two years earlier. Given that the elderly couple hadn't given her much use lately, they certainly wouldn't have that many hours on them since the rebuild.

After checking the fuel lines and battery hookups, I went back to the main controls, turned the key and fired her up. She huffed and complained but then turned over. A cloud of blue smoke pumped from the exhaust pipes, but after a few minutes, the exhaust turned a lovely light grey and I stopped thinking nasty thoughts about the piston rings. While she idled, I moved around the main deck feeling the throb of the engines underfoot, untying her and throwing the ropes onto the dock below.

I pulled her into reverse, and nursed away from the dock and pilings. I'm sure it was my imagination, but I thought I heard her sigh audibly. Happy to once again be out on the water. A boat tied up should only be a temporary state.

We trundled past the docking slips and into the inner harbour. She hadn't been out for a long time, so I kept the speed down to two knots. Chugging along leaving almost no wake, I looked at the Island across the harbour thinking of Paul, and felt a little unworthy.

As we made a large circle inside the harbour, gulls wheeled overhead and other small pleasure craft plied back and forth. During the circuit I checked the autopilot and depth sounder. After passing the Eastern Narrows we glided slowly past the concrete piers of the docklands while I listened for anything from the engines I didn't like. We came about and soon began to pass in front of the sugar refinery and the lakeside hotels. I moved up the rpms a little to test her a bit and the engines surged her forward. As we neared her docking, I brought her speed down again. I eased her in through the narrow entrance of the marina, past the other boats and outer slips until she was level with her own. I spun the wheel and set the left engine in reverse. She turned as if on a spindle and nestled into her docking space. After I cut the engines I jumped down to the dock and made her fast. The broker waited until I was back aboard to start the real pitch.

"So! She's a ready craft isn't she! A bit old, granted, but very affordable. You won't find another like her at this price," he said affably.

I pulled the sales sheet out of my back pocket. They were asking forty-nine thousand. It was a great price for the boat, but I hoped I could do a little better.

"Well, she is a good boat but she's over 40 years old." I sucked at my lower lip a little. "And it's going to need at least twenty-five thousand to put it right."

No, no. I wouldn't say nearly that much. Ten thousand at the most," he protested.

"When was the last time the bottom was hauled?"

"Well, I…I'm not exactly sure but I can easily find out for you. I could contact you through your agent…"

"I have no agent. The bottom is going to have to be stripped and refinished and re-coated. The decks will have to be totally redone. The foredeck has to be stripped and re-caulked. The throttle and steering cables have to be pulled and replaced. The interior is almost all original, which is quaint, but most of it will have to be replaced. The engines have been rebuilt, but hardly used. That means they haven't been pushed at all, so I don't know how good the rebuild was. You're welcome to have a marine and mechanical survey done, but that's what it needs for starters."

"Well," he backpedaled, "I'm sure the owners have taken all that into account given the low asking price."

"How long has the boat been on the market?"

"I believe just this year."

"Well, it's coming up to end of season. If they want to sell her this year then I'm willing to offer thirty-one thousand. I'll want a title search and the marine survey thrown in."

He stiffened perceptibly. Probably because I had just chewed through a considerable part of the percentage he had been looking forward to.

"Mr. Birnam, I can assure you that though, as you say, the boat needs some attention, I'm quite sure the owners will not go to that price."

"We both know they don't use her much. We both know most people don't want a boat this old. We both know most people don't want one with a wooden hull – too heavy. I'm here and I'm serious. Give them a call from your office. I'll wait right here. And tell them I'm also willing to offer more than half in cash as a show of good faith."

His appraisal of me changed suddenly. Maybe he had been a little hasty in his earlier assessment of me. He said he would find out but assured me again of his lack of confidence. He retreated to his shore side office while I took another look.

She was definitely a good piece of boat, and with a little elbow grease and application, she could be beautiful. Putting that much money down was going to take a big bite out of what I had come home with. The money I'd saved working under the table was sizable, for me anyway. It was a lot to put down all at once, but I didn't think I was going to find a better deal any time soon.

I hopped down onto the dock and walked over the suspension bridge connecting Harbourfront with Pier 4. His office was in the low pier building beside the docking slips. I could see him through the window talking desultorily on the phone. He saw me coming, said a few words I couldn't make out through the open window, and cradled the receiver.

His office was comfortable with the usual nautical nonsense hanging on the paneled walls. There was a fake fishing net with brightly coloured glass floats and a row of desiccated cork floats strung like a necklace on a piece of grey rope. There was a harpoon affixed to the wall behind his desk. A couple of antique-y brass running lights sat on the filing cabinet. His desk was awash in paper.

"As I thought Mr. Birnam, the owners are not very happy with dropping the price so much. They would be willing to go to forty-two thousand, but that's as low as they want to go."

"Alright, I understand," I said. I did some fast calculations in my head. "Tell them I'll go to 38 solid." I watched his eyes narrow a little. I wondered if he might take the bait. "Because I don't have an agent, that means you get to keep the entire commission. The usual is what, two-and-a-half points? So take three-and-a-half and put the rest against the purchase price. I'll let you sell them on the deal. You and the owners can fill out the papers at any final value you want. With your commission based on asking or actual, whatever. I won't be reporting to anybody what I paid for her."

He began to reach for his cellphone again. "But," I said, "I still want the marine and mechanical surveys and title search supplied. And for the extra money I'll want the docking fees paid through until next August. The tie ups are year-round here, yes? Good. And for all this, I'll give them half of the agreed upon price in cash tomorrow with the balance to be financed. You have the necessary information to arrange for the financing. And I'll want you to arrange a line of credit secured against the craft to pay for the repairs. Let's keep it all under one umbrella."

He couldn't help himself from smiling involuntarily. I didn't want to haggle any more than I had. It was the best that I could offer and I didn't think I could push any farther.

As he began to make the call I said "I'll leave you to it. You have my number. After you work out the details with them I'll come back whenever and we can discuss the transfer."

I left his office hoping the extra spring in my step didn't show too much. I crossed the bridge again and looked down on her from above. She would be a beautiful boat if someone would give her the care she deserved. I freed the helmet from the lock mounted under the seat and pulled it on. I started the bike and took one last look at her as I put my gloves on. When the revs calmed to idle, I dropped the bike into first and drove up Queen's Quay, heading for downtown.

# Chapter 10

When we were kids, our scout troop visited the local police station on a field trip. It had been a small neighbourhood station with tall polished oak doors letting onto a massive wooden desk that seemed forty feet high when we were small. There had been hard wooden benches flanking the waiting area. I could still remember how when one of the cops had asked us all some question, Chris had given him a smart aleck answer and I had laughed. The cop had smiled and said why didn't we all follow him to check out the cells. It was a small station with four holding cells in the basement. The cop invited Chris and me to go into one of the cells and see how small it was. As soon as we went in, he closed and locked the gate behind us, rattling the door to show the others how secure it was. Then he had invited everyone to another part of the station and left Chris and me there for the balance of the tour. We were probably only in there for fifteen minutes, but we started hollering after two. When the cop came back to let us out, he knew by the looks on our faces that he'd made his point.

The police station I was walking into that afternoon could have fit the entire station from my youth in its lobby. Revolving doors gave way to a polished terrazzo floor with a large brass Metropolitan Police logo set into the middle of it. Uniformed and plain-clothed officers moved quickly past me, disappearing down corridors and into offices. I walked up to the desk sergeant. I hadn't known where to begin when I had called, but somebody at the police switchboard suggested I talk to the homicide squad out of 52 Division.

The sergeant glanced up from his paperwork. He was a beefy guy in his early fifties with a red face, mutton chop sideburns and a thick mustache.

"Good morning, I said, "Could I see the detective in charge of the accidental death on the Island the other day?"

"May I ask the nature of your business? Do you have information concerning the accident?" He spoke in the practiced and clipped manner of every police officer I had ever met. And he had the same unmistakable accent of my father.

"Newcastle?' I asked.

He cocked his head and then beamed at me. "Pretty good," he said.

"My father was a Geordie," I said, returning the smile.

"Good for him! Now, who was it you were wanting to see then?"

"I don't know. The man who died on the Island was an old friend of mine."

"Well, give me half a minute and I'll find out for ye."

He motioned me to take a seat in the waiting area and picked up the desk phone. After a brief conversation, he called over to say somebody would be with me by and by. The bustle in the station continued unabated as I sat wondering how to approach the problem.

In my limited time on the cops, we were taught to be a closed-mouth bunch except with our own kind. It came with the job. I had been one of that kind but that was unlikely to curry any favour. Too short a time and too long ago. But if they thought you might have something helpful, they were trained to cozy you until they knew what it was.

A man in shirtsleeves came out of one of the offices and walked up and talked to the desk sergeant. I saw the sergeant nod in my direction and I stood as the man walked toward me. He looked to be about forty, as tall as my six feet and fit. His shirt had two vertical creases down the front, military style. His tie was still done up and his shirtsleeves were rolled up over his forearms. I tried for friendly and stuck out my hand as he strode up.

"Jonathan Birnam."

"Detective Kelly." His handshake was firm and dry. "What can I do for you Mr. Birnam? I understand the deceased was a friend of yours. I'm sorry. Is there something you can tell me that would help us with our investigation?"

"Well, in truth," I said, "I don't have any information for you, but I wondered if you might have some for me."

He folded his arms across his chest, cocked his head and said. "Really? Well, we'll see. Exactly what were you hoping for? You probably realize we're not big on talking about open cases around here."

"I assumed as much. I guess the thing is, I don't believe that my friend died by accident and I wondered if you did."

He stared at me for a moment. "Perhaps we should talk. My office is this way." He led me down a hall with offices on either side. Phones rang, doors opened and slammed shut. We came to a door with his name stenciled in black lettering on the stippled glass. He opened the door for me and motioned me to sit.

"Something to drink? Coffee, water?"

I said no thanks and he said he'd be back in minute. It was more like twenty. His office was neat. Two steel filing cabinets sat in the corner with a potted fern on top. There were citations and diplomas framed on the wall behind the desk, which looked like it had been organized with a T-square. Everything was perfectly aligned to the edges. There was a silver picture frame off to one side with a smiling blond woman and a couple of towheaded children. A phone with fifteen or so lines sat on the desk blotter, the lights winking on and off intermittently. The light in the room came from an overhead warehouse-style lamp and through a bank of glass bricks to the left of the desk.

I heard the door open behind me and he came back in apologizing for keeping me waiting. He had a mug of steaming coffee and a couple of pieces of paper stapled together, which he put inside a file folder on his desk.

"Now, then," he said, leaning back in his chair and absentmindedly twirling a pencil in one hand, "You said you don't think your friend died by accident. What do you mean by that?"

"Exactly what I said. It's none of my business as far as you're concerned, I know that Detective. I've been away for a long time. I came back because another friend of mine, Christopher Allinson, died about three weeks ago. I didn't make it back for the funeral. I've been back less than a week and lost another friend, the second one inside of a month. The coincidence is bothering me."

"I see. And I'm sorry to hear about your other friend. But what exactly are you basing your assumptions on? Do you have evidence that we should know about?"

"No, I don't. That's why I came to see you."

"And why would I know?"

"'Cause you're a big city cop." His face clouded over and I thought we were done. Then he realized I was kidding him, and his face broke into a grin.

"Yup, that's right. I am a big city cop. Got a badge and everything. It's official. So you'll forgive me Mr. Birnam …"

"Jonathan."

He nodded. "Jonathan. You'll forgive me Jonathan if I have a little trouble understanding what you're basing any of this on. I should also add that I realize that you're upset over the loss of your two friends, but without anything to go on, I don't know what I can do for you. Our investigation is proceeding and when we know more, I'm sure the papers and TV will carry it."

"Can I ask what happened on the Island? What I've been told and what I read online…"

"Told by who?"

"Whom," I said, smiling. "The objective form of who. Whom."

He gave me a half smile and said, "Love having my grammar corrected."

I grinned and said, "My old friends all kept in touch while I was gone. I saw them the other night and one of them told me. Laura, Paul's wife, called and told him what happened."

"I see. And this man's name would be…?"

I shrugged. "An old friend. What I'm wondering is whether you're treating Paul Hobbs' death as an accident or as something else."

He opened the file folder on his desk and pulled out the sheets of paper. "Jonathan Parker Birnam. 195 centimeters, 180 pounds. Brown hair, green eyes. No distinguishing marks or tattoos. No criminal or arrest record."

He began to rattle off my education and the years. "Graduated high school. Joined Army Reserves same year. University of Toronto, HBSc Criminology. Applied to Metropolitan Police Academy following graduation. Accepted for enrollment August same year. Did the 24 and did them well. Graduated 4th class Constable. Two years working your way up. Good arrests, clean service. Wrote the detectives exam. Before you could be promoted you quit. No reason given. Quit reserves same year, again no reason given. After that …?" He dropped the papers and spread his hands. "After that, I have no record for you. No address, no telephone number. Where did you say you were Jonathan?"

"I didn't." I paused and smiled. "I figured you'd still have my information on file."

"Well, that's almost far back enough to have been on the microfilm records. But I hear we're almost caught up with digitizing everything." He placed the papers back in the file folder. "Seems you leave a lot of things without explaining why."

"Uh-huh. Well, Detective Kelly, I won't take up any more of your time." I stood to leave.

"Jonathan, we were just getting started, I thought. Have a seat and we'll talk more about all of this."

"I'll come back maybe, when I have more to bring you."

His voice dropped 10 degrees. "Mr. Birnam, do you need reminding you left the academy? You're not an officer. I hope I don't have to tell you not to interfere with this case in any way."

"Probably not."

"Probably not isn't good enough."

"Well, Detective. I leave a lot of things with no reason given. But I have a knack for being a pain in the ass and I'm without purpose these days." I stood and took my jacket off the back of the chair.

He looked at my levelly. "Don't be a pain in *any* ass that involves homicides under my purview ... "

I nodded and left but by the time I got out to the sidewalk I knew it had been an amateur play. I had learned absolutely nothing, and had probably only succeeded in pissing off a Detective. I hadn't learned a thing about Paul or Chris, all I knew was that they still had me on record.

Maybe they should simply microchip us when we're born. Somewhere convenient like on the back of the hand. Then whenever someone needs information about us — have our credit checked; find out what our grade point average was; what our sexual predilection is — simply scan the chip. Tell you everything you need to know. There is absolutely no way to escape the all-seeing eye. Orwell only missed it by a few decades.

I drove back to the apartment in the late afternoon. When I had showered, changed into some old shorts and had a cold beer in hand, I checked my phone. It seemed they had another way to trace me. I was now the proud owner of the Trojan.

# Chapter 11

"Friends, family members, will you please bow your heads," the minister intoned. His words echoed through the vaulted openness of the stone church. St. Johns' Anglican sat high above the Hollow mostly screened by tall pines and maples from the ugliness the Hollow had become. When I had grown up not far from here, the Hollow, a valley in the north of the city, had contained an exclusive enclave of old homes in one corner and diagonally across York Mills Road in the opposite corner, a golf course. In the centre of the Hollow was the huge white building with the grandiose fountain in front, The 4000 Apartments, where until recently Chris' mother had lived; and across the street, the Jolly Miller, a tavern from the turn of the century. That was it. But that was a long time ago. Now it was filled to capacity with condominiums and uninspired office buildings. What had been mostly trees and ravines and dirt paths to ride a bicycle on had become polarized glass, rebar and stressed concrete.

Inside the cool of the church, the service continued. Paul's casket was polished oak and brass; a wreath of lilies and greenery lay atop the coffin. The nave of the church glowed with candles and resonated with solemnity. I was sitting in a pew up front with Mack, Jason and Ron along with two other pallbearers who worked in Paul's office. I glanced behind me, scanning the crowd quickly and saw Katherine, Jeff and the kids a few rows back and across the aisle. Jeff lifted his chin in hello and Katherine gave me a half-smile. Laura, whom I had met only an hour before, sat with her children in the pew across from us. Behind her were Paul's parents and beside them, another elderly couple I took to be Laura's folks. There were a lot of faces I didn't recognize. The ushers who had directed everybody to their places were evidently more work colleagues.

The minister finished the formal part of the service and began to bring it to a close.

"I know that Laura would want to thank you all for coming," he said. "Looking around this church, I see that Paul was rich in the manner in which we should all be blessed." He nodded his head toward her and the kids. "Rich in the love of family."

Then he spread his arms to encompass the rest of the congregation. "Rich in the comfort of friends. And now, he is with our almighty Lord, rich in His care. May the spirit of the Lord be with you."

"And also with you," returned the assembled.

"May the peace of God which passeth all understanding, keep your hearts and minds in the love of God. And in doing so, make His spirit to shine upon you, and keep you in his everlasting care."

"Amen," said everyone but me.

The organist began to play a psalm as the six of us stood. The congregation stood up with us and watched silently as we lifted the casket off of the wheeled trolley and began the procession through the church. As we reached the back of the church, I looked over to the far side of the last pew and saw Detective Kelly with his head bowed.

We passed out of the dark cool of the church and into the warmth and sunlight of a bright afternoon. I could hear Laura and the kids walking behind us, crying. We moved slowly down the stairs, trying to keep the casket level. At the base of the stairs we set it on the edge of the rollers lying in the bed of the hearse. The driver and attendant rolled it in, secured it, and closed the rear door.

We stood with our arms around each other's shoulders for a moment as the hearse moved to the front of the procession and waited for the rest of the mourners. Mack left to ride with Laura and the kids in a waiting limousine and Ron and Jason said they would see me at the cemetery and went off to Jason's car.

"Mr. Birnam … ?"

I turned to find Kelly standing behind me. "Jonathan, Detective. And it was good of you to come. You knew the funeral was today?"

"Well, us big city cops are not without resources."

"Never thought you weren't."

"About the other day…"

"Detective, I appreciate your coming. And I'd like to talk more as well but another time. Not the time, not the place."

He tilted his head slightly. "You're right. Another time."

"Are you coming to the interment?"

"No, I have to get back."

I pulled out a pen and a piece of paper from my wallet. I wrote down the address of the apartment.

"I'll be here for one more day. After that I'll let you know where I'll be." I allowed myself a smile. "You can add it to my file."

He nodded and put the piece of paper in his jacket pocket. We shook hands and I turned and left him standing in front of the church steps. I got into the rental car I had taken for the occasion and followed the procession of cars down the long driveway to watch them lower my friend into the hard ground.

# Chapter 12

Mack had closed The Breakers for the night and we were all there for the wake. A lot of people from the last few years of high school, now with spouses and kids, even a few old teachers had shown up. Laura had tried to pass on the evening, but Mack had evidently talked her into it. Now she was smiling for the first time all day, stroking the hair of her kids absent-mindedly while they slept on the banquette beside her and talking with her parents and in-laws. I had been introduced to Ron and Jason's wives, both of who said they had heard all about me. Countered with the usual don't believe everything you hear. Parried with oh don't worry, it wasn't very nice anyway.

It was tiring answering the same questions with the same replies. I stepped outside and took a table to myself on the patio with a fresh bourbon. The amber liquid moved sinuously through crushed ice as I leaned back in the chair and lit a cigarette and exhaled towards the sky. There was the sound of a woman clearing her throat and then I heard a familiar voice behind me.

"Haven't you given that up yet?"

Jesus.

*The mirrored ball revolved over our heads throwing dots of light everywhere - the floor, the ceiling, on the faces of the everyone dancing, on the faces of the ones lining the walls of the gym. She had her hands around my neck; I had my hands in the small of her back. Crinkled paper streamers spread out from above the spinning ball, draping gently, and then rising to the catwalk and the running track that ran around the upper level of the gym. The music pounded down us from the speakers set high on stands flanking the DJ.*

*"Every love song… on every TV,*
*And Hollywood told me… it should be beautiful and sweet,*
*Like watching Soul Train… with Marvin Gaye on,*
*But baby it hurts to love you,*
*Baby hurts to need you too…."*

Spring dance. Last dance of the year. The end of the school year was about five weeks away. The doors to the gym were open and every once in a while; a warm evening breeze would wash in and lift the streamers slightly.

"What are you thinking about?"

I had to bend closer to hear what she said clearly. "What am I thinking about?" I repeated.

"Yes," she said slowly in exaggeration. "What…are…you…thinking …about?"

"Um, I don't know." I had to practically shout over the music. " I was thinking about the summer. You know, jobs and all that. Have you decided what you're doing for the summer?"

"Well, kinda. My parents said if my grades were good enough this year, they were maybe going to pay for a course in Italy. An art course. My Mom says it's not that expensive. The school over there has a dorm and everything. It would be kinda like camp."

Yeah, except the camp would be in Europe. My heart sank, but I tried not to let it show.

"Really? Italy. Wow, the whole summer?".

"No, not the whole summer. Just seven weeks."

Seven weeks! "Oh, just seven weeks." Mr. Cool. "What about the rest of the summer?"

Oh, probably hang around the house, maybe go to my cousin's cottage for a week or something. What about you?"

"Like I said, I'm still thinking about it. My folks say I have to get a job. Pull my share and stuff. You know, maybe house painting or landscaping or something."

She knew there wasn't the kind of money in my family for European art schools so she nodded her head enthusiastically at my plans to be responsible.

A breeze floated in from the open doors and pushed wisps of her hair in front of her face. I reached up and hooked them back behind her ear again, feeling the downy softness of her neck as my hand brushed past. She laughed and grabbed my hand and

*spun herself out on my arm in a little pirouette. I smiled and turned her around the*
*small space on the dance floor we had to ourselves.*
*…Baby it hurts to love you…baby it hurts to need you too…*


What do you do when your past walks up behind you and taps you on the
shoulder? I could almost hear the Fates snickering in the corner.

I stood and turned around slowly. "Well, I've got to have one or two vices left,
don't I? Just to keep me interesting?" I turned all the way around as I finished
speaking, smiling a grin so wide that it threatened to cleave the top of my head off.

"And are you under the impression that's it's your vices that make you interesting?"

Tara smirked at me with an arched eyebrow. She'd hardly changed at all. Some
new laugh lines around her brown eyes and wide mouth. Her matching brown
hair was no longer curly but long and straight with a little gray working its way in.
I was pleased to see she wasn't doing anything about it. She looked trim and lush
all at the same time. Looking at her made me feel like it always had, as if the air
around us was cleaner, the light around us purer. I opened my arms and she
stepped into them. We hugged for what seemed like an eternity and it wasn't
enough. She broke gently from our embrace.

"So, you gonna buy a pretty girl a drink, or what?"

"Oh, I'm sorry," I said. I scanned the patio with my hand to my eyebrows. "Is
there a pretty girl here?" She jabbed me in the solar plexus. The air whooshed out
of me and we both laughed. I pulled out the chair opposite mine and held it for
her while she sat.

"Well," she said. "I see some things have changed. Quite the gentleman now…"
I moved around the table and sat down across from her. "I was always a
gentleman," I protested.

She laughed the way I remembered, spiritedly, with her whole self. "You were
many things Jon, but gentleman wasn't one of them."

Oh, really," I said. "Well then, things have changed. I'm very cultured now." I
said, affecting an English accent. "Quite the gentleman, if I may say."

She laughed again. The waitress saw my signal and Tara ordered a white wine
spritzer.

"Really? A spritzer? Perhaps with dinner we can order an unassuming little Chardonnay. Something citrussy, yet gentle on the palate with just a hint of oak and an undercurrent of the sun-dappled grassy meadow across the river? And then you can destroy it by adding soda."

"I was unaware we were dining together. And I had no idea you had become so uncouth on your travels. Isn't travel supposed to broaden one's horizons? Don't you know that to be truly cosmopolitan, you need to embrace all that the noble grape has to offer?"

"I'm all for enjoying the noble grape, I'm just against destroying it with fizzy water and fruit."

"Oh, shut up" she said laughing. The waitress arrived with her drink and put it down in front of her. She picked up her wineglass and grandly made to leave. "I think I'll find someone less barbaric to drink with."

I reached up and grabbed her arm. Touching her skin galvanized me the way it always had. Like tiny electric shocks running across the surface of my palm. She looked down at my hand with that mischievous arched eyebrow, smiling. She lowered herself back into her seat. When she took her first sip, she stared at me over the rim of her glass. I felt like a fifteen-year-old on a date with an experienced woman. She had a way to make me feel foolish and blessed. The patio seemed to dim, the other conversations muted.

"So," I started. "You've been back since May?"

"You seem well informed. Have you been stalking me?"

No, just trying not to think about you, I thought. I explained what Jeff and Katherine had told me.

"Oh, that's right! I was talking with Katherine at Chris' funeral. I was there, out west for ..." she paused and tilted her head, counting up the time, "eleven years. When you say it like that it seems so long. I guess it was a long time," she said, looking down at the table.

"Yeah, a lot of time has gone by. A lot has happened."

She nodded in agreement and looked through the windows into the bar. I could see her eyes coming to rest on Laura and her kids. "Yes, a lot has happened. Jon, I'm sorry about Paul. And about Chris too."

I shrugged. "Thanks. I wish to hell I'd talked to both of them before, but it didn't work out. Anyway, tell me about you. What's been going on with you."

"Well, let's see." She began to tick the points off on her fingertips. "I've been married to the wrong man. I've been from one end of the country to the other. Both my Mom and Dad have died. I'm getting divorced and I'm living in my parent's house." She laughed too brightly and looked up from the table with her eyes shining. "Gee, am I leaving anything out?"

I reached across the table and lay my hand on her forearm not knowing what to say.

"Sorry, Jon," she said. "I guess it's just the day. The funeral. Funerals," she corrected.

"Hey," I said, "let's take a walk?" She nodded, so I fished a twenty out of my wallet and slipped it under the bottom of my glass. As we stood, I saw Mack look over at us from inside, his face etched with an ear-to-ear grin. I winked at him and Tara and I went out into the night.

We ambled slowly along Queen Street. It was just after closing time for the stores. I could see the shopkeepers behind their locked doors counting the day's receipts at the tills. There weren't many people on the streets, but there was a fair bit of traffic cruising up and down, so we wandered south towards the lake down a side street, the lovely Beach homes lining each side. Most of the area had been settled in the early twenties. Some of the homes were grand old family places while others were tiny converted former cottages that had been built near the turn of the previous century as lakeside retreats. We walked without speaking, the quiet rustling of the trees replacing conversation. At the bottom of the street, there was a small park that separated the houses from the boardwalk. Tara and I crossed the park and turned east, away from the city lights, walking slowly down the wide wooden boardwalk that followed the curve of the beach. The lake was calm with little waves cresting ten feet out and then bringing small foam up to the sand. Tara was first to break the silence.

"So you've been away for a long time as well. You never came to visit me on your way?"

When I had lived in the mountains and then in Vancouver I'd always known where she was. In my more honest moments with myself, I would admit why I'd headed that way. How can you keep something beyond arm's reach without knowing where it is?

"I knew where you and Daniel were living. I got your letter before I left, but I … I guess I just never found the time. You know … I worked as much as I could when I was out west so I could finance going down to the States, and…" my voice trailed off. It wasn't any easier to say to her now what I couldn't say to her then.

"No, no I understand," she said letting me off the hook. "I know you would have come to visit if you could have." Her words seemed filled with understanding. "You got the invitation didn't you?"

I shook my head noncommittally without saying anything. "Mmmm, I thought so. I was sure you would come if you'd gotten it. It wasn't the same not having you at the wedding," she laughed. "Maybe it was an omen."

I smiled at her weak joke but didn't reply.


*The rain had finally let up. It had been drizzling incessantly for four days. But that's what it did on the coast. It just rained. Suited my mood. I had the invitation in my breast pocket. Jesus I just couldn't escape her. No way. I wanted to, but no way. So I stood leaning against the bike as the limo pulled up at the bottom of the stone steps. The street was bathed in sunshine. The rain had made everything clean and new for her day. The bike and I were in the mouth of the alley, a dark line of shadow separating me from the bright white stucco church across the street.*

*The bells began to peal as the doors opened and everybody poured out, forming two groups on either side of the stairs. I pulled the collar of my jacket a little higher and hunkered my chin down a little farther. Everyone started throwing rice as the couple stepped from inside the church and into the sunlight. The groom smiled broadly and shook hands with his best man and the minister. The bride hugged her bridesmaids, then the bridal party all posed for pictures; the photographer moving from vantage point to vantage point taking shots from all angles. She was wearing an understated off-white dress. No veil, no train, no crinoline. She had some kind of wrap around her shoulders. Her hair was up with wisps trailing down to frame her face. A casual breeze blew one of those wisps across her face. The groom smiled at her and hooked the wisp of hair behind her ear. Behind my sunglasses, my eyes stung and my chest was tight with want.*

*After the photographer was through, the couple linked arms and descended the steps. The bride lifted the hem of her dress slightly as she negotiated the stairs, exposing the promise of her tanned calf. When they reached the bottom of the steps, the bride turned her back to the crowd and threw the bouquet backward to the throng. The groom bent down, out of sight behind the limo, the bride looking down at him and laughing. He popped up again with her garter taut between his hands and snapped the elastic up into the crowd.*

*Everyone cheered as the couple kissed long and deep and then bent their heads to get into the car. The limo started up and drove slowly away as everyone descended the steps of the church waving at the receding car.*

*I sat astride the bike and kicked the sidestand up with my heel. It was time to leave. I checked to make sure the big pack, tent and sleeping bag were strapped on tight and turned the key. The border was only forty minutes away. I made it in twenty-five.*

"Yeah," I said. "I'm sorry I couldn't go, but I was already on my way south when I heard. And I'm sorry it didn't work out for you two."

"Don't be. I'm not. No, no, it wasn't terrible. He didn't hit me or cheat on me, at least not as far as I know." She paused and sighed.

"You know, our first year or so was wonderful. We had this little apartment. It small and awful but it was ours. We were both working. We didn't make much but it didn't matter, we were happy. Then Daniel got this great opportunity at work. They put him in charge of his entire division and he started working all these hours. He was really proud of his position and he got this huge raise. We moved into a bigger apartment, in a high-rise on the harbour. After a year or so we bought a house. It was a cliché. He, the successful businessman and me the bright, shining wife."

I watched her face as she talked it out. She was looking beyond me, recounting the time.

"After a while, Daniel was making enough that I didn't have to work. We talked about starting a family. So I quit my job and played house."

"Did you quit because you wanted to or because he wanted you to?"

"I don't know." She smiled to herself and lifted an eyebrow. "That's the question I guess, because that's when things started … started being … I don't know, not great. Anyway, we tried to get pregnant and we couldn't." She paused for moment as we continued walking. "We saw specialists and there were drugs to take …" she laughed, "these weird exercises and … anyway it, um, it never did take, I guess."

She was silent again for a time. I didn't break the quiet. We were coming up to the Leuty lifeguard shack, the only building on this stretch of sand. She banged her shoulder into mine to push me off the boardwalk and we walked down to the water's edge, wobbling in the soft sand in the dark. There was an off-leash dog run near the lifeguard shack with some large flat stones beyond it at the water's edge. We stepped over a tumbled-down bit of plastic fencing and picked our way across the sand. We sat down next to each other on a wide slab of rock, quiet, and stared out at the lake.

"So anyway," she said finally, "Daniel was working crazy hours and I was lost inside this big house. We started to see less and less of each other. He was coming home late, you know, we'd talk a little but then it was bedtime, and our … well, trying for kids … had made … well, things changed there too and …"

I nodded to try and help her from being embarrassed. It happens to the best marriages. Expectations and pressures begin to take the joy out of the pure physical. What used to be healthy and thrilling becomes mundane and mechanical. What used to enliven the spirit becomes a reminder of how it used to be. Eventually you realize that maybe it's nothing more than the difficulty of splitting, of telling the family and deciding what is whose, that keeps couples from doing what they really should. Maybe, if there is such a caveat, in any emotional situation the hardest thing to do is usually the right thing to do.

"So after a while, I moved to another bedroom, and Daniel worked even harder. We'd have these dinner parties for his work and they'd all talk and laugh about people and things that I didn't know about. We were strangers to each other. We had to come back last year for my mother and when we got back to the coast, I think we both knew that it was over. I just … took a few things that were special … and here I am." She smoothed hands down her thighs roughly, as if to slough off bad memories.

"OK, your turn. Make me laugh."

So I told her what I had done with the last decade of my life. And I made her laugh. I invented crazy characters, exaggerated victories and underplayed failures. I made myself the hero in countless happenings and spun the life that I had looked for rather than the one I had lived.

"…so I was in Chicago, and I heard about Chris. I was thinking about heading home anyway, and that sealed it."

"And now what are you doing? You've been back what, a week? Do you have a place to stay?"

I took her question as innocent, though I wanted an implication.

"Yeah," I said, "I'm covered." I didn't want ~~her~~ to tell her about the boat yet. "I don't know yet what I'm going to do. I have money saved so I don't have to rush into anything yet."

"But what will you do?"

It was like old times again. We were a couple of teenagers talking about summer jobs in specific and life in general.

"Jesus babe, I don't know. I haven't held the same job for more than a couple of years my entire adult life. I've never really worked for anyone before. Yeah, there were foremen and owners and captains and people above me, but every job I had I pretty much worked alone. Went my own way. If I was taking groups into the mountains, I was in charge. When I first got to the States, I spent more than half a year fixing up an old hunting lodge in the high ground for a developer and didn't see or talk to anyone except when I went in for supplies."

"How long were you by yourself?" Tara asked.

I thought about the time. "Uh, it took me almost eight months to rebuild the place."

"Eight months! You were alone in the mountains for eight months? My God, what did you do?"

"Wrote my manifesto, stockpiled ammunition ..."

She laughed and bashed my knee with her hand. "I'm serious, what did you do?"

"I don't know, I worked, I guess. The place was a disaster and it took a long time. I finished fixing the roof and the outside walls before the snow came. And then during the winter I redid the interior, the electrical, the plumbing. Sometimes ..." and I stopped myself.

"Sometimes, what?"

I paused. "Well, sometimes, the repair you need to do on yourself is best reflected by repairing something else."

She was silent as she thought. Then she looked away from me and at the water, nodding her head in understanding. "And you were alone the whole time?"

"Yeah. But I don't mind being alone. When I worked charter, I didn't deal with the owners except occasionally back on shore. I like being self-reliant. So whatever I do from here on in, it's going to have to involve being self-sufficient."

"Autonomy?"

"Exactly. Being entirely responsible for yourself, answering only to yourself. Nobody looking after you and nobody in control of you."

"Doesn't sound like it leaves room for anybody else," Tara said.

"Sure it does," I replied. "I'm not saying there's no room for anybody else. But I think that somehow, you've got to make yourself independent of others. What they think of you, how you earn your living, whatever. If you don't live your life freely, then you make yourself beholden to others. And I don't want to be beholden to anyone."

"Why not?"

"Maybe because the only person I can trust is me."

Tara laughed. "That's a little heavy, isn't it?"

I smiled back in return. "OK, OK maybe a little. But how many times have you made decisions based not on what you wanted, or what you thought was best, but on what somebody else wanted."

"Lots of times," she said, shrugging her shoulders.

"And how did those work out?"

"I don't know, sometimes good, sometimes not so good."

"So how would those moments have worked out if you'd gone your own way?"

"Who knows?" she answered. "Maybe better, maybe worse. But you can't go through your life being that selfish. I mean, how could anyone live with that?"

"Maybe the right person would let you live your life on your own terms. Maybe you need to be sure of what's important to you. See yourself in terms of you and not someone else."

"I've never had that. I was always somebody's daughter, or somebody's girlfriend, or somebody's wife."

"Well, if you want it, now's your chance."

"I don't think I can do that."

"Why not? What's to stop you?"

"It's easier for you," she said quietly.

"Why should it be easier for me?"

"Because you've always been that way. When we were kids, I spent all my time going to parties, or cottages, or I was away doing things that my parents paid for. You were always here doing summer jobs. You put yourself through college. You always struggled. And you always kind of scared me."

"What do you mean I scared you?"

"I don't know, Jon. You had this ability to focus completely on what you wanted. If you wanted something, you never wavered. You went after it until you got it."

"Not everything …" I said, looking hard at her.

She saw me staring and smiled uncertainly. There was a small silence and then Tara looked away.

"That was so long ago," she said.

I leaned closer and whispered, "Not for me it wasn't."

"You really did scare me, you know."

"Why did I scare you? Because …"

"Because you were so … so fierce about everything."

"No I wasn't," I said, staring at the foam at the water's edge.

She put her hand and my arm and squeezed gently. "Yes, Jon. Yes, you were. Maybe you don't remember, but I do. You were so focused on being, I don't know, the person you wanted to be I guess, that you overshadowed whoever you were with."

"What, the pure and unyielding force of my incredible personality?"

She laughed and shook her head at me. I tried to smile back but our conversation was getting too close to the dangerous places I didn't want to tread near. I tried to joke about it.

"I was just too much was I? I always knew I was too much."

"Well, you were too much for me," Tara said.

That was it. It was out of the cage now.

"Well why didn't you tell me that, then."

"I tried. Maybe I didn't try hard enough. I didn't know I just …" she paused, taking a deep breath. "I know now after spending my life seeing myself in terms of other people, my parents, my ex-husband, you're absolutely right, it's time to …"

"Time to …"

"To take control of my life. Of me. I need to feel like I can manage to … like I'm capable of being my own person. Like I can give myself the things I need to be happy. That I can choose my path. I've got a new job starting in September. I'm going back to teaching."

"Really?" I said.

She nodded her head excitedly. "Art, French and English at a small independent school near my parent's … near my house. I've got to know again that I can look after myself."

"Autonomy?"

She smiled quietly at me and nodded. "Yes, autonomy."

I smiled back and held out my hand. She looked at it for a moment and then tentatively put her hand in mine.

"I'm sorry if I scared you. That wasn't my intention. Believe me, I definitely had other intentions."

She laughed quietly. "And what are your intentions now?"

"Well, I can say with a fair degree of certainty, they're still not honourable."

She laughed again and squeezed my hand.

"You should understand something. A long time ago, OK I came on … a little strong. Though it seems not strong enough because…" I shrugged my shoulders and smiled. "I had a sense then that maybe ... I don't know, maybe I realize now that it was too much. Too much for ..."

"Jon, we were kids then."

"I know that. I know that," I said nodding my head. "And now we're not. Listen to me, you deserve the truth." I waved my hand generally out to the water. "I've been mostly stumbling around out there since I left. I've had some good times and I've learned a lot. I've had some lousy times too when I didn't learn enough. But I'm back, and I'm back to stay. I'm getting settled in again. And there are some things I have to take care of first. Maybe after I'm done, if you let me, I want to…"

"Jon," she started.

"I know I'm being a little scary again. I've heard everything you've said. And I understand. Whether you want to hear it or not, my feelings haven't changed. I still…"

She put her fingers gently against my lips. "Shut up," she said. She kissed me gently and I felt her breath, sweet with wine as she brushed her lips across mine, barely touching. She looked at me with searching eyes, searching maybe for the people we had been when the world was ours. Before knowledge. Before disappointment.

I reached up and caressed the side of her throat. She tilted her head to catch my hand between her chin and shoulder and held it there with her eyes closed. Then I lifted her chin and kissed her. I felt her lips part and her breath come faster as she kissed me back.

We were sixteen again and dancing with crêpe streamers above us. And the circle we danced in was ever closer with no end to her spins and infinite laughter. We were both surrounded and alone, and there was only each other. There was water sound and the rush of tilting sand. There was promise and play. There was time and no time. There was Tara and night and heat and rebirth.

We held each other in graceful gratitude, as two people foundering after so long adrift.

# Chapter 13

I called the car rental company first thing and told them I wanted the car for one more day, then I drove from the apartment to Katherine and Jeff's and started moving my past into my present.

In their laundry room storage area, I sat going through the boxes I had left behind. They were faintly musty smelling and the white cardboard had yellowed over the years. I annoyed a lot of spiders pulling the boxes off the shelves and dropping them to the bare concrete floor. I opened them one by one and then started making save and trash piles.

I found old letters and photographs of Katherine and me as kids. I found my old Boy Scout sash that I'd saved because I had earned all the badges. I found my diplomas from high school and university. I found my written driver's evaluation I'd taken at sixteen, the paper soft and blistering at the folds. I found embarrassing clothing that couldn't possibly have been stylish at any point in history. I found some treasured shirts and sweaters that I wouldn't part with if my fashion life depended on it.

I found lucky rocks. I found the brightly painted clay dishes I had made at school and had given my parents one Christmas.

There were boxes of CD's and books by Fitzgerald, Faulkner and Salinger. I found essays with A's and B+'s in red ink. I found a lot of terrible poetry.

Sentimental bastard. I saved almost everything.

I took the boxes to keep out to the car and piled them in the trunk and back seat. Then I tossed the trash bags into the containers in the crawlspace under the front porch and drove down to the lake.

The Trojan sat high in the water, waiting for me. I had phoned the broker to confirm the details and had brought the cash down payment as promised. I went to his office first to sign her over. After some grumbling, he made out a receipt for the cash. I checked with him that the dockline telephone and freshwater lines were still hooked up. We had agreed that as of the fifteenth the new services would be transferred to me when the new name became registered. In the meantime, the old couple had said to leave everything until then as long as I was prepared to take care of any long-distance charges. I initialed in the appropriate spaces to agree to their conditions, then signed the notarized transfer. When he offered to walk me over to the boat for a final inspection I told him it wasn't necessary. He shrugged and handed me the master and two copy sets of ignition keys, two sets of keys for the sliding glass doors at the back of the main salon and another set for the door that led to the lower controls from the side. Finally, on a piece of his letterhead, he wrote down the electronic code for the slip gates that kept curious pedestrians from walking down to the boats at night.

I went back to the parking area to begin to load the boxes from the rental car down to the dock. Along the way, I stopped at a chandler's store and bought sandpaper, sealer, paint and brushes. Just because the new name wasn't officially registered yet didn't mean I couldn't make her my own. Within an hour I had everything stowed into various closets and cupboards. I pulled off my sweat-soaked shirt, changed into a pair of faded shorts and grabbed the paint. After clambering over the back rail I dropped down onto the teak diving platform. A couple of hours of masking and carefully sanding off the old paint was followed by resealing the area. Then using a stencil set of letters, I scrolled the new name in place. I stood back as far as I could to examine my handiwork. Jumping up and down with pride occurred to me but that would have been embarrassing. I packed everything back up and padded into the galley. Pulling open the fridge, I found six frosty bottles of Grolsch, that great Danish lager with the porcelain flip top. Attached to the front bottle was a little note from the elderly couple wishing me well and hoping I had as much fun with her as they had. I hoped so too.

I took the note and stuck it onto the front of the fridge then took a bottle with me through to the main salon. I grabbed my cell and made a quick playlist with Esperanza Spalding and Kendrick Scott, plugged it into the stereo unit and pressed random and then I went up the stairs to the fly bridge to toast my new domain. I popped the porcelain top and took a long pull on the bottle as the music filtered through the speakers set below the fly-bridge panel. It was noon on a bright Sunday and the other pleasure boaters were polishing their brightwork, mopping the city grime off their decks and the other hundred assorted little jobs that come with boat life. A few looked at me uncertainly and then waved tentatively. I sat down in the fly bridge captain's chair with my feet propped on the controls and raised my bottle in hello. The sun stung my bare shoulders and back. I put the bottle in the holder beside the control panel, lit a cigarette, leaned back and laced my fingers behind my head.

Chris and Paul. Chris and Paul. Chris had been killed in late July. Little more than three weeks later, Paul had died on the Island. I swiveled the chair a little so I could see the Island on the other side of the harbour. Small craft bobbed in the water, the sunlight turning reflections a hopeful blue.

Chris had been heading home from his usual Sunday night with his mother and had wiped out and died in a car crash. Paul evidently went to the island and had drowned? They had both died by accident while doing something they did every week.

There was something Ron had said after Paul had died that had bothered me. Who did they hurt? I had been gone awhile. I didn't know what Chris had done in the intervening years. What he had done for a living. Who did he know? Was he living with anybody? Had something soured in his life? Paul had worked as a lawyer; was married with two little girls. That's all I knew. I didn't know enough.

I took another pull at my beer, stuck it back in the holder and went below to get the phone, killing the music at the same time. That was going to have to be changed…. Who was going to know what I needed to know? Mack was the obvious choice. He sounded like the social convener with his access to tickets for baseball and hockey games. And Mack seemed close with Laura. Close enough anyway that he was the one who looked after things for her when Paul died.

There was Ron and Jason. I didn't know how plugged in they were to Chris and Paul. And there was Kelly. We were both going to keep the promised date but it was probably best to stay away from him for the time being. He had no reason to help me. In fact, I knew that his only priority was to clear the cases — solve them and file them. So far, I didn't even know if he was investigating what happened on the Island. He hadn't seemed to know about Chris and if he did he was playing it close to the chest. So Mack was top of the list with Ron and Jason close seconds. The only other person I could think of was Nick, Chris' brother.

I phoned Chris' mother's apartment, hoping to catch Nick there as I had when I'd first arrived. The phone rang and rang until the message kicked in. It was Nick's voice saying to leave a message for his mother and somebody would get back. I left my cell number and told Nick to call me when he could. I drained my beer and padded below again and got another. When I was topside again the phone was ringing.

"Jon, it's Nick," he said. "Sorry I just missed you, just got in."

"Hey Nick. Thanks for calling back. Listen, could I buy you a beer? Have a chat, about Chris."

The question took him a little aback. Nick and I weren't friends, just acquaintances by family. "Uh, yeah, I guess. Where're you calling from?"

"I'm way downtown, down by the lake."

"Well, I got no wheels right now. It's in the shop. Can you come to me?"

"Sure, how about The Miller?"

"Yeah, great. How long?"

"Give me an hour. I have to ditch a car first and pick up my bike."

"Fine, I'll see you there, say… four-thirty?"

"Perfect. Thanks. I'll see you in a bit."

I snapped the lid back down on the Grolsch, went below and put it back in the fridge. Gotta love a beer you can re-seal. I changed into some jeans and a T-shirt in the master stateroom. My helmet and leather were in the trunk of the car. After locking her up tight, I walked over to the rental in the high Sunday sun and headed uptown to return it to the agency. Once the car was paid for and the keys returned to the guy at the desk I went out to find my bike. She was sitting inside a fenced-in security area where I had left her that morning with the rest of the unused rental fleet. It was a bright day and the seat was boiling hot. I lowered myself gingerly into the saddle and started the engine. Within minutes, the temperature gauge was crawling past where I usually liked to keep it. I reached over and flipped the toggle switch I had installed in the plastic panel that surrounded the small instrument cluster. Even liquid-cooled in-line fours need air running over them on hot days. After having one too many uncomfortable moments sitting in Florida traffic, I had installed a secondary fan behind the cowling to bleed off the heat whenever it was necessary. I heard the fan start to whir and felt the heat rush out the side vents in the lower fairing. When the temperature had dropped to an acceptable level and the engine was idling just right, I put her in first and rolled out of the parking lot.

Forty minutes later I pulled up at The Miller. I mounted the stairs and glanced at the patio area. The place had changed, and the Miller had gone uptown since I'd last been. The tables were full of Sunday drinkers either soaking up the sun or hiding from it under colourful umbrellas. The apartment building was right across the street so I assumed he'd be on time, but I didn't see him on the patio. I pulled open the door to the bar and stepped into the cool of the air-conditioning.

As my eyes adjusted to the dim, I scanned the room. When I'd come here as a teenager for underage drinking there was a long bar down one side with a brass step rail and spittoons at either end on the floor. Classy. There were only two beers on tap and none of the beers served back then came from anywhere other than North America. Now there were a dozen taps lined up behind the bar, with attractive signs advertising two kinds of English cider and some fine European lagers hanging over the mirror that ran along the wall. Not a Budweiser in sight. In the old days the main bar area was scattered with tables and chairs with hardcore bar types throwing back chicken wings and potato skins and staring at the silent images on the TVs dotted around the room. Now couples and groups of men and women in business casual sat over grilled chicken wraps and vegetarian burgers in pitas.

Nick was sitting in a booth on the wall opposite the bar, drinking from a nearly full pint glass, an empty one beside him, and watching the TVs. A wrinkled pack of cigarettes sat beside him. He saw me just as I reached the booth and smiled and stuck out a paw.

"Jesus, the ghost of Christmas past. How're you Jon?" Nick said.

We shook hands as I slid into the seat opposite him and put my helmet, gloves and jacket on the cushioned wooden seat beside me. The years hadn't been kind to Nick. Even back then, he was a dumpy kid, florid and out of shape. He was still big; a fine pattern of veins crisscrossing his nose and cheeks, and he had filled out even more in the years I had been away.

"Hey Nick, good to see you again. How are you holding up?"

"Ah! What can I tell you? I'm hangin' in." He smiled weakly and took a gulp of his beer. The waitress angled over to us from the service area at the end of the bar. She reached over and plucked Nick's empty glass from in front of him. I ordered a pint and she sauntered away with more hip swing than she needed.

"You look good, Jon. Stayin' in shape. Jesush, I wish I had your luck buddy, I just sheem to get bigger n' bigger." He grabbed his middle with both hands and his fingers disappeared in the folds of flesh and shirt. "So what's doin' Jon? You been away for a while right? I think Jeffy said you was down in the States. What, you workin' down there?"

"Well, I left for a short trip and it turned into ten years."

"Oh yeah? A three-hour tour..." he sang, laughing, and then finished in a wet coughing fit. The waitress returned and put my drink down harder than she should have, causing it to foam over the rim. She apologized and bent over the table to wipe it. Nick stared down her open top while she wiped up the spill, then raised his eyebrows at me and smirked. He watched her weave her way through the tables back to the service bar.

"Not bad eh, Jon? You want some, I'll bet you could. She's never given me a look-see like that before."

"Hey, Nick? Give me a break."

"Hey yourself, what's your damage? She's a great piece of tail is all."

"Listen to me Nicky. I didn't come here to check out the help." I leaned over the table, closer to him. He smelled like he'd been drinking since he woke up. "I need to talk with you. I need to talk with you about Chris. Are you willing to do that and forget about the waitress?"

"Yeah, yeah. Jesus, what're you so serious about? I didn't mean nothing."

I sighed and rubbed the back of my hand along my jawline. "I'm sorry. Look Nick, I've been gone a long time. I lost touch with Chris. Then I get a call saying he's dead. Just like that. I come back and within a week I lose another old friend. So, I'm a little short on patience but that's my fault. But you want to sit here and get drunk and leer the waitresses, go ahead."

"Aright, aright. Jesush! Whatever Jon, whatever, you know?" He raised his eyebrows at me and nodded at his empty glass. I signaled the waitress to bring one just for him and breathed deeply.

"And I don't want to sit here all day while you get wrecked. I'm sorry about Chris *and* your mother."

"Hell, d'you go see her? How d'ya think *she's* doing?"

"What happened the night Chris had his accident, Nick?"

He sat in silence for a moment, his eyes focusing and defocussing on the tabletop. When the waitress brought him another, at least he didn't leer at her. Progress.

"Ev'ry Sunday for about two months I guess, Chris was comin' over for dinner on Sundays. I've been livin' at home again for about a year. Lost my job out at the plant, got downsized. So I moved back until things got better, you know? Anyways, Chris starts comin' for Sunday dinner. You know he didn't... hell you been away so you wouldn't know... but Chris didn't come around much... just the holidays an' shit like that. So, he starts comin' by to see Mom again. And she's happy as hell to have him around again, regular you know?" He looked sourly up at me. "I been there for her whenever she needs, and she gets all... when he comes back once a friggin' week..."

"I'm sorry Nick. It's just one of those things. The ones you don't see all the time. Absence..." I shrugged my shoulders at the obvious.

"Yeah, well whatever. Anyway, all of a sudden he's comin' around again. Bein' real nice to me and Mom. Lookin' after things for her like her medicines and whatever else."

"So what happened the night of the accident?"

"Ahh..." he shook his head, clearing the cobwebs away. "It was just the usual Sunday dinner. He came over around six. We had a few beers in the living room, talkin' and stuff. Then Mom brings out dinner and we ate. I was meetin' some friends later so I left around ten. Then I get home real late, like in the morning, and Mom's sittin' in the living room with a couple of cops. An' she's cryin' and wailin' that Chris's dead. An' the cops ask me where I been and I tell 'em. An' they get pissy about maybe I had too much so I told 'em to get out and leave us alone. Anyways, so they go and Mom 'n me are sittin' in the living room and then..."

Nick began to tear up. I didn't know him well enough to offer any consolation so I stayed silent.

"Anyways, so she's cryin' and then she calms down all of a sudden. She gets this real quiet look on her face and asks me why I'm cryin'? So I say well, cause of Chris. An' she's cryin' but she's not makin' any sounds and she says who's Chris?" He balled his fists and ground them into his temples for a moment. I waited. "Jesus... anyway, so I called the ambulance, and they come and take her to the hospital and..." The tears were flowing freely now. They slid down his cheeks and hung at the end of his chin.

"Anyways, so she had a... had some kind of stroke... and she's in and out now. Mostly out. Doctor said the shock has sped up the dementia." He sniffed and rubbed his hand under his nose and across his cheek, then wiped his hand on his pant leg under the table.

"I'm sorry Nicky. I'm really sorry about your mother. It's not fair."

"Your goddamn right it in'nt fair. Fuckin' cops an' ev'rybody else."

"Listen to me Nick. What was Chris into? What was he doing?"

"Whaddya mean what was he doin'?"

"I mean what did he talk about? Who was he seeing? What did he do for a living?"

"Why you askin' all these questions? You're no cop."

"Not trying to be one. Chris was my friend. I've known him and your family since we were all kids. But I lost touch with everyone and everything when I left. I'm just asking you what he was like. I have no idea about him. What he did. Who he did it with. Tell me about him."

"I told you already he didn't come around forever, an' then he was there. He started hangin' around more. I don't know, he never said nothing about nobody special. Sometimes he had a girlfriend, sometimes he didn't I guess. He didn't talk about nobody special." It came out "shpeshul". Nick was losing the battle with coherence.

"What did he do Nick? For a living?"

"Uh, he was," he searched for words. "A whaddya call it ..." Nick snapped his fingers impatiently, effort furrowing his brow. "An investment, money guy, you know?"

"What, he was an investment dealer, a banker, a trader, stockbroker?"

"Yeah," he said, his eyes swimming in confusion, "one of those trader guys. Stocks an' shit."

"He was a stockbroker?"

"Yeah. Offered to get me into some sure things. I never had the money for it so I couldn't never do it." Nick's eyes began to close on their own and he struggled to keep them open like a long-hauler fighting fatigue on the highway.

So Chris had become one of the money boys after all. I thought back to when we'd all made our university decisions in high school. When we graduated, almost three-quarters of our class had gone to business college. Chris had gone to one of the universities outside the city, had stayed on to do a Masters and then was offered some position by a local firm. By the time he had come back to the big city to chase the big money, I was somewhere in the Dakotas chasing something more elusive.

I called the waitress over to see what the damage was. Nick asked for another, but she looked at me and shook her head. He saw her head shake and sighed. Then he put his head slowly down to the table and rested his head on his forearm. A moment later he began to snore softly.

"It's OK," she said. "Nicky's a reg. He does this all the time."

I offered to help her with him but she shook her head again.

"It's slow today. There's no game on tonight, so it'll be slow for a bit, at least inside. And he'll look after himself in a little while. He always naps for a bit then pays his tab and leaves. Same old same old. Besides, he's had a bad time what with his brother and mom an' all. It's OK," she said.

I pulled enough money out of my wallet to cover both tabs, added an extra twenty, and thanked her for looking out for him.

"No trouble. You take care of yourself, we'll take care of Nicky."

She knew exactly how Nick thought about her. Clearly she had served him enough to know he was a drunk, and she was more than prepared to cut him off when the time came. Yet despite his coarseness, despite his sloppy behaviour, she was still willing to show him compassion.

I thanked her and shrugged my leather jacket on. She told me the extra twenty wasn't necessary. I didn't know how to explain that it wasn't enough. I smiled and pressed it into her hand, grabbed my things and left. When I looked back, she was stuffing the twenty I had given her into the sleeping Nick's shirt pocket.

I spun the bike back down to the lake after stopping for some groceries and wine on the way and parked it in the shade of one of the pier buildings. I locked the steering column and wandered over the causeway and down to the docks.

Despite the generosity of the waitress, my encounter with Nick had left me feeling sad and grimy. Once I was aboard and the food stored away, I stripped off and took a long, hot shower. After toweling off, I pulled out one of the few bits of clothing I had brought back from Florida – a treasured pair of white sailcloth pants with a drawstring around the waist. It was still hot in the early evening so I skipped a shirt and rescued my earlier-opened Grolsch from the fridge. I started the music again and went up to the fly bridge. Most of my neighbours were beginning to pack up and head back to their homes and condos. There didn't seem to be many live-aboards. They lugged their weekend bags and garbage up the gangways and over the bridge. I sat in the captain's chair with my bare feet propped on the console and watched them pack their cars out on the street, then head back to wherever they lived their real lives.

Nick had whined about it not being fair. It looked as though life had been unfair to the entire Allinson family. Father died early, youngest son killed in a car wreck, mother debilitated by a stroke, and the eldest son reduced to incoherence.

I didn't want to think about it anymore. I went down to the galley and took a couple of boneless breasts of chicken out of the fridge and marinated them in some lemon pepper, tarragon, garlic, olive oil and balsamic vinegar. While I made a salad with honey dressing I browned the chicken on the stove top. I opened a bottle of Gigondas and splashed some into the pan to deglaze it, then tossed the pan into the warming oven to finish it off. After pouring myself a healthy glass, I wandered aft to the lower sun deck.

The sun was falling behind the western edge of the Island beyond the small city-centre airport. I moved past the table and chairs and leaned my forearms on the aft rail and watched the ferries plying the harbour, bringing people from a day at the Island. Tomorrow was going to be question-and-answer day. I knew what to ask but I needed a little time to think about the approach. I was in danger of pissing off a lot of people I knew, people I cared about.

A light breeze from the west kept the heat from becoming stultifying as well as sweeping away any night bugs. The timer sounded on the stove so I put my glass down on the table and went forward. I assembled my dinner in the galley and as I was searching for cutlery, found two cut-glass holders and a box of candlesticks. I stuck a candle in one of the holders, grabbed the bottle and headed back to the sundeck with my dinner. I set the candle on the glass topped wicker table and fished in my pocket for my lighter. The candle flickered a little in the breeze and then settled into a low steady flame.

I felt now, for the first time since arriving, that I was back. Back in the city of my youth. Back on the water. A cloak of contentment settled over me and tension ebbed from my shoulders and gut. I ate my dinner and watched the sun dip imperceptibly towards the far end of the lake as the newly named *The Saracen* rolled gently against her moorings with the wake of each boat that made its way past the mouth of the marina. When I was done I dropped the dishes into the sink and returned to the aft sun deck with my cigarettes. I lit one and inhaled deeply, holding it in my lungs then letting the smoke drift slowly out. When I took another sip of wine, a small exhale of smoke became trapped on the surface of the dark crimson liquid, eddying back and forth, looking for escape. Watching the gray smoke as it drifted languidly out of the wineglass and trailed away on the evening breeze, I sat on the aft sun deck thinking of nothing and everything. Turning over problems in my mind and then discarding them.

I toasted the sun as it slipped out of sight beyond the lake's edge and sat a while longer in the gloaming. When I couldn't keep my eyes open any longer I went to bed.

*The Saracen* creaked and sighed against her lines, shifting back and forth in her berth. And I fell into sleep, mercifully without being chased by visions of my dead friends with melting scarlet faces.

# Chapter 14

I woke up in the predawn grey to a hissing sound on the deck above me, and it took me a few moments to realize it was only a slashing rain. Rainfall on a boat deck makes a lulling sound all its own and I hadn't heard it since Florida. I smiled. After pulling on some sweatpants I made my way to the galley and put on some tea. When it was made, I took the steaming mug into the main salon and watched the rain bounce off the sundeck and accumulate along the back edge, then roll its way down to the scuppers and out into the marina. As the storm cell passed overhead, heading east, the rain gave way and I could see the orange promise of a clear day on the horizon.

I went back to the master stateroom and grabbed a pen and paper from the chart desk. Sitting back in the salon I made a diagram trying to connect the dots into some kind of pattern. Chris had been a financial consultant/trader/whatever. Not married, no kids. According to Nick he had been an absentee brother and son until some point before the accident. Then he started coming around. Being friendlier, looking after his mother's needs. Then there was Paul, a lawyer of some variety. Married to Laura with two little girls. I got up and grabbed the list I'd lifted from the funeral home. They lived in Cabbagetown, Paul and Laura Hobbs, on Winchester Avenue.

I glanced out the port side. The rain had stopped completely and the concrete wharf was already drying in patches. I cleaned up the galley from last night's dinner and stored everything away. Then I showered and dressed and headed out with a rag to dry off the bike. While it warmed up I swept the accumulated water off the seat and tank and got the worst of it off the steaming exhaust pipes. Then I stowed the rag in the tiny space under the seat and headed off.

Cabbagetown is a sweet little pocket in the core of the city that holds a fine collection of Victorian Era homes. Many of the homes had been built to house the families whose men worked in the old Gooderham and Worts distillery down near the east ports. At the time it was a very poor part of town and the staple for most of its denizens was boiled cabbage. Now the homes were for the most part restored to splendour by their new owners. It was now an exclusive enclave now with the average price for the smallest houses well above a million. They came in all sizes; eight-bedroom mansions on acre lots, their gables and porticos dripping with wrought iron work and authentic gingerbread trim to the more modest single-family homes with their definitive brickwork and pillared front porches to the two-bedroom dollhouses known as the Wellesley Cottages. The neighbourhood became an island unto itself, surrounded on all sides by 1970s social-housing experiments gone wrong. It always had that oasis feeling to it because no matter how you approached Cabbagetown, you first had to make your way through the messes of St. James Town and Regent Park.

Paul and Laura's place was one of the grander homes near the Necropolis, an ancient cemetery that bordered the Don River and the Riverdale petting zoo. As I drove up in front of the house, a yellow daycare bus was pulling away from the curbside. When it had left, I saw Laura standing on her front porch waving to the bus. She watched me as I set the stand and pulled off my helmet. It took her a second and then I saw her register who I was. I hoped she knew a little more about me than as just one of the pallbearers of her husband's casket. And I hoped she wouldn't mind some difficult questions from a virtual stranger. I crossed the street and opened the low wrought iron gate at the foot of the front garden.

"Hi Laura," I called. "I hope it's all right. I just stopped by to say hello, see how you were doing."

"Jon?" she said, as if testing my name to see if it fit. "That's really very nice of you. Will you come in for a coffee or something?" She waved her hand indeterminately over her shoulder toward the open door and when I nodded, she preceded me into the house. I closed the heavy wood dark blue door behind me and put my jacket and helmet on an oak coat rack with a seat in the middle below an oval beveled mirror.

It was a centre-hall plan featuring a wide wooden staircase rising in front of me with an ornate wooden hand-railing painted white and a crimson carpet runner down the centre. To my right, through two French doors, was a parlour with two wingbacks turned toward the fireplace. There were two silver torchiere floor lamps with cream-coloured shades flanking the front window, which was draped in deep red velvet curtains. An antique reclining couch in a pale gold colour sat in front of the window with a white cat curled up in the middle of it, asleep in a ray of sunshine. To the left was the dining room with a cherrywood dining set that looked like it would seat a football team. There was a matching sideboard against the wall with crystal decanters full of scotch, rye and port on its top. The sunlight coming through the windows bounced through the decanters and sent prismed rainbows up the wall. There was a grandfather clock at the top of the stairs on the landing, which ticked sonorously, the sound filling the front hall. The house spoke of wealth and professional interior decorating. She led me down the hall past the stairs. On the walls were framed pictures of her and Paul. Alone when they were younger; on a beach somewhere with palm trees; in front of the Eiffel Tower; and then with kids when they were a little older; at the swan boats on the Island, paddling a canoe on some northern lake. Happy times.

We walked into the kitchen, which had an island in the centre with a pot rack overhead, dangling copper cookware. There was a copper exhaust hood over the range top against the wall with a stainless-steel backsplash. The countertop was done in grey ceramic to match the slate tile floor. Another pair of French doors off to the side led out onto a sizable deck. I could see the garden beyond defined by a seven-foot-high boxwood hedge. It was a lush garden with a flagstone path meandering down its centre, small statues on pedestals at intervals along the path's edge.

"Coffee?" she asked.

"Tea, if you wouldn't mind."

She smiled. "I would prefer, actually." She put the water on to boil, then pulled two oversized mugs down from a cupboard. I cringed inwardly as she dropped a tea bag in each cup instead of making it in a pot. When the water had boiled she poured it into the cups and offered me milk and sugar, both of which I declined.

"Why don't we sit in the back?" she said. She led me through the doors and we sat at a black wrought iron patio set with a canvas umbrella on a wooden pole rising out of the middle of the table. There was birdsong from the other side of the hedge, but otherwise no sound.

I complimented her on the garden and the house. She smiled her thanks, holding her mug in both hands up to her face, not saying anything.

"So, how are you?" I asked.

"It's hard to know really," she replied. "It comes and goes. I think it's somehow worse for Lily and Elizabeth. They keep asking where Daddy is, when is he coming back. They don't understand it all yet, at least not completely."

I nodded but didn't say anything. I sipped my tea. It was terrible but it was hot.

"The police offered to help with grief counsellors and social services people, but I want the girls to understand it from me. Does that sound selfish to you?" Her eyes were glistening.

"No, it doesn't sound selfish at all. They should hear it from you. Know it from you."

"Mmmm," She nodded her head and dabbed the corners of her eyes with a crooked finger. "I'm sorry Jon. I barely know you and here I am telling you sad things and crying in front of you. I never got the chance to say thank you for helping after Paul … after the accident."

"I was glad to able to do something for you, and for Paul."

"You two were close when you were at school?"

"Yeah, fairly close. We didn't start out as friends but we ended up that way. All of us did."

"That's good. Paul used to talk about you and all the guys when he and I first met. You left a little before that I think."

"I've been away ten years."

"Yes, that would have been just around the same time then."

I smiled at her self-consciously. We were making the small talk that people make who don't know each other at all but feel they should. We had one common connection but we didn't share it. I had known him as a child long ago, and she had known him as an adult. We were exhausting the topic already.

"Laura, I need to ask you some things, I hope you don't mind."

She looked at me innocently, like I was going to ask her where she got the car serviced.

"When Paul had his accident," I started, "I imagine the police asked a thousand questions?"

"Yes, they wanted to know everything. What he was doing on the Island in the middle of the day? I told them he often went once a week. Did he always go to the same place? He always went to Ward's because the beach was quieter. Were we having any kinds of problems? No, everything was, well, the usual couple stuff like everybody else, but we were fine. Stuff like that. Why?"

"Did they ask about his work. Anything going on at the office?"

"Yes, they asked about everything. Paul recently changed his practice. While he got a lot of satisfaction out of helping people with citizenship issues, he wasn't really fulfilled, I don't think. Even though he was very good at what he did."

"What did he do? I'm just trying to get a sense of him that's all. I lost touch when I left and I really only knew him when we were kids and then in college."

"Well, Paul used to work for a boutique firm specializing in immigration law. It paid very well…" she waved her hand around the garden and at the house. "He loved helping people. It was the nature of his work. So we talked about it. Just last month, he started his own firm. I was proud of him and he seemed … lighter." She smiled at the memory.

"So how did you two meet?"

"We were set up by a girlfriend of mine."

I smiled and nodded, saying nothing. "I'm in retail, I've got a boutique down-town but right now I'm taking as much time as I need. I've meeting with the executor tomorrow to figure everything out."

"Did you ever meet Chris? Chris Allinson?"

She nodded. "Sure. We used to see Chris all the time. He'd come for dinner sometimes or he and Paul would go and shoot pool downtown. Actually for the last few months, he hadn't been by, but Paul said he was very busy with work. Why? Why are you asking all these things?"

"I'm sorry Laura. I'm not trying to upset you. It's just, well I can't believe that both Paul and Chris … I just have questions. I just want to know what happened."

Whatever control she had left broke in a torrent. "What happened! Four days ago, my husband died!" she cried.

She got up too quickly from the table, jarring it with her hip and knocking over the two mugs. She looked for a moment at the liquid dripping down from the metal edge of the table and then spun and ran inside the house. I could hear her crying inside until the closing of a door cut her off. I righted the mugs and swept the worst of the spill off the table with the edge of my hand. After ten minutes she came back, her eyes red-rimmed and her shoulders curved in sorrow. She was holding three business cards. Sitting down across from me again she offered the cards to me over the table.

"I'm sorry I…Here," she said, handing me a buff-coloured card with black lettering. "This is Chris's business card. It was in Paul's desk. If you have any questions about Chris, you should call his office. I don't know very much about what Chris did." She handed me the second card. It was nicer than Chris's with the name of the firm debossed on a linen stock. "And this is one of Paul's cards, from the old firm." The address was on Bay Street in Commerce Court. She handed me the third card which was less austere than the first two. The address was on Richmond East. "His new office is here. He could bike there …" Tears began to well up again.

"Thanks," I said, "I'm sorry. I didn't mean to …"

Laura cut me off. "No, I'm sorry Jon. I'm sorry I blew up at you." She shook her head to clear away the thoughts. "I just … I just have trouble thinking about anything complicated right now you know? I mean if I focus on ~~the~~ feeding the kids or cleaning the house I can lose myself in it. Yesterday, I was wiping the counter after dinner and looking out the window and Lily came in to ask me something. And I didn't hear her, I just kept wiping the counter and then she started crying because I didn't say anything I guess, and she ran up to her room and slammed the door. I heard the slam and went upstairs and told her not to, like I'd told her a thousand times before. And she was crying and saying why wouldn't I talk to her, and where was Daddy? I didn't even remember her in the kitchen. I didn't hear her. It's not fair to them."

"It's not fair to anybody, including you. They don't understand it yet. You said yourself that when they know, they'll know it from you. And no need for apologies, Laura. Besides, if you can't chew out an almost perfect stranger, who can you chew out?"

She smiled and I stood to leave. "Listen, thanks for giving me the time," I said. I looked at the spilled tea drying on the iron table top, "… and the two sips of tea were really nice as well."

Laura laughed, in spite of herself. "I promise the next time you visit I'll wait 'til you finish your drink before I explode," she said.

We wandered back through the house, the missing husband and father a presence in the empty rooms. She shook my hand at the door.

"Please do call Paul's office if you want. I'm sure after you tell them who you are, somebody will help you."

"I will. Thanks."

We shook hands again, hers cold in the morning sun. When I pulled away from the curb, she had her hands thrust deep in her pockets and her shoulders braced against a chill that wasn't in the air. I rolled over to Parliament Street, stopped and pulled off my helmet then dug out my cell. I decided to try Chris' office first. I called the number on Chris' card and the secretary who answered flipped me to her boss. I told him who I was and asked if he could give me ten minutes. He stalled me, doing the important man of business routine, and finally suggested we meet in the coffee shop on the main floor of the office building in a little while if I promised it would only take a few minutes. I told him I'd be carrying a helmet if he didn't recognize me at first and thanked him for his help, then I headed downtown to the financial area.

The offices were in a long six-story building near Bay and Wellington. I saw the café banner on the north side of the building, so I bumped the bike up over the curb and parked it just off the sidewalk beside the windows. When I got inside he was already standing and smiling at me. He was a little shorter than I was, probably in his late forties, with a thin frame and eyes set too close together. His hair was cut in a semi-Julius Caesar flat to the head style. He was dressed in a glen-plaid suit that fairly radiated monied confidence.

"Jonathan right? Sam. Sam Powell. Great to meet you!" He was vibrating with enthusiasm, like a tiny dog. He motioned me to sit across from him and handed me one of his own business cards. A girl came by the table and I ordered an Earl Grey.

"So you're an old buddy of Chris, eh? Terrible, terrible thing. We sure miss him around the office. Terrible. So what can I do for you Johnny?"

"It's Jon or Jonathan," I said.

I raised an eyebrow at him and watched him make the mental note. He was typical of the breed. He would file away how I wanted to be spoken to and make sure he used it whenever he needed to make me at ease. They are everywhere. The ones who size up people and situations in order to get the maximum personal benefit from every opportunity. You almost can't blame them though. They're being churned out of universities and community colleges like sausages: uniform, mass-produced, and you don't want to know what's really in them. The whole construct of modern business doesn't proceed from the idea of the better mousetrap. It proceeds from the notion that you can take a better mousetrap, produce it cheaper offshore with necessitated inferior production quality, sell in quantity to the distributors, and provide a warranty which is calculated to expire the day before the mousetrap falls apart.

The girl returned with my tea and I thanked her and paid for it.

"I want to know what Chris did."

"What Chris did?"

"Yes. What kind of financial work did Chris specialize in? Were all his clients satisfied? Did he have any big deals that went south on him? Did he leave anybody hanging?"

He winked at me conspiratorially. "You on the job there Jon?"

"Why, you want to see my gun?"

A crease of concern crossed his face. For a second, he actually thought I had one. The look was gone again almost as soon as it had appeared. I couldn't believe Chris had been a friend of this dolt. He realized he was being put on, so to hide his embarrassment he laughed big, leaning back in his chair.

"Nice one, Johnny. Almost had me there."

"Definitely had you, and it's Jon or Jonathan."

"OK, whatever," he said dismissively, waving his hand in the air like my insistence was a trifle to him. "Chris was working with me on the pooled accounts."

"A pooled account?"

"Well, we call it the 'Balanced Future Program'." He made exaggerated quotation marks in the air when he said it.

"What does that mean? What's the 'Balanced Future Program'?"

"OK, what you get is you take two portfolio managers with different styles. Chris was quiet. I like it a little riskier, a little more out there, if you know what I mean. Ragged edge. So we tag team it like … good broker/bad broker."

With effort, I didn't roll my eyes and forced myself to look fascinated. "So these two portfolio managers work for you, say. Everybody thinks that rich people move their money all over the place getting into all kinds of risk potentials. But the richer you are, the more conservative you are. People who do well in their investments do it slow and steady. That day-trading stuff years ago is strictly for people who like risk. And rich people don't like risk."

"So let's say you're this guy and you want your money to grow and take care of itself and you. So two managers get together and move your money into different asset classes, Canadian equities, international equities, bonds, mutuals, whatever. Now, these two managers have very different styles, so that depending on what the market is doing, if it requires slightly more aggressive behaviour, or a little more laid back, everything balances out. The two styles will be in or out of favour depending on what the market is doing."

"So there's less volatility then. Less fluctuation."

"Exactly. Remember, rich almost always means conservative. They want safety of capital. You're an investor and you give us ten million to put to work. OK, so we put together two sharp managers who watchdog your ten million for you. Now the markets are a little unstable, and you've only got one manager keeping an eye out. Let's say that guy moves you into something that drops by only four percent."

"A $40,000 loss."

"Bingo. Half a Range Rover. So me and Chris, working together but with independent preferences and skill sets, make sure that if you're a little down on one asset class, you're up on another. And if we're shooting at fifteen points growth annually, which is possible with that kind of capital, then unless something really goes wrong, the money tap just keeps on pouring."

"So did anything go really wrong?"

"What do you mean?"

"I mean Chris was a successful fund manager. Working for some high-profile, very well-off people …"

"Hey now, I can see where you might be going and there's no way. After Chris died, the auditors and lawyers were all over our records. I mean we were good. We made our clients a lot of money. And we made the firm a lot of money. And we did very well ourselves. Shit, you ever been to Chris' place? That condo didn't come cheap, pal."

"So?"

"So, the cops have been all over the financials as well as asking all their goddamn questions. Chris' exec assistant went on vacation right before the accident. We still haven't got all the forensic accountants out of the goddamn office yet. It's a pain in the ass I can tell you."

His callousness had pushed the wrong button. "And I can tell you," I started, "that Chris' brother in a spiral. That I just came from talking to a woman who is drowning in grief. People a lot worse off than you. So I'm having a little trouble feeling sorry for you."

He held his hands up defensively. "Hey, hey. Me and Chris were friends," he said.

"Then show it." I got up and left.

Outside, I cranked up the bike and headed back to *The Saracen*. Once aboard, I changed out of my riding clothes into fresh gear. It was only eleven in the morning and already it was scorching outside. I paced around the salon thinking about what I just learned — mostly nothing. I felt like I was out of my depth. I needed somebody to talk it all out with. I picked up the phone and called Mack at the bar.

# Chapter 15

We sat on the patio before the lunch service started. The staff moved around us, hurriedly wiping down tables and unchaining the stacks of plastic chairs against the wall. Mack watched them casually, making sure nobody was dogging it.

"So what's up?" he said.

"I saw Laura this morning and she gave me Chris' old business card. And I just met with his old partner to pick his brains."

Mack nodded, blowing across the surface of his steaming coffee. "And?"

"And aside from the fact that there wasn't much to pick, it seems Chris was a straight guy. Doing well."

"Hmm, hmm. You surprised?"

"No. I would have been surprised to hear anything else. So the partner said the forensic accountants have been crawling all over this thing since Chris' accident and nothing's out of place."

"So far ..."

"Yes, so far."

"So what are you going to do from here?"

"I don't know yet. I need to find out more about what happened to Paul."

"And Chris…"

"Yeah, Chris too. But Chris died almost three weeks ago. Paul is…"

"Fresher?"

"Yeah, as awful as that sounds. I need to have another chat with Kelly."

"Who's Kelly?"

"Detective downtown. I talked to him just after Paul died."

"And what did he have to say?"

"Not much. We got into a little belly bumping. He pulled my files and knew about my quitting the force."

Mack put his coffee down and stared away cross the street. "He know why you quit?" I shook my head. "Did he say anything about Paul? Investigation continuing?"

"He wouldn't say anything definitive, just warned me to stay out of it. The Island, public place, people will want to know how and why."

"So you gonna get into it with this Kelly again?"

"I hope not. But he's the best one to ask right now. He's plugged in."

He took a sip of his coffee. "Why you doing this, Jon?"

"What do you mean why? I thought you agreed with me that this doesn't feel right. Why should two of our friends be dead so soon after one another? Why should two guys who knew each other their whole lives suddenly be dead?

Mack blew his breath out in a rush. "Jesus Jon, I don't know."

We were quiet as the last of the staff checked their stations, wiped condiment bottles, restocked glasses. There was something going on here but I didn't know what it was. A situation I was getting used to.

"Listen, I'm going to head. Talk to Kelly again," I said finally.

"See if you two can keep your peckers in your pockets this time?"

"You silver-tongued devil you."

Mack laughed and stood with me. I stuck my hand out and we bumped fists. "Lemme know what happens, huh?" he said.

"You got it. I'll be in touch."

I started the bike and headed back downtown. I decided to stop first at *The Saracen*, think about the approach and call ahead in case he was not there. I parked the bike off the street and locked the helmet under the seat. As I walked over the bridge from the pier building to the slips I glanced down at *The Saracen* below as I peeled off my leather jacket. When I had left that morning to go see Laura, I had opened the small hatch on the foredeck to let the day's heat escape and closed and locked the larger one. The small hatch was held open by two steel sliding rods set inside the hatch-edge. It was too small to fit through so I figured I didn't have to worry about someone breaking in as the rest of her was buttoned up tight. The tiny hatch was closed now.

I stopped frozen on the bridge. Had I closed the hatch before going to Cabbage-town? No, I hadn't. Had the old couple I'd bought her from forgotten about lending a set of keys to somebody? Maybe. I ran the rest of the way across the suspension bridge and down the stairs. As I rounded the stairs, a man appeared on the rear sun deck. He was dressed in a black windbreaker, jeans and white runners. He had thick black hair swept back and high with long sideburns that came down to his jawline like Elvis and he was wearing leather gloves. Elvis poked around the rear deck and then he must have heard my footfalls because he looked up and saw me. By that time I was through the security gate and was pounding down the ramp as fast as I could. *The Saracen* was docked three slips over from the gate. I turned and bolted along the connecting dock, making sure I didn't trip on the electrical and water lines that were spooled at each tie up. I saw Elvis vault over the side rail onto the dock and start running in the other direction, towards the concrete breakwater at the far end of the marina. As I passed *The Saracen* I jumped up and looked above-decks and didn't see anybody else on my boat. I dropped the leather jacket on the dock as I ran past and kept after him.

As Elvis neared the end of the slip, he slowed down when he saw there was nowhere to go. Where the last slip stopped just before the breakwater, there was a six-foot gap and beyond that, hanging on heavy chains, was a huge tire, the rubber scarred and gouged from unsure boat pilots. There was a green beard of algae clinging to the tread area that touched the water. Elvis jumped the gap running and landed on the inside rim of the tire, which shuddered under the impact, sending ripples across the water and knocking some of the algae loose. He scrambled up the tire and onto the breakwater. Then he reached inside his jacket and pulled out an automatic.

I hadn't seen a handgun up close since I'd left the force but we were close enough that I could see it looked like a Beretta nine. Regardless of the manufacturer, it was big enough to put a sizable hole in me. The blue finish gleamed dully in the sunlight. He didn't point it at me, but held it in two hands at arms-length; tight to his body so nobody else would see it. I skidded to a stop, my breathing laboured from sprinting. Elvis grinned at me and stood there for a moment catching his breath. Then he stowed the weapon back inside his jacket and walked quickly around the other side of the pier building. I heard something with a big engine start up and after a little peal of rubber, the sound faded down Queen's Quay.

I jogged back to *The Saracen*, retrieved my jacket from the dock and went aboard. The lock on the sliding glass doors off the rear deck was ruined. The pry bar he must have used had bent the locking hook clean off. At least he hadn't shattered the glass, that was civil of him. The salon was upside down. The couch was tipped over, the cushions tossed aside and its bottom fabric slashed open. The blue jacquard chair and the two chairs that matched the couch were in a jumble in the corner. The bulkhead shelves had been swept clean with a forearm, framed pictures and books spilled onto the carpet.

The galley cupboards had been emptied and tossed into the salon. I was careful to avoid the few smashed dishes and glasses lying on the tiled floor of the galley. I went forward to find the master stateroom was turned over as well. Clothes had been pulled from the cupboards and thrown in a heap across the bed. The chart tubes were empty, my nautical maps all over the jumbled bed. The drawers of the desk had been emptied, notepads, pencils, compasses and course plotters strewn everywhere.

The medicine cabinet contents in the master bedroom head were smashed in the sink. The forward compartment was a disaster. The lower locker contents had been spilled through the doorway and into the hallway. My intruder must have closed the small forward hatch to keep the noise down. Only the guest stateroom and second head had escaped serious injury.

I guess I had caught somebody's attention.

"Gee, welcome home," I muttered.

# Chapter 16

I sat in the interview room behind a table brutalized by coffee stains and age. The officer taking the information was young — maybe twenty-one, fresh to the job. He was writing on a lined yellow legal pad. There was a sheaf of incident reports waiting for the information to be transferred there once he had it straight. This was the fourth time we'd been through it.

"So you chased the man and he ran."

"Yes, he took off."

"And he didn't say anything to you."

"No, he didn't."

"And he was wearing a black jacket, denim jeans and running shoes." They weren't questions anymore, they were statements.

"Yes, jeans, black nylon jacket, runners, gloves."

There was a knock at the door and Kelly stepped into the room. He leaned against the wall by the door and folded his arms across his chest. The constable turned to look at him and Kelly just pointed his chin at me to tell him to keep going. I nodded at Kelly who stared back at me.

He checked his notes. "And this man also pointed a gun at you."

"No, he didn't point it at me. He just pulled it just to show me he had it."

"And you stopped chasing him."

"Yes. I was out-calibered," I said.

Kelly snorted quietly. The kid looked up from his writing and narrowed his eyes at me. Tough.

"Do you own a firearm, Mr. Birnam?"

I smiled up at Kelly. "Do I own a firearm, Detective?"

He looked back at me. "Not one that's registered. Not in my records."

The kid looked at Kelly then back at me. I smiled broadly at him and spread my hands. "See, I'm just a concerned citizen who got broken into. I'm just trying to do the right thing, officer."

"And you didn't just call the police right away because …"

"Because my boat was a disaster. I had to wait for a locksmith to come and redo the door. And I felt like putting it all back in one piece again before I called you helpful lot," I said.

"You should have contacted us first, sir. There could have been valuable evidence that you've now destroyed. Fingerprints and so on."

"I already told you he was wearing gloves," I said wearily.

Kelly leaned forward off the wall and said, "All right, I think we're done here. Constable, why don't you go fill out the report and make sure I get a copy."

"Yes sir," the kid said quickly. He stood to leave and thanked me for coming in. When the door shut behind him, Kelly took his chair.

"So, have you been a busy boy?"

I smiled at him. "Nope, not me. I seem to remember being told to stay out of active investigations. I'd never want to step on anyone's toes like that."

Kelly regarded me dryly. "Yeah. Well, if you wanted to stir the pot I guess you succeeded. Not many people I know getting their places tossed and having guns pointed at them who keep to themselves."

"Nobody actually pointed a gun at me. Honest, Detective."

"Yeah. Whyn't we go to my office and continue this little chat."

"That'll be fun."

Once in his office, we took our places on opposite sides of his desk. It was still laid out perfectly symmetrically. There was a note in careful handwriting placed just under the desk blotter with the slip number for The Saracen.

I nodded at the slip of paper. "Keeping an eye on me?"

"Just keeping up to date," he said.

"You want to add a phone number to that?"

He pulled the note out a little farther from under the blotter, showing my cell number written up the side.

"Well gee, I have plans this evening, but I'm free Saturday," I said.

"You're not as funny as you think you are. Sit tight a minute," and he got up and left the office. A few minutes later he returned with a tall, attractive woman with long dark hair. She had fine steel-rimmed glasses on and was dressed in a loose-fitting blouse and a dark blue skirt that hugged her hips. Nice hips too, I noticed. I stood when they came back in like my parents had taught me and waited for Kelly to introduce us. He didn't so I sat down again.

The woman followed Kelly behind his desk as he sat and propped herself against the wall behind him.

"So, what have you been doing with yourself, lately?" Kelly asked.

I looked from one to the other. "A little of this, little of that," I replied in kind.

"Meaning...?"

"Meaning, are we all playing show and tell?"

"We'll see. Let's hear what you have to say first."

"Since the funeral? Well, I've talked to Chris Allinson's brother."

"Nicholas Allinson."

"Yeah, Nick. We talked about Chris, and what he'd been doing all these years. I talked with Laura, Paul's wife. Same thing, old times and what's been happening lately. I talked with Chris' old partner at the firm he worked. That's about it."

"And what did you find out?"

"Not much. The guy I talked to and Chris were a team at the office. They worked together on something they call pooled accounts. Since Chris died, the accountants have been poring over the paperwork, but nothing seems out of place. So far, I can't find any reason that Chris or Paul would be killed. So far, it looks like coincidence."

"But you don't see it that way."

"No I don't. By the same token, if something's out of place, they're not going to tell me anything. So if something is off, then it's going to be up to the forensic accountants to find it. How good are they?"

He grimaced and glanced back at the mystery guest. She nodded but didn't say anything.

"Fair question. They're good. Very good. But understand that Metro's forensic accounting team doesn't have the manpower of the Feds. The guys who work that detail usually have to give it over eventually, especially if it's deep. If they find something that looks like it runs deep, if it's big enough, then there's a criminal department at the CRA that takes care of running it down ultimately. And I've heard they're good but like all government arms, it's never easy dealing with them. Anyway, I'll put in a couple of calls and see where we are," Kelly said. "What else?"

"Beyond that I don't know anything else. I don't know enough. Nick said Chris had been coming around the family more often before the accident. I don't know if that means anything. Laura said everything between her and Paul was great. And the partner at the office said that Chris was a successful fund manager who did well by the company and the company did well by him."

"But for some reason, someone tosses your boat," said Kelly flatly.

"Yeah" I replied, "I don't know. I don't even know how it's connected, if it is. But I've got nowhere to go if it's not."

Kelly was silent, twirling a pencil slowly between thumb and forefinger. He glanced back again at the woman who was staring at the floor. When she looked back up, she eased herself off the wall and came around the desk to sit beside me. I turned back to Kelly.

"OK, your turn," I said.

"What do you think we should say to you?" Kelly asked.

I glanced from him to her. "I don't know. Let's start with how handsome I am."

Despite herself, the woman beside me laughed. "No."

No, you won't tell me or no I'm not handsome. I can't be gorgeous and brilliant?"

"Or either."

I looked at Kelly. "Ouch."

Kelly broke in. "Birnam, shut up."

I smiled, turning back to the woman. "So if you can't tell me how you really feel about me, tell me something safer for both of us. How about your name. Or not, and tell me the details of how my friends died? You know, an ice breaker ..."

She regarded me quietly for a moment, sizing me up. There was no reason why either of them should say anything. But the fact that I was sitting in Kelly's office meant the ongoing investigation was probably stalled otherwise they wouldn't be giving me any time. And we all knew it. The woman sighed and handed me a business card to introduce herself.

"I'm Detective Sergeant Walsh," she said as we shook hands. "I'm the lead investigator on the death of Christopher Allinson. When DS Kelly said you were coming in to make the complaint about your boat being broken into, he suggested I come down. What I have to tell you will not leave this room, is that understood? If I read about anything in the media, I will have you up on charges, do I make myself clear?"

"Eeek," I said.

She looked at Kelly with exasperation. "You were right. He is annoying."

I grinned and said, "Just keeping the mood light. Look, the fact that you're willing to talk to me means you've already decided to trust me. So you'll forgive me if I think you don't need to overcompensate, Detective. I wouldn't compromise your investigation. I used to be on the job so I know what's at stake. Maybe I want to find out what happened more than you do."

She raised an eyebrow and opened her mouth to say something, then changed her mind and thought for a moment more and began talking.

"I was brought into the investigation several days after the accident. When the accident team went over the crash scene, their findings were... inconclusive," she started. "There was one set of skid marks. Christopher Allinson died from blood loss. By the time EMS arrived, he was already gone. The car was badly damaged in the accident and all but consumed in the ensuing fire. The rear of the car took it the worst. Rear windshield shattered, rear axle was left up on the street." She paused and looked at Kelly, who nodded his head in agreement. "There were no witnesses to the accident. EMS figured they couldn't have done much for him anyway."

As I listened, I watched her talk. She wasn't squeamish about anything she was saying. But I noticed she called Chris by his proper name. Perhaps it was a way of depersonalizing him.

"So if the back was so wrecked, did somebody rear end him and drive him off the road?" I asked.

"As I said, Mr. Birnam, there was one set of skid marks and no witnesses. The accident reconstruction team said that the damage to the rear of the car probably happened because he spun out. There was no paint transfer we could find from another car on Christopher Allinson's. The car was a ruin. So far everything I've said is what was reported in the media. Are you sure you want to hear the rest?"

"Yeah." And she told me the details of how Chris had died.

"Jesus," I said quietly after she was finished.

"Mr. Birnam, are you all right?" she asked.

"Yeah." I blew air out slowly through my teeth.

"Now, last week … your other friend on the Island," said Kelly.

"Papers said Paul drowned," I said looking at the floor, trying to clear my imagination of the image of Chris impaled and dying and then burning. "They said that maybe you think he went in to cool off and drowned by accident."

"Well, that's what we told the papers," said Kelly.

"And …" I said, looking up at him.

"And he was already dead when he went in the water."

I lifted my eyes and stared at the ceiling, concentrating on breathing. Kelly ran a hand up his cheek and around the back of his neck, massaging hard while he continued.

"ME's office said his lungs were clear. People who drown don't have clear lungs. There was blunt-force trauma to the back of his head. There were lacerations on his arms and back and his chest was crushed; now much of that could have been caused by the ferry. When the guy on the Island ferry saw the body, they weren't able to stop it quickly enough. The body was trapped between the front of the boat and the dock. We're still waiting for the final report on that. There were particles of moss on his back so we're checking the Island, but there are about a million trees on it. We found his ID with some articles of clothing on the beach. His wife said he used to sometimes cycle down to the Island. His bicycle isn't at his house, and we haven't found it on the Island yet."

"Stolen?" I asked.

"Probably, by now. But we're looking just the same. If it was stolen, it'll turn up eventually. His wife said it was expensive and they registered the serial number," he said.

"You told her about how he died?"

"No."

"No? What do you mean, no?"

"I mean when she came to ID the body, she was in tough shape. I didn't want to make it worse by telling her how it happened. We showed her a face shot.

After the autopsy, the ME had a word with the funeral home. I'm told they did a good job."

"Christ…" I said shaking my head in disbelief.

"Now then, when all the reports are in, I'll meet with Mrs. Hobbs and give her the full tilt. She knows we're investigating it as a suspicious death, but that's all she knows for now." He looked at me hard. "That's all she needs to know. You follow?"

I nodded in agreement. "Yeah, I follow."

"Listen to me," he said, leaning forward and nodding at DS Walsh, "we're going out on a limb sharing this much with you. We all know we don't have to tell you anything."

"So what," I said flatly. "You're stalled and you think I can shake the tree a little."

"What I think is that I pulled your records and read through them. You were doing well. Damned near top of your class at the academy. University grad in Crim. Your evals were excellent across the board. You were fast tracking. You wrote the detective's exam. Near perfect. You were about to be promoted after only a few years. Then you pulled the plug."

"I'm not some pet project."

"Don't flatter yourself. Why'd you walk?"

"I had my reasons."

"No kidding. I can read."

"Wasn't just that."

Walsh cleared her throat loudly to interrupt.

"Personally I don't think you can do anything to help us except stay out of our way. We are the professionals. You are now a civilian. However," she said, exchanging a glance with Kelly, "when the Detective spoke with you before, given your experience and the fact that the deceased were friends of yours, he anticipated that you might try to involve yourself." She looked down, crossed her legs and smoothed some wrinkles out of her skirt.

"And," she continued, "we felt it would be irresponsible not to reassure you that we are doing our due diligence as regards the deaths of your friends."

Kelly nodded his head and took over the explanation.

"There aren't that many murders a year in Toronto, maybe fifty or sixty, which is almost nothing for a major urban centre."

"And…" I said.

"Most of them are either gang-related or family disputes. Every once in a while, people get shot at nightclubs. As much as it pisses us off we kind of accept it, it's part of that scene. What I'm driving at is, in my experience, with homicides in this city, there's usually an arrest within a week. Because usually the case is clear-cut. I'm not bragging when I say this, but the force clears its homicides, on average, within four days. Like I said, most of the murders that occur in this city are not premeditated and finding the perpetrators is usually fairly routine," he said.

"Then how come these ones are taking so long?" I asked.

Kelly's face shut down and Detective Walsh jumped in, "These investigations are being handled concurrently from here. The Detective and I are working them in concert."

"In other words …?"

"In other words," Detective Walsh said, "we think they are connected as well, so let us do our jobs. If Christopher Allinson and Paul Hobbs were murdered, we'll find out who did it."

"Look, I appreciate you being up front with me." I turned my attention to Kelly. "And worrying for Laura's feelings …"

"What else would I do?" he said, grimacing.

"Yeah. It carries weight. So thanks for telling me what you didn't have to." I stood and looked from Kelly to Walsh. "I'm not looking to get in your way on this. But I'm still going to stumble around this thing until I know happened."

"We figured you would. Just don't stumble around so much that somebody actually points a gun at you. Don't get in our way, and do nothing to compromise our investigation. You get anything, you bring it to us." He jerked his thumb at the door. "Out," he said.

# Chapter 17

I met Tara up in the parking area at 6:00. She said she'd be driving a burgundy Ford, her parent's old car. I was leaning against the bike when she pulled through the gates and parked beside where I was standing. I was wearing my old sailcloth pants, sandals, a blue cotton shirt and I looked fabulous. I held the door open for her as she got out and beamed at her as she came in for a hug. She was wearing a yellow cotton summer dress with a braided rope belt loosely tied to show her hips and a cream-coloured wrap around her shoulders and I felt light-headed just looking at her. Her hair was down and the summer sun was bringing out some light freckles on her cheeks and nose.

"Would it be uncool of me to say 'Wow'?" I said.

"It would actually be expected of you."

"Wow."

"Thank you, young man. So, are we going to the Terminal Building for dinner?"

"Nope."

She rattled off the names of some of the hotels that flanked the water's edge.

"Nope."

"Another romantic walk by the lake?"

"Sorta."

We walked across the suspension bridge holding hands, around the corner and down to the security gate. I punched in my access code and the gate unlocked with a clang.

"Jon, where are we going?"

"C'mon."

We walked the three slips over and down the finger slip beside *The Saracen*. I stopped at the steps and smiled at her. She looked at me, then at the boat, then back at me. Comprehension spread across her face and her eyes crinkled in amusement.

"No."

"Yup."

"This is yours?"

"Yup."

"No."

"Yup."

"Oh, my God."

"Yup."

I went aboard and she took my hand as she followed after me. I gave her the grand tour. She gave me little squeals of pleasure and amazed looks.

"How did you … when did you buy this?" she asked.

I told her all about the sale and the deal I got on her. We went into the salon and I poured us each a glass of red wine. I showed her where the stereo was with my phone plugged into it. As Tara sorted through my playlists I cast off the lines and pulled up the rubber docking fenders. She put some Kamasi Washington on and I led her up to the fly bridge. The twin Chryslers gave a throaty roar starting up that made her jump and then laugh with excitement. Tara went forward of the controls and leaned against the fibreglass bulkhead above the foredeck while I worked *The Saracen* out into the harbour. I spun her west and we moved through the western gap, past the Island airport and out into the lake. The water was evening calm and there was a hint of wind coming from the south. The sun was still high enough to throw heat and the breeze from the moving boat felt good. Once clear of the gap I moved up the rpms slowly, making sure to keep the engines in sync. The added speed blew Tara's hair softly around her face as she came back up to the fly bridge.

"My God, Jon, this is great! It's a beautiful boat!"

"*She's* a beautiful boat, *she*. There are rules you know."

She laughed and I felt my chest tighten with pleasure. "OK, OK. *She's* a beautiful boat."

We cruised along at a snail's-pace three knots, moving slowly west. After a time I spun her back toward the far side of the Islands. By now the night lights in the downtown high-rises glowed vibrantly as evening settled over us. I checked the chart and headed for the area I had already picked out. About a mile offshore, but still within view of the city was a shoal that would take an anchor and was well clear of the shipping lanes. When we reached the spot on the chart, I checked the depth on the sounder. Then I went forward and tossed the big Danforth anchor over the side. When the chain stopped, I gave it an extra fifteen feet until the anchor re-snugged itself. I let the tide turn *The Saracen* slowly on the anchor until the bow was pointing southwest. I went aft and tossed the other anchor, making sure it was firmly set as well, then I went back to the fly bridge to join Tara. She was half-slumped in the passenger chair, her head back and eyes closed, feeling the setting sun on her face. I sat in the captain's chair and swiveled it around to watch her. After a moment she crooked one eye open and smiled dreamily.

"Mmmmmm ..." she said.

"I'll make a note of that in the log. First passenger, very satisfied."

She sat up slowly, took a sip of her wine and beamed at me. "I don't know what to say. My God Jon, what made you buy this?"

I smiled back at her. "Well, the best time I can remember in the past little while is when I was in Florida. I had this job for a few seasons on a charter boat. Big one. Sixty-five foot. I lived aboard and took tourists out six days a week for the owner. Fishing charters mostly, out to the edge of the Gulf Stream. He was too old to run her anymore, but he didn't have anything saved for his retirement, so I ran her for him. It was a pure time. Elemental. Everything depended on the weather. On reading the water right. You know, making sure a following sea didn't overtake you or reading the colour of the Stream to see what it was going to do that day. And at night, after I had everything stowed and rigged for the next day, I used to sit up in the fly bridge. I'd talk to the other captains on Charter Boat Row. We'd get together and complain about the tourists. Laugh about the sport dummies who couldn't do their own rigs to save their lives."

"It doesn't sound so bad. So why did you leave?"

"I wanted something more, I guess. That sounds weak." I reconsidered. "I was pretending, maybe. It was a good life, but it wasn't ..."

"Enough?"

"Yeah. But more than that, it wasn't mine. It was a life that I only pretended to. Like going into a store and trying something on because you like the way it looked in the store. But then you get home it doesn't look good on you anymore or doesn't fit quite right."

"You were always so responsible when we were kids. But you had to be," she said.

"Yeah, I know. And all those years on the road were a reaction to that. When I settled in the Keys for a spell, I did it because, well, because it's a perfect place. The sun, the spring storms that come howling up from the Bahamas, the rawness of it. Have you ever been?"

"No, I've never gone, but I've always wanted to."

"Well, the quieter Keys, you can be on beaches and get the feeling sometimes that nobody has ever walked there before. Pristine sand, wind and water, no sign of man."

"But you decided to leave."

"Well, I felt I needed to leave. It took some time but I realized that maybe my place was back here. This place has changed." I paused and stared back at the city, gently rising and falling a mile away. "It's gotten bigger since I've been away and I don't really know it that well anymore. But despite that, it feels more like home than anywhere else. And I never lost the love of the water. Loved being on it and living on it. I love the simplicity of it. I knew when I got back, it was going to have to be a boat."

"And here it is!" she laughed.

"And here it is. So what about you. What are going to do with the house?"

"Well, it's all mine. The mortgage was paid off ages ago. I'm living for taxes and utilities now."

"What's it like living there again?"

"Kind of creepy-comfortable. My parents didn't change it at all. Everything's still the same. My room still has the same wallpaper from when I was a teenager, for God's sake! Ewwww!"

I laughed and reached over and poured her some more wine.

"C'mon," I said. "There's cookin' to do."

We went below and talked while she watched me make dinner. I had some marlin steaks marinating in olive oil on the counter. I ground up some fresh basil and coriander seed using a mortar and pestle and dredged the steaks in the mixture. I put some new potatoes on to roast and when they were close to being done, I pan fired some asparagus in lemon and garlic. While I grilled the marlin on the barbecue that was bolted to the rear railing, Tara made us a table on the rear deck. I opened another bottle of wine, a Tokay Pinot Gris from Alsace, and we sat and ate by candles in the twilight.

After dinner, when everything was cleaned up, we wandered hand in hand back to the rear deck with the last of the wine and stared at the city bobbing up and down.

"So now that you're settled, what are you going to do?" she asked.

"Do? You mean, how am I going to become a productive member of society?" I asked.

She laughed and shook her head. "When I saw you the other day, you said you had some things to take care of."

I knew I was going to have to bring it up with her eventually. Now seemed as good a time as any. "I'm going to find out what happened to Chris and Paul."

"What are you talking about? Jon, they both had horrible accidents."

"No babe, they didn't. I'm not sure about Chris yet, but I know Paul was murdered."

"What are ... how do you know?"

"I didn't believe they could both go like that. I've talked to the police already. Paul didn't drown, his body was just thrown into the water."

"My God!"

"Yeah. I know. Who would want to do that? It seems unbelievable that ... I don't know." I shook my head. "I think back to when we were kids. When we used to play pick-up baseball on Thursday nights, I can see us as kids in my memory. Laughing and running the bases. Taking it so seriously if we were losing. It was so long ago and I think, you know, the innocence of that time. Those little kids. Thirty-odd years later, two of them are dead. It's hard to reconcile that time with the now."

"I know, Jon," she put her hand on my forearm and stared out at the water. "It's not nearly as serious but I'm living back at the house I grew up in. I can remember being a little girl there, and then I realize I'm actually a near-divorced woman."

I held out my hand and she took it in hers. "When I think about what we talked about as kids, growing up to be, I don't know," I laughed, "cliché things like firemen and astronauts."

She arched an eyebrow at me. "Or police officers?"

"Yeah, or cops." I looked at her and felt that electric thrill of somebody special knowing your old secrets. "We all romanticize our past. Comes with the territory. But I think as kids, we didn't know about the limits of adulthood. We'd look at the sweep of the sky and know there were no boundaries. Except getting home in time not to get grounded. I mean we didn't think about it those terms, but in hindsight I guess that's what it was. As we get older, life becomes so complicated that just staying human requires a massive effort. But we didn't know that then."

"Dreaming of the simplicity of youth?" she asked.

"Yeah, maybe a little. But mostly I'm trying to reconcile who we were with what we became. At least what Paul and Chris became."

"Are you making judgments?"

"Yes. But I think I'm entitled to."

"So what do you think about what they became?"

"I don't know exactly. But I can't shake the feeling that the people they grew into is somehow responsible for what happened to them."

"So you disapprove?"

"Not exactly. I still have to learn more. Outwardly it looks like Paul was a happily married guy with two kids. Laura seems very grounded and a good person. He was good at what he did. Successful. Respected."

"And what about Chris?"

"Chris? I only know that he was doing well at the firm he worked for. I spoke to this twit he used to work with who told me that Chris lived in some spectacular condo somewhere. His mother's in a home and Nick was almost no help. I'm going to have to figure out another way to tap into his life."

Tara was quiet for a moment, then smirked at me. "And what about you. Do you disapprove of yourself?" she asked in mock serious tones.

"Me? No, I'm above reproach," I said, returning the smirk.

"Really?"

I laughed. "I'm susceptible, like anybody else. A life without self-reflection is not worth living, etc… We're all responsible for creating an image for ourselves that makes us comfortable. I am as guilty as anyone else in trying to maintain an image that suits me. I have this idea of what I am and I try to live up to it as much as possible. And I tell myself I don't need the things I secretly covet. Now you, on the other hand are a different matter." I leaned over and poured the last of the wine between our glasses.

"Oh?"

"Yeah. You're a mess." Smiling fatuously, I got up and ambled back into the galley to get another bottle while she yelled imprecations at me from the rear deck. It took me a moment to find the wine I wanted, but by that time Tara had come in off the deck and crept quietly up behind me. She slid her arms around me and rested her head between my shoulder blades with a small sigh. I put the bottle down and hugged her forearms tighter around my waist. We stood that way for a minute, not speaking, feeling the deck roll gently beneath our feet.

Finally I turned to look at her, moving her arms around me so we didn't break the hug. She kept her head on my chest, the top of her head snuggled under my chin.

"Tara?"

"Mmmmm."

"You OK?"

"Mmmm …"

"Something wrong?"

"Shhhh."

She stirred finally and looked up me. Her eyes shone with knowledge and secret promise. She seemed to make up her mind about something and nodded almost imperceptibly. Then she put her hand on my chest in a wait-there gesture and went forward to the master stateroom. I stood in the galley like an uncertain teenager, then I heard her call me. Trying to quiet the butterflies in my stomach, I reached over to the lower controls and flicked the switch on for the running lights fore and aft. Then I went forward down the hallway.

I opened the door to the stateroom. The only light was the small map light over my desk. It threw a small circle of light on the harbour chart I had pulled down earlier. The rest of the room was in semi-darkness. Tara was lying naked on her side, one arm under her head, the other resting along the length of her. Looking at her, I felt like I had never seen a woman before. Her back was to the light so the details of her were in shadow. The side of her face touched by the light was calm and smiling. I slowly undressed while she watched. When I was naked as well she regarded me for a moment, then she stirred and stood and walked around the bed, keeping the light behind her. I opened my arms and she folded herself against me, the firm softness of breasts and belly sending shivers through me. I trailed my fingertips from the nape of her neck to the small of her back then slowly up and down her spine. Her breathing changed, coming faster. She reached down, guiding me, and we were suddenly joined in that ever-the-same-ever-new immediacy.

I picked her up and she wrapped her legs around me. Turning slowly I sat on the edge of the bed with her in my lap. *The Saracen* seemed to rock below us in sweet counterpoint. And as her time became closer, she gripped the small of my back harder and ground us together. When release arrived, she cried my name and hugged herself to me, straightening her back so our upper bodies were co-joined as well.

Staying with her, I lay us slowly on our sides as our breathing mellowed and our exertion cooled. She lay with eyes closed making small happy sounds while I stroked her hair. I rolled over onto my back, gently bringing her with me, and laid her head on my chest. I could still feel her small after-contractions as she settled herself.

"Jon ..." she said quietly.

"Yeah?" I whispered. My voice was still a little hoarse.

"How ..." her voice drifted.

"Since forever. That's how long."

"It's not too late?"

"Anything this side of dying isn't too late, love"

"Mmmmm. But I wish..."

"What do you wish?"

"I wish that we'd done this sooner," she giggled.

Laughter exploded from both of us, and I hugged her to me. This girl/woman that I had known forever. And that I was bound and determined never to let go now. We laughed until our stomachs hurt and our jaws ached. As our amusement subsided and I stroked her back lightly, she realized I was still hard inside her.

And so we began again that slow intimate rocking that creates a knowing between two people that no conversation or shared history can engender. That unison movement that changes everything at once and forever. It was just as strong for her the second time as the first had been. But this time our being together was a little more certain, less trepidatious. She was more adventurous this time, finding and offering pleasures, chuckling to herself in enjoyment. As she came to the edge again, she held herself briefly, then allowed herself to tip over and I joined her in her deep and lasting release.

After some quiet gentling, she rolled over and we fell naturally into spooning each other, her head tucked under my chin. I held her, stroking her side until I heard her breathing deepen and her body gave small twitches of self-relaxation. When she was asleep, I eased myself out of bed and padded naked through *The Saracen*, turning off the lights in the galley and the salon. I went fore and aft and checked that the lines were snug and the running lights were all aglow. I stayed for one final smoke above-decks, staring at the night sky and thinking about boundaries. Then I went below and contoured myself around my lady again and followed her into sleep.

# Chapter 18

The next morning, Tara and I had breakfast at anchor, and then I dropped her back at the marina. She said she had a day planned and with a saucy grin she agreed that more time below-decks was a good thing, but there were appointments to keep. So after some humid goodbyes she drove off home, honking the horn and waving out the window at me.

When I got back, I reattached the water and electrical lines and noticed my cell had a missed call on it but no message, with "No Caller ID." I wasn't sure where to start again with Chris and Paul, so when in doubt, do something else. I called over to the chandler's store and yes, my new fly bridge panel had arrived and I could pick it up anytime. I wandered over to Pier 4 and picked up the new panel and a box of brass marine decking screws.

I took my phone out of my pocket to find I'd missed another call but it was a blocked caller and still no message. I went below and dug out my cordless drill, counter-sink bits, wire cutters and electrical tape. Once topsides I pulled the old rusted screws and worked the faded and scratched panel free. After unhooking the wiring harnesses for the gauges and the ignition from behind, I unscrewed all the chrome rings and gave them each a polish. I lifted the new panel into place to make sure it fit properly then, satisfied, I inserted the gauges one at a time through the pre-cut holes and tightened them down with their newly shined rings. Once I had the harnesses reconnected, I installed the ignition housing and turned the key to make sure everything worked. Then I pre-drilled new screw holes with a counter-sink bit and drove the bright brass screws down through the new mahogany panel. While I worked, I turned over the questions in my mind.

I needed a way to tap into Chris' life and past. The more I thought about it, the only person who was going to be able to help was Nick. When the new panel was firmly screwed in and wiped clean I called him but there was no answer. After I had showered and dressed, I picked up the phone and called Chris' brother again. This time Nick picked up but he sounded like he was still in a fog.

"Nick, it's me, Jonathan."

"Mmmmmrhph, unh, yeah, yeah, Jon. Whassup?"

"Listen, what happened after Chris' accident? Where did all his stuff end up?"

"Hang, hang on a second," Nick replied. He made a small grunt of effort and I heard bedsprings creaking. There was stifled yawn and the sound of Nick rubbing his hands on his face to wake up, then he came back on.

"Yeah, sorry Jon, what'd you want again?"

I sighed and said, "What happened to all of Chris' stuff after the accident? What happened to his condo?"

"Oh, uh… I'm still waitin' on the insurance and the lawyers for all that," replied Nick. "His company told me they'd look after that stuff. Said they'd get the best price for the place and pass the money to Chris' lawyer. But they gimme a key for one a' those storage places. I ain't been down there yet. Say there's boxes a' clothes and furniture there."

"How would you feel about letting me go down and have a look?" I asked.

"Uh, well, maybe sure, if ya want. I dunno what's … why you want to go there?"

"I just thought there might be something there that might help, that's all."

"Well, I'm goin' down to see Mom today."

"OK," I said, "why don't I meet you there? I'll borrow the key from you and go check things out while you're with your Mom."

"Yeah, yeah, OK. How 'bout an hour?"

I checked my watch. "Perfect. I'll see you in front at eleven."

We hung up and I went to the master stateroom to collect my keys, jacket and helmet. As I came back down the hallway, my cell rang but when I picked it up, there was only silence at the other end. After repeated hellos I gave up and hung up.

I set to work cleaning up the galley from our breakfast. Once everything was clean and stowed, I picked up my things and locked up the side doors, thinking about the guy I'd chased off my boat. It was probably time to think about installing an alarm. At the very least, it was probably a good idea to figure out a way to turn off the fuel system to slow up somebody who might try to steal my new home. I went forward to the guest stateroom and took a short-handled mop out of the wardrobe, unscrewed the cloth head and lay the doweling handle in the track of the sliding glass door. It would do until I had the time to create something more high-tech.

Once *The Saracen* was firmly buttoned-up, I walked over to the parking area and started the bike. I swung astride, dropped her into first gear and went along Queen's Quay and then north on York Street. Because of the plantings that ran down the centre of University Avenue, I had to go a little north, pull a U-turn and come back in the southbound lanes. The traffic was flashing past in all three lanes so I bounced the bike onto the curb and parked on the sidewalk. I watched people in hospital gear go in and out of the buildings, most of them just coming out for a coffee, milling around the broad stairs in the sunlight.

I heard a voice screeching behind me and turned to look. Walking down the sidewalk were two identically dressed women; from the look of them a mother and daughter. They were both wearing gray track pants and white sneakers. Over-sized white T-shirts hung outside their pants and were cinched tight at the waist by brightly coloured windbreakers, making the bottom of the shirts billow out like mini-skirts.

The girl, who was probably in her late teens, had the top of the hoodie she was wearing over her head and tied tightly. As if on cue, she would walk ten paces then stop in her tracks, turn her head and hurl nonsense curses at her mother. Every time she turned, before the daughter got a chance to start in on cue, the mother would open the red and white umbrella she was carrying and cower behind it until the tirade was over. Then they would both shuffle down the street until something new occurred to the girl, and they would begin their dance all over again.

As they came level with me, I heard the girl scream at the opened umbrella. "... an' you got no idea ... no idea ... look at me ... look at me with your big red eye pointy red eye ..."

The strange family moved past me and the mother closed the umbrella and dragged the girl up the stairs into a hospital and through the revolving doors. There are some people born into this world who have never stood a chance.

After a few more minutes of waiting, I saw Nick come huffing up the street, sweat glistening on his forehead from the effort. He saw me and half-waved, then put his head down and continued his trek up the street. When he finally got to me, he was breathing hard and struggling not to gasp. He leaned one hand on the tank of the bike, forcing me to re-steady myself so that we both didn't topple over.

"Hey! Hey Jon. How's it going?" he panted.

I couldn't help myself from smiling in sympathy.

"Hey, Nicky. You OK?" I said, resting a hand on his damp shoulder and repressing a laugh.

"Yeah, yeah, I'm OK. Just gimme a ... yeah, yeah." He bent over at the waist, trying to catch his breath and laughed a little at himself. "Man I gotta do some-thin'. This is getting' embarrassing."

I laughed with him and said, "You all right?"

He nodded and straightened up.

"Yeah. Hooo! Man, it's a scorcher today," he said staring up at the cloudless sky and holding one hand up to shield his eyes from the sun. He reached around and rummaged in one of his back pockets, coming out with a key. It had a paper tag attached with a fine gauge, twisted wire. On one side was printed the name and address of the storage facility. On the other side were two numbers — one six digit, the other, a three digit.

He handed me the key and said, indicating the information printed on the tag, "OK, there's the address. It's a place down on Eastern at the corner of Cherry Street. The guy at Chris' office said there's a big green sign in front, can't miss it. The six numbers are the code to get the gate open. This number is the locker. I met some guy from the office and had to sign some kinda inventory list. I haven't been down there."

"Thanks, Nick. I'll get the key back to you."

"S'OK. Take your time. I'll get it from you whenever. Like I said, I got no reason to go down there," he said.

I reached over and turned the key to fire up the bike. Nick stood on his own two feet as the engine caught and started. I pulled my helmet on and pushed up the visor.

"Thanks again Nick," I said. "I find anything interesting, I'll be in touch.

Give my best to your Mom."

He nodded and glanced up at the long-term care facility towering over us.

"Sure thing, Jon," he said slowly, still looking up.

I rolled off the sidewalk and bounced the bike gingerly down onto the road, trying not to scrape the plastic moulding protecting the underside of the engine. Then I pointed it south and drove down towards the docklands.

The storage facility was right where Nick said it would be. He was right — there was a large green sign and I didn't miss it. Parked on cinderblocks to the right of the entrance was a large industrial trailer, the kind you see at construction sites; that acted as the office for the place. Facing the trailer, on the other side of the tarmac, were four parking spots. At the end of the short driveway was a large steel gate on wheels and tracks. I pulled up beside a keypad that sat on the end of an iron pole. After fishing in my pocket for the key and consulting the number scrawled in black pen, I punched the six-digit number in and hit the pound key as per the instructions. The gate shuddered and the chain attached to the base of the gate began to retract, rolling open the steel barricade. When I had enough room, I drove the bike through the opening and read a large map on wooden pilings, looking for the entrance into the building nearest the locker.

Once the bike was parked and locked and my gear was stowed in one of the hard bags bolted below the passenger seat, I ambled over to the elevator and pushed the call button. The area near the elevator was littered with bits of paper that had been blown in by the wind and trapped by the cinder block walls. There were two large, flat rolling carts in one corner with tall push handles at one end and were each big enough to hold a couch with room to spare.

The elevator arrived. I stepped on and hit the button for the fourth floor. When I got up to the fourth and the doors opened onto a darkened passageway, the air was surprisingly cool and had the flavour of being trapped. As I stepped off, I must have tripped some sensor, because the overhead lights began to flicker and then blazed into life.

A giant number four was painted in orange on the wall facing the elevator and below it, two arrows pointing in opposite directions indicating which way the numbers went. I followed the left corridor, checking the numbers on the rolling steel doors. The place was a maze, and after two wrong turns, I finally stumbled across #436, mostly by accident, the number stenciled on the metal door in glossy black paint.

A big, steel Master lock hanging from the bolt barred the way, but the key Nick had given me fit and the bolt moved back with a squeal borne from lack of use. I yanked on the rope that was threaded through the flange at the base of the door and it rolled up on its tracks.

I felt around the edge of the doorway until I found the light switch. The two banks of fluorescents hanging from the ceiling on chains flickered and then caught, casting their even yellowed light over a space roughly twenty by twenty. Whoever had packed the room had been very organized about it. There were a series of boxes marked Kitchen 1 through 5 and then sub-labeled "Dishes" "Glasses" "Plates" etc., which were stacked in the left-hand corner of the space on the bare concrete floor. Beside the kitchen boxes was another series that listed dining room china, utensils and candles. There was a four by eight sheet of beveled glass with two hammered steel workhorses that I assumed was a dining room table. Six wooden framed chairs, the seats and backs in black upholstery, sat beside the sawhorses. Three area rugs had been rolled and tied with string and were resting atop the boxes. Wrapped in plastic were a couch and matching love seat in a steel gray fabric. They were of the squared-off, Japanese-inspired design that was popular in minimalist circles. I saw several black lacquered end tables and a matching coffee table stacked carefully on one another. Beside them were two large brushed-steel urns filled with fine sand and had what looked like dogwood twigs sticking out of the sand in fan arrangements. A series of tall thin boxes stood on end and probably held framed artwork.

In the back right corner was a mattress sheeted in plastic, a bedspring, iron side rails and header and footboards done in brushed steel. There was a set of bedside tables, a dresser and an armoire in dark wood. Beside them was a box marked "Linens & Pillows." Four tall boxes with a rod fitted across the top of each indicated they were full of hung clothing. There were a number of boxes marked as containing books which were stacked on a grey desk that had been modeled on that spare 1940's style of industrial furniture. I pulled out the desk chair and sat, swiveling slowly and looking around the storage room.

I'm not a materialist by nature, but for some reason the fact that Chris' entire living environment could fit in one small room was depressing. Then again it would take a considerably smaller space to fit all of my personal possessions. I turned the chair completely around and began pulling out the desk drawers one by one. They were all empty except for a few rubber bands and paper clips, which rattled back and forth.

There was no date book or calendar of appointments in any of the drawers. Presumably it was all electronic anyway. Then why wasn't there a computer here? Nick said he had signed an inventory prepared by Chris' office. I closed all the desk drawers again and turned back to the room, slowly scanning the written demarcations on each of the boxes. At the bottom of one of the book stacks was a box marked "Photos." One by one I pulled the upper boxes off and stacked them aside. The box I wanted was the same size as the others in its group except it was more compact, only two feet deep. I picked it up and put it carefully down on the desktop. It was sealed with clear packing tape, so I pulled out the key to the bike and sliced through the tape down the seam, between the two wings of cardboard. After pulling open the four panels I began removing the contents. There were a couple of photo albums and a dozen framed images, along with a couple of glossy prints with the faint horizontal patterning that comes from a home colour printer, which hadn't made it into frames yet. It occurred to me again to wonder who had packed Chris' things after the accident and it also made me start to wonder why they had been so meticulous.

I opened each of the albums and according to whatever was on the first page, closed and stacked them in rough chronological order, then I started with the one on top. The cover was made of heavy dark brown leather with tan stitching.

The first page had a happy, smiling baby with bright eyes and open mouth, staring quizzically at the camera. One of standard small personal studio shots. It was followed by a succession of shots of Chris as a very small person. There was a series of over-exposed images of the baby Chris being washed in a tub placed in a kitchen sink underneath a window. There were pictures of him and Nick as kids in front of Christmas trees; bundled up in snowsuits in the family driveway; wet grins and plastered hair in a lake somewhere.

I skipped the rest of the first album and went to the second. I opened the cover and found myself staring at our school class picture from third grade. There were about thirty of us, with the girls ~~were~~ all dressed in neon coloured skirts that went below the knee, the boys in collared shirts for the occasion. There were Chris, Ron, Paul and Jason all grinning like idiots. Down in the lower right corner was an eight-year-old me smiling uncertainly at the camera. I had an embarrassing haircut and a button-down shirt. I shook my head, smiling and cursed my mother for dressing me funny. As I turned the pages, Chris' grade school years unfolded before me. Action shots playing Little League and junior soccer, at the zoo and on summer vacations. Each segment was broken by our successive class pictures, grade four, five, six. I turned the pages and watched us all age.

The third album was filled with pictures from junior high and high school. Pictures of me began to crop up outside of the year-end class pictures. There were snapshots of me, Paul, Mack and Chris at St. Mary's on our boards doing wheelies, jumps, and slaloming through mini orange cones. There was a series of shots we'd done as fake crashes. Mine showed me crumpled in a bricked corner of the building, ketchup dribbling from my mouth and my board stuck between my arm and my side as if I had been impaled. I thought suddenly of how Chris had died and my stomach did a slow lazy turn.

The next album seemed to start in grade eleven. There was a picture of Chris, Mack, me and a giant Ron all wearing goofy grins and ripped and soiled uniforms after a game. The out-of-focus scoreboard in the background above the bleachers was clear enough to say we'd won. After that was page after page of Chris standing beside his old Honda. It looked like he'd covered every possible angle, including lying in front of the car and shooting up at the front grille. Then the shots of his girlfriend in high school started. After the first page or so I skipped ahead until I was past them. It didn't feel right. Without his permission, it didn't feel right to look at him in happy times with an old girlfriend. We should have been looking at these together and saying remember when.

The final album seemed to cover the university and post-graduate years. Off-kilter shots of Chris and his friends at the campus pub getting drunk. Pictures of Chris with different people from different years in different seasons; summers away and at home. Halfway through, the album showed graduation and the years that followed. I closed the book and skipped past two more albums and picked up the last one. He hadn't had time to name it yet, though it was full of photographs.

There were pictures of Chris on vacations overseas with the usual architectural standards — cathedrals, monuments and the like. In every picture that he appeared in he was always alone, as if they had all been done with the timer or with the help of some passer-by. There weren't any shots of him with somebody else. It bothered me vaguely that there were damn few photographs of Chris looking happy with someone else. I began to wonder who had taken the few photographs of him. Then that was it. The albums stopped. The framed photographs were a mixed bag of old family shots from childhood, some deep contrast black and whites of landscapes that may have been original or may have been commercial. The unframed photos were black and white shots of the city at night taken from a high vantage point – probably the condo.

Moments frozen in time. I remembered listening to an interview years ago with Richard Avedon, the portrait photographer. He had called photography the sad art. He'd said that photographs never actually told the truth, unlike what the cliché tells us. Photographs are liars; they show a glimpse, a fragment, a sliver only, of a person or a time. Photographs miss the larger issue by concentrating specifically on one tiny moment. All of Chris' albums taken together charted a timeline but missed the life. I had been there for some of those moments as a supporting player. And the man whose story they tried to tell was off-stage now. Social media has replaced Avedon's idea more tidily and likely more dishonestly.

But why wasn't there a computer here? I could accept the firm keeping the work one but everyone, annoyingly, has multiple devices keeping us jacked in. So where was his laptop? Tablet? Cell? The printer had been hooked up to something, so where was it?

I picked up the three photo frames that were yet to be filled. None of them were still in store packing and they each had mattes under the glass and backing boards. Two of them had hanging wires installed and the third a hinged table stand. The table stand frame was easiest to open. I flipped the metal tabs and pulled off the backing. The hard matte card had the usual furred paper damage made from pulling tape off. I popped the backs of the hanging frames and they too had the evidence of images removed. Didn't necessarily mean anything, but maybe it did. And it still bothered me that there were no electronics.

I searched through all the boxes this time and still came up empty. No cell, no tablet, not even a charging cable.

I spent another half-hour putting everything back and pulling the furniture back from the walls to see if anything was worth digging out. All I found were little plastic dishes with dusty mouse poison in them. I put everything back where I had found it, then turned out the lights and closed and locked the door on his past.

# Chapter 19

We were in her parent's house. Her house now. End of the street overlooking Sherwood Park. The small bedroom was stifling in the night heat. I opened the tall double hung windows and heard the rustling of the trees below and thought about all the time I had spent down there as a kid. I turned and looked back at her from the windows A breeze came in and billowed the little-girl curtains that hung on either side.

"Yikes," I said.

She was lying naked on her front, her knees bent and her calves scissoring the air. She lifted and turned her head and propped her chin on her hand.

"Yikes?" she said.

"Yeah, yikes."

She laughed, sat up on the edge of the bed and held her arms out. I walked over to her and dropped to my knees so we were the same height. Running my hands over her shoulders and down her sides I cupped her bare backside on both sides, pulling her closer. We stayed that way for a minute and then her stomach made a tiny gurgling sound. She laughed, embarrassed, and curled up into the fetal position, hugging her legs to herself and burying her head into the tops of her knees.

"Still hungry?" I asked, laughing.

Tara nodded her head and gave me a look that was lecherous by anybody's standards.

"OK then, up you get," I said. "Point me to the kitchen and I will try to satisfy your hunger."

"Oh, you've already done that," she replied, smiling. "But you can make me dinner though."

I gave her a light whack on her bare haunch and pulled her up off the bed. She moved across her bedroom and took a crimson terry-cloth dressing robe off the hook on the back of the door and put it on. I pulled on a pair of her track pants, which managed to go all the way to mid-shin on me. She laughed at the way I looked and took my hand and led me down the corridor. The last time I had been in her house had been in high school and the place hadn't changed at all. The walls of the hallway and upper landing were painted turquoise with tall white baseboards and crown molding running around the ceiling. The banister that led down the carpeted stairs was thick with years of paint.

We went through the center hall and down the corridor to the kitchen. Tara showed me where all the pots and pans were and then she went back to the bar in the dining room and made us each a drink. When she returned, she had a Dubonnet for herself and a neat Bourbon for me. We touched glasses and I took a sip, the liquid making a very pleasant burn down to my stomach.

"Jesus," I said laughing, examining the interior of the fridge.

"What?"

"My God woman, what do you survive on?"

The fridge was near empty. There was a tupperware container with some pistachios, a carton of skim milk, a stick of butter on a plate, a chicken breast wrapped in cellophane and a big bottle of orange juice. I opened the crisper drawers and found a couple of cloves of garlic, a yellow and a red pepper, an onion and two apples.

"What do you mean?" she said giggling in mock self-defense.

"How am I to work my magic with such paltry offerings?" I asked. Tara shrugged and smiled so I said, "All right then, a little clean-out-the-fridge pasta."

I put some water on to boil and started Tara on shelling the pistachios. I found a paper bag in one of the drawers so in went the peppers and then into the oven to roast. When the onion was peeled and chopped I slow simmered it in virgin olive oil. After it became translucent I threw in a little brown sugar to help caramelize it and then added the sliced chicken. When it was browned I peeled and tossed in the peppers and pistachios with some chopped garlic and dried tarragon. Tara sat on a stool at the counter and watched me, sipping her drink.

"So," she asked, "where did you learn all this?"

I smiled over at her while I stirred. "I don't know, here and there. I tended bar for a while and for a couple of months I shared an apartment with the chef from the restaurant. I picked up a few pointers. Besides, I like doing this. Like doing it for you too."

"And I like you doing it for me," she said leaning over and giving me a kiss on the cheek.

I strained the linguine in a colander and then threw the pasta and the pan contents into a ceramic bowl. After coring and slicing the apples I tossed everything together while Tara set out two plates and some candles for us. I served up our dinner and she poured us each a glass of wine.

"Do you know you're very handsome when you're domestic?"

I smiled at her as we clinked glasses. "I'm handsome even when I'm not domestic."

"Yes you are," she said, leveling her eyes at me. I held her stare until she laughed self-consciously.

"Tell me about your day," she said.

I tasted dinner first. Not awful. "Well, I spent most of the day in a storage locker going through all of Chris' things. There were a bunch of old photo albums that I went through — his whole life laid out."

"And..."

"I got kind of restless. It didn't feel right looking through all his stuff. His clothes, furniture, boxes of knick-knacks. His entire life was compressed into this tiny room."

"So what bothered you about it?"

"Maybe I'm not used to snooping, I guess. There's something else too. I can't put my finger on it. But it feels like, like there's some kind of satellite circling around. Something that has touched every part of all this. Something still affecting everything. I mean, the police are taking so long because there appears to be no connection. So either they're no good at what they do or it's so goddamned complicated that they haven't sorted it all out yet. They won't tell me what they know other than they think both Chris and Paul died under suspicious circumstances and what the details were. It's like, I don't know, it's like Kelly wants me involved but only a little. Like he needs to control me. At the storage place, it looked like a couple of images had been taken out of frames. There were no electronics, nothing. Not even a television. And everything was packed like it had been organized by a retentive. Like somebody had gone through everything very carefully before it all got stored."

"Have you talked to the police about this? What's his name again?"

"Kelly."

"Yes, Detective Kelly. Did you talk to him after your search?"

"No. There's nothing to tell yet. Besides, the last time I spoke to him, he didn't seem too enthused that I was still poking around as much as I am. But there's still this, well, feeling of disconnect... from Chris, partly 'cause he's gone. But also, I can't shake feeling the inter-connectedness of everything; that the two deaths are part of the same thing, but I can't find the connection"

"Maybe that's just you," she said. "I mean, you've been gone a long time. You're not sure of the things you used to be sure of. Maybe what happened to your friends is just a terrible coincidence." We ate in silence for a time, then Tara asked, "So what are you going to do from here?"

"Keep plugging away, I guess."

She pointed her fork at her plate and said through a half-mouthful, "This is very good by the way."

I winked and smiled at her. "OK, I know Paul was definitely killed by someone and chances are so was Chris. The police know this but nothing's moving beyond that. So, were they killed by the same person? Were they killed for the same reason? It doesn't make sense. I mean, if there is a connection wouldn't that lead straight to whomever did it? Or, maybe whoever did it doesn't care. Now, Nick was out the night Chris was killed but I think he said he was out with friends and no doubt the cops have cleared him."

Tara looked at me while I talked it out and her concentration was total. I couldn't help but lean over and kiss her before going on.

"So, were Paul and Chris connected in some way other than just old friends? Maybe Paul acted as counsel for Chris or Chris' company. Laura said Paul went out on his own just before he died so Chris might have hooked him up with some business to help him get started. So maybe the connection is Paul's firm."

"Have you been there yet?"

"No, not yet. Laura didn't give me many details. With Paul dead, maybe the company died with him. Laura gave me one of his cards, so a phone call or an office visit would answer that question. The house that she and the kids live in is spectacular so he made a ton of money before hanging out his shingle. The office was a downtown address."

"Will you go to his office next, then?"

"Don't know, but probably. Whatever I find, I'm going to keep on poking away at this until it's finished."

"Well, I can think of no one better to do that," Tara said laying her hand across my forearm.

"Thank you milady."

"The knight in shining armour. Shall I wrap my scarf around your lance?"

"I've never heard it called that before. Could we finish dinner first?"

She laughed and gave me the lecherous look again. Then she dropped her fork with a clatter and, laughing, ran upstairs with me chasing behind.

# Chapter 20

The next morning, thinking about my burglar, I picked up an electronic brass shut-off valve from the local marine supply store and spent a couple of hours in the engine compartment installing it. It had only two settings – off and run. I installed the valve on the main fuel line and then ran split wiring to a switch to the main control panel as well as one at the topside controls. I mounted the switches out of sight under the lip of each panel. I also set LED lights into each panel below the ignition. The tiny light would tell me whether the valve was open or closed. If the shut-off were left in the open position, the light would glow. That meant toggling the switch would turn off the fuel supply and the engines would go dead as soon as whatever was settled in the lines was exhausted. If the valve were already shut off, the light would be out. Flipping the switch would prime the carburetors, and would allow the gas to flow freely. At least it offered a little piece of mind if somebody tried to steal my home.

I finished screwing in the switch on the fly bridge panel when my cell rang. I went below to answer it, but when I picked it up there was nothing but dead air. The display said Unknown Caller. After repeated hellos I gave up and was just about to hang up when I heard a muffled roar that sounded like an engine starting up, through the receiver. I said hello again, but there was still no reply. I hung up and went back to the fly bridge to collect my tools.

I stored them away in the cupboard off the hallway down below and the phone rang again. The display said Unknown Caller again. This was getting annoying. Again I picked it up and the phantom caller stayed silent. I could hear a big engine idling in the background so I just kept saying hello over and over again as I went back up the fly bridge. Finally my caller hung up on me. I thought about blocking the number, but whoever was calling was persistent, if silent. Maybe if they finally did speak I might learn something. When the phone rang again I just let it ring while I bent over to pick up the little bits of cut wire that had fallen on the deck in front of the panel. Let them wait. Almost immediately it started again so on the fourth ring I picked it up but didn't say anything. We stayed that way, neither of us speaking, for a good half minute, when I heard the sound of air brakes being released with a hiss. I suddenly realized that I had heard it twice. Once muffled through the phone, and clearer, though more distantly, over on Queen's Quay. I heard it accelerating, and then, as if on cue, a brightly painted tour bus appeared from in front of the Radisson Hotel and trundled down Queen's Quay. My phantom caller was still with me so I went below quickly and shut the sliding doors to keep out the noise, then I went to the below-decks controls, gave two fast taps on the air horn and heard them remotely through the receiver. Whoever it was hung up on me. I dropped the phone, locked *The Saracen* and walked quickly off the slips and over the suspension bridge. When I was up and over, I jogged the hundred yards to the tour-bus stop on Queen's Quay. Nothing but tourists milling about. No one looking at me, or obviously not looking at me. I turned and went back to the boat. As I pulled myself up onto the rear deck my cell buzzed. I checked the messages and a hushed female voice said "If you are who you should be, 2:00pm, Allan Gardens, Palm House."

Allan Gardens is a small park in the middle of downtown, with a glass-topped Conservatory. Built in the 1860's, it squats in Victorian splendour in a park populated now by some of the downtown core's unfortunates; the underfunded and the self-medicated.

The original magnificent Horticultural Pavilion was destroyed by fire just after the turn of the century, but the Conservatory escaped mostly unscathed. The main body had several arms attached to it after the fire, which now house the tropical plant and cool plant areas, but the most beautiful part of the Conservatory is the domed Palm House; a delicate iron frame that rises about seventy feet and encloses ponds, fronds, and statuary. Majestic ferns and palms stretch their leafy fingers towards the glass dome that makes up the ceiling. Gravel paths meander through the lush foliage with benches placed every so often for quiet reflection. I had been standing about thirty feet from the main doors, screened by a broad fern, since one-thirty. On a weekday afternoon, there wasn't a lot of traffic — the occasional person wandering in with a bag lunch; elderly couples tottering in, fanning themselves in the humid air.

Finally at five minutes to two, a woman walked in. She was tall and thin with a severe but pretty face, maybe mid-thirties. Good, high cheekbones and full lips. Her eyes were almost black, the skin below them was hidden under makeup and was pouchy, like she hadn't slept well lately. Her long blond hair was piled up in a loose bun, the darker roots showing around her ears and at the back of her neck. She was wearing gray wide-leg pants with upside-down V cuts at the cuffs, an open-necked white blouse, and she had a light gray cotton jacket over her arm. Monochromatic. She wore a gold necklace with a locket around her neck. She was a little unsteady on the gravel in her heels.

I kept her in my sight while keeping myself out of hers. She walked the paths, trying for casual, but belied herself by constantly looking over her shoulder. She came to a bench beneath a towering fern and sat. Her eyes searched the paths and tried to peer around trees. I let her stew for a bit. Nobody had followed her in. And nobody who looked potentially dangerous had preceded her. After a minute or so, I walked around the curve in the path and into view. She heard the stones crunching under my footfalls and turned her head to me as I came around the path. I walked up to her and stopped in front of the bench, looking down at her.

"So, who should I be?" I asked.

She regarded me quietly. "You look like your picture, a little older, but same," she said. Her English was good but there was a strong accent that I couldn't identify.

"I'm sure you look like yourself, too," I said.

She smiled but didn't say anything.

"You have me at a disadvantage," I said leaning closer. "Who are you?"

"You come to the point, don't you?" she said.

"Ordinarily I love it when mysterious women invite me for illicit afternoon assignations. But the last couple of days have made me edgy, I guess. So, mystery woman, who should I be?"

"You should be Jonathan," she said

"Well, isn't that a happy coincidence." I kept my voice light while I scanned the paths for other people and listened for sounds of approach. She saw me looking around and began to do the same. When I was satisfied nobody was watching us I sat down at the other end of the bench and waited. She returned her gaze to me.

"I was not sure you would come," she said.

"Well, you went to a lot of trouble to ask me on this date. The least I could do was turn up. Besides, I'm a little curious."

"About what are you curious?"

"You know who I am. You know where I live, despite the fact I've only lived there a couple of days. I'm curious about where you get your information. And I'm curious about why you went through that rigmarole to get my attention. You have an over-developed sense of the dramatic."

"I am just trying to be careful," she replied defensively.

"Careful of what? Of whom?

She didn't answer. She unfolded her jacket partly from around her arm and reached into the inside breast pocket. She came out with a photograph and placed it face down on the bench between us. I picked it up and turned it over and saw it was a picture of her on a rocky beach with a smiling, freckled man. The man was sitting on a huge driftwood log and she was sitting in his lap with one arm around the man's neck. He had both arms wrapped around her slim waist. His hair was shorter than it had been when I'd last seen him. But the grin was the same. Chris.

I was quiet as I looked at the picture for a minute. Then I put it down on the bench between us, waiting for the man in the picture to introduce us. She smiled down at the picture and I watched contrasting emotions play across her face like cloud shadows racing across a field. Finally she stirred and looked up at me.

"My name is Karolina. Karolina Magyar."

I scanned my memory of the guest list from Chris' funeral. I didn't remember her name and said so.

"No, I couldn't go. It wasn't possible."

"I had an excuse. I was a thousand miles away. Why couldn't you go?"

"If I had gone I ... I must say goodbye to Christopher in my own way."

I nodded. I knew how she felt. I hadn't been able to say goodbye to him in the officially sanctioned way either. Surrounded by others who had cared for him. My grief had been private as well.

"Karolina," I asked gently, "why did you come and find me?"

She smiled quietly and said, "Christopher talked about you many times. He used to say that ... how did he put it? That when you and he were friends, that it was innocent."

I shook my head. "What you mean by innocent."

"Christopher said that when you were children, he told me how you used to sit and talk somewhere."

"Sherwood Park," I offered.

"Yes! That is it, Sherwood Park! And you used to talk about many things. He said that his friendship with you, how did he say it? Brought out best in him. I wish that I had known him when he is a boy. To grow up with him. We did not have enough time." She shook her head in embarrassment. "Does anything I say make sense?"

"Yes. We were good friends. We talked about lots of things. We were kids and it was a long time ago now."

I didn't know what else to say to her about it. Trying to explain why you're friends with someone almost makes the feelings sound trite and unremarkable. The reasons people become friends are myriad, and the reasons that people become good friends can be remarkable while at the same time impossible to describe.

"So tell me about you and Chris," I said.

She looked at me warily. "Why do want know about us?"

"Hey, you got in touch with me, remember?

"Yes, I did. I am sorry. I wanted to meet you. Christopher talked about you many times. Christopher and I were together only for six months. But they were very beautiful; he was ... he missed you when you were gone. He said once that he did not know why you left, but that it was good that you did. It kept you away."

"Meaning what, exactly?"

She shook her head. "You seem like a good person, Jonathan. Christopher said you were. And I am happy for him that he had a friend like you. I wanted to meet you, but I also wanted to tell you that you should stop what you are doing."

"Look," I said. "I don't want to be rude, but, frankly, who the hell are you and how did you know where to find me?"

"No," she said firmly. "These things do not matter. There are things that I cannot tell you. I will not tell. But that you should forget about what happened. Keep your good memory of Christopher."

She stood to leave. I stood up with her and grabbed her arm as she began to turn away. "Not enough, Karolina." I squeezed her arm a little tighter. "Who sent you to warn me off?"

"Nobody send me. I just ..."

An elderly couple came around the corner of the path. She had her arm through his and they were talking quietly to one another about the verdant plantings around us. I let go of Karolina's arm and the couple smiled and nodded at us as they passed.

With a downward glance Karolina said, "I know Christopher would have" she searched for the word, "appreciate what you are doing. I know that he would want you to stop. For your sake, Jonathan. Be the friend to Christopher. Leave the memory alone and good."

With that, she turned and followed behind the elderly couple. When she came to an exit path, she stopped and looked back at me. I was still standing by the bench. She dropped her gaze and then turned and walked away. A moment later I heard the street sounds outside amplify momentarily, then with a hiss of the closing door, they were silenced. She had left the picture of her and Chris behind on the bench. I picked it up and put in my shirt pocket as I sat heavily on the bench. I wasn't going to follow Karolina because I knew I wasn't willing to push as hard as I thought I would have to get her to talk to me. But I wasn't going to leave it alone either. So was that what she really wanted? The reverse psychology of everything was beginning to hurt my head. Was she the one missing from the empty frames? Was she really his ex-girlfriend and did that mean I was supposed to listen to her and drop it? Or had she set Chris up somehow and was responsible for what happened? Now my head really hurt.

I left the Palm House and crossed the park to where I'd left the bike. I opened the nylon tank bag and took out the card Laura had given me. Paul Hobbs, Solicitor and Counsel. I rubbed the embossed characters on the card between thumb and forefinger. I climbed aboard and fired her up and pulled on my helmet.

There was an underground parking garage below Paul's office building. At the base of the ramp was an automated ticket machine but I edged the bike around the gate arm, and parked near the elevator in a thin space near a giant fan unit.

It was a 19th-century brick and beam building with a freight elevator. I took the elevator up to the lobby and found the glassed-in directory panels on the wall to double-check the suite number. There was no nameplate showing Paul's firm. I pulled the card from my back pocket and checked the address again. Right building, so? I went up the stairs and checked each floor. At the top floor I walked the halls and followed the numbers until the corridor terminated in a set of wooden double doors. There was adhesive residue on one of the doors where somebody had pulled off a sign. As I reached for the handle, the door swung open suddenly and a yellow cleaning cart worked its way through the opening, followed by a small woman in a light blue uniform. I smiled at her and held the door wider until she had cleared out of the way then stepped past her into room.

"No business," she said as the door closed behind me. I waited for to her say something else or tell me to leave but she just wandered away, the squeaky wheels of the cart rolling off down the hallway.

The reception area had a large curved perforated steel and laminate desk and two chairs in the corner with a square glass table between them. There were no magazines on the table or artwork on the walls. I walked behind the reception desk but there was no phone, only the cord poking through a hole in one of the steel legs. The desk was spotless.

Beyond the desk was a shelf affixed to the wall and there was a perfect circle of water damage left by a planter or a vase. Somebody had once had an office here. Beyond the reception area were three offices, all with window views and what was probably a boardroom at the corner of the building, which had the best view of the bunch. Every room was devoid of furniture or any ornamentation. Paul was dead less than a week and if this was his old business, not only had it folded up around him, it was gone without a trace.

# Chapter 21

Since Paul's office had been a dead end, once I was back aboard I checked everything I could think of online but found no Karolina Magyar listed in the city directory or on social media. I then tried all the outlying municipalities but came up empty again, so I called Kelly to see if he had any ideas. I gave him Karolina's name and told him about my conversation with her. He said he'd see what he could do, so I paced the salon impatiently until he called back ten minutes later.

"Magyar, right? M-A-G-Y-A-R?"

"Yeah. I think so."

"I ran her through DMV and got nothing. I checked everywhere I could think of, but nothing. I'm gonna run ~~through~~ her through the system, see if there were any arrests."

"She had a strong accent, eastern European maybe. You got any friends in Customs?"

"No, but I can make an official inquiry. What are you thinking?"

"She must have come here from somewhere. Can you run her past Passport Control? She said she'd been with Chris for only a little while. So I guess you can start there and work backwards."

"Can I?" Kelly said sarcastically. "All right, I hear anything I'll let you know. Keep in touch." And he hung up.

I called The Breakers but the bartender said Mack was out at a supplier's. I thanked her and dialed Laura at home. It was killing me not to ask her if she knew about the empty office but she had enough to deal with right now.

"Yes, Jon, what can I do for you?" she asked.

"Listen, Laura I'm sorry to bother you again, but do you know where Chris lived?"

"It's no bother," she said, "I think it might be in Paul's phone. Can you hang on?"

"Jon? OK, here's the address; do you have a pen? Yes? OK, it was a condominium. Downtown, near Jarvis and Bloor. Chris lived in the west tower of The Palisades, penthouse. And…"

"And what?"

"Well, there's three phone numbers. Not sure what they all are. Maybe one is an office?" She gave me all the numbers that she had.

I thanked her and hung up. I called the first number that Laura had given me. A toneless computer voice told me the number had been disconnected. I called the second number and a different, equally toneless voice told me I was out of luck. Then I called the last number. The phone rang four times and a voice answered.

"Hey, this' Chris." I felt my stomach drop when I heard his voice for the first time in a decade. "Sorry I'm not here right now. You know what to do." Just before the message ended there was the sound of giggling in the background that was quickly cut off. There was a pause and then a sustained beep.

The silent message system waited for me say something across the years. I terminated the call and put my phone down gingerly on the table beside the sofa. I stared at it defocused as it dared me to pick it up again and leave Chris a message. When it rang again I jumped. It was Kelly.

"I've got a Karolina Magyar entering through Halifax in June of last year. She came in on a student visa and a Hungarian passport. Customs says that they've got no record of her either renewing her visa or leaving Canada. But there's no big surprise there. Says it happens all the time. There's a lot of illegal immigrant traffic through the East Coast. Somebody comes in with a proper visa, they figure it's all right. Not much they can do if somebody disappears after that."

"So they've got no address on her?"

"File says she was supposed to be staying with a family. When the requests for confirmation on the expired visa came back unanswered, they sent somebody to the address she'd provided. Turned out the place didn't exist."

"What, so they left it at that?"

"Yeah, I'm a little surprised too. But the guy told me they've got bigger problems than that. One small fish goes missing, doesn't send up enough flags to worry about. Like I said, they've got bigger problems."

"OK, listen I've got three numbers here for Chris Allinson. Can you look them up?"

"Yeah, gimme the numbers."

I reeled out all three numbers to him and he put me on hold while he went to look them up. He came back on after a minute and a half.

"All right, first number was a cellphone, billing address on Bloor, checks out with what we've got in the case file for the accident as his primary address. The number has been disconnected. Second is an old cellular number, same again, disconnected. Phone records show the billing address for both numbers was the condo. Third number we didn't know about. It's not listed under the condo address. In fact, it's not listed to him at all. The reverse says it's a telephone number listed to an Ontario Business Registration number and a billing address uptown — 257 Amber Road. You know where that is?"

"Yeah, I do. I grew up a few blocks away." I shook my head, confused. "But Amber Road doesn't have houses that go that high. They stop around 190."

"I don't get it."

"When we were kids, me and Chris used to skateboard at a place called St. Mary's Catholic School with Paul and a bunch of others. St. Mary's is on Amber Road at the end. The street dead ends at St. Mary's, so I don't understand how the numbers could continue."

"Unless they developed the area on the other side of the school and continued the name."

"Yeah, maybe."

"So what about this Magyar woman?"

"I have to find her and talk to her again. She knows something. Enough to tell me to back off, anyway."

"Get me her picture and I'll have it distributed. Maybe we'll get lucky and we can bring her in for a chat," he offered.

"I'll send it to you now." I said.

We hung up after I promised again to keep in touch. I took a picture with my cell and texted it to Kelly. Then I tried Mack at the bar again. He was there this time.

"What's goin' on?" he asked.

"This and that. What's shakin' with you?"

"Just trying to keep the suppliers in line. I got this produce guy who's got the best prices and his stuff's always fresh, but he's got a bad habit of putting his thumb on the scale, if you know what I mean. I had to have a talk with him this morning. He's shorted me the last two deliveries. That's my excitement, anyway. The romantic bar trade," he laughed. "Hey, Jason phoned last night. Wanted to know if we all wanted to get together for some cards on Friday night. You in?'

I wondered if Jason was still the player he'd been in high school. I hoped he'd faded a little otherwise I was in trouble. "Absolutely. What are the stakes?"

"Nothing a high-roller like you can't handle. Texas Hold 'Em, hundred in, blinds double every hour." Mack said, rolling off the hip poker-talk.

"Where and when?" I asked.

"I gotta see us through dinner here first. How about nine, nine-thirty at his place?"

"Done," I said. Mack gave me the address and after a little more small talk we hung up.

I spent the rest of the afternoon with a caulking gun and some marine silicone sealer working on the foredeck. I cut away all the old sealant and cleaned the edges of the thick fibreglass with a marine degreaser. I went below under the foredeck and opened the access panels set on each side of the bulkhead. The leaks on the foredeck had left some minor water damage on the inner hull. I excised the small areas of rot and screwed in some fresh oak pieces, and then sealed them. When I was back topside, I bleached and cleaned the foredeck, then set to work with the caulking gun. By eight o'clock, the foredeck was resealed and polished clean. The final sanding and urethane coat of the teak decking could wait now until another day. I rewarded myself with another Grolsch. I made myself a couple of sandwiches and washed them down with the beer. After one more satisfied look at my handiwork, I showered and fell into bed with a pleasant muscle soreness to serve as a reminder of working hard on my new floating home.

# Chapter 22

The morning arrived clean and bright and I was sitting in the captain's chair on the fly bridge with a steaming mug, watching the sun dancing on the inner harbour. There wasn't any real traffic — the ferries had only just begun to run, so the calm was mostly disturbed by only the occasional water taxi moving from the mainland to the island and back. I had slept deeply but since waking up my mind churned with everything that I had learned lately.

The girl had come out of nowhere. How the hell had she found me? Somebody had pointed her at me. But who and why? And going through Chris' possessions in that depressing concrete bunker had left an impression as well. Everything had seemed so small and cheap, stacked up on itself in the dusty little room. Nick had said the company had provided him with the inventory. Maybe the dolt who had been Chris' partner would have something more useful to say than trying to impress me with what a financial sharpie he was.

I went below and found the card Laura had given me. After sidestepping the secretary, I got through to the man himself.

"Johnny!" he cried like I was the best thing that had happened to him today. "What can I do ya for?"

"After our talk the other day, you got me thinking about some things. Wondered if I could buy you a drink after work?" I said. Mr. Congenial.

He faltered for a second and said, "Yeah, sure. But how 'bout I buy. Why don't you meet me at my club? I'm gonna leave early today, get in a sail. You know the RCYC? On the Island? So how about 4:30? You can take a ferry over and walk, or there's a launch."

"It's OK," I said, "I've got a way to get over."

"Good, good. I'll leave your name at the front desk. If I'm not back when you get there then grab a seat in the lounge and order whatever you want."

"Fine. Four-thirty then," I replied. We hung up and I sat back and thought about what to do with the day. The Calvinist work ethic in me was attempting to ruin my doing nothing. After another mug of tea and some careful consideration, I decided that I could afford to ignore what few responsibilities I had. I uncoupled everything and took off for a day of cruising. After clearing the Eastern Gap I chugged out into open water and turned east toward the Leslie Street Spit and Ashbridges Bay. I moved her rpms up and again noticed the slackness in the throttle cables. Mental note to self: order more cables. Despite that though, the engines surged up and pushed the heavy craft smartly across the water.

I passed into the small bay that comprises the Beach. From my perch in the fly bridge I could see the boardwalk and the Leuty lifeguard shack. There were joggers and walkers and families with strollers plying the boardwalk and the concrete path that ran parallel to it. I made Bluffer's Park Marina with the tall sandy cliffs rising behind it around noon and docked her in the visitor's area.

After making her lines fast, I went ashore and had a burger and beer lunch in the sunshine on the patio. Most of the other folk on the deck overlooking the marina were much older than I, enjoying their golden years.

I was back aboard and heading back toward the city by two. I went the long way around the Island, stretching my cruise out, the sun strengthening my quickly fading Florida tan. Once I was clear of the airport runway, I swung her into the Western Gap. According to my watch it was only half past three, so I brought her speed well down and pointed her casually at the Royal Canadian Yacht Club building in the centre of the islands. She wallowed a little at slow speed as the Island ferries kicked up their wakes.

When I was a hundred feet out, a teenager dressed in starched white shorts and a blue golf shirt bounded down onto the dock and waved me over to a slip large enough to take *The Saracen*. I nuzzled her into the berth and gave her a quick bang in reverse as forty-seven-foot cruisers don't just stop on a dime, and she settled. The kid tied up the lines I threw to him and inquired as to whether I was a new guest. I told him no, that I was here to see Mr. Powell, Mr. Sam Powell. He practically stood at attention at the name and said that he would be pleased to look after my boat, and gee what a beautiful boat it was. I thanked him and went below to change out of my cruising shorts. When I was dressed for success in khakis, blue madras dress shirt and boat shoes, I closed her up and headed off.

The main building of the RCYC would not look out of place on an antebellum plantation. Built in a perfect square, the clubhouse sports wide wooden posts that hold up the second story porch, which runs the entire perimeter of the building. From the broad wooden front steps, you have a perfect view of the harbour and the downtown skyline. It probably makes the membership feel all warm and cuddly that they can enjoy their whiskey sours within sight of the financial towers that pay their dues and initiation fees.

An information board in the main lobby listed Powell as Treasurer of the Governing Board. It also mentioned two upcoming regattas that I didn't want to miss and that tickets were going fast for the End of the Summer Dinner and Dance, which was sure to be the social highlight of the season. I found the lounge and took a stool at the end of the long polished bar. There were a couple of afternoon sailors in a loud group at the other end. The bartender left them and came down to me, polishing a cut crystal tumbler as he walked. I ordered an Eagle Rare, neat, and he nodded and left to make the drink. The group at the end called the bartender over and nodded at me and spoke in low tones. The bartender glanced at me and shook his head then left them to return with my drink.

He put a leather coaster down in front of me with a gold club logo on it and placed the heavy tumbler. The amount was generous and my first sip burned heavy with sweet fire.

"Sir," the bartender said, "the gentlemen at the end wish to know if you'd like to join them." There was loud laughter as one of them slipped halfway off his stool and had to grab the bar edge for support.

"Do you think I should?" I asked.

He smiled and said, "Up to you, sir."

I stuck out my hand. "Jonathan. And it looks like I'd have some catching up to do."

"Edward," he said, shaking my hand. "About two hours' worth."

"Tell them thanks, but I'll pass."

"Very good." He looked back at them and shook his head, then went to a position halfway between the soused group and me and made busy work. There was more laughter as one of them got up and lurched the length of the bar.

When he pulled up beside me, he leaned a casual and unsteady arm on the bar and said, "Hey pal, whyn't you wanna have a drink with me and my buddies? You're new here, right? Whyn't you come and meet the boys?"

He was bigger than I was, with spiked blond hair and a barrel chest, no doubt the bully of the group. He had a strange half-Australian accent that he wavered in and out of. I was hard to tell whether he was an ex-pat or a pretender. And he punctuated each question with a finger-jab to my shoulder.

I smiled at him and said, "No thanks, I'm just here to meet somebody."

"Oh, you gotta date?" he asked mockingly. "Who with?"

"Sam Powell."

"Sammy? Sammy Powell? Yeah? Good guy Sammy. So who're you?"

I casually hooked my foot onto the barstool behind him and pulled it quietly away from him. "Just a guy," I shrugged.

"So you know Sammy, eh? Helluva guy."

"How do you know him?"

"Sammy? Oh, Sammy's old school. Hooked me up with some great invest ... invest ... deals."

"Really? How nice for you."

"Yeah? So listen, guy, you gonna have a drink with us while you're waitin' for Sammy-boy?" Again with the finger-jab.

"No thanks," I said. I motioned the bartender for another drink.

He half-turned and shook his head at Edward with a big grin and told him not to bring me another. As he turned back to me, I knocked his leaning arm off the edge of the bar. His expression changed as he flailed for balance, tangling his feet in the stool I'd pulled out behind him. He cracked his forehead on the edge of the bar and down he went, taking the stool with him. His mates erupted in laughter as he dragged himself up again, rubbing his head. Just then, Powell came through the doors, overdressed in yellow wet-sailing gear.

"Hey boys! Whaddya say?" he said loudly. My new friend took his attention off me and looked back at Powell. The bartender came back and replaced my empty tumbler with a fresh drink. He grinned at me and then went back to his neutral position ten feet away.

Powell waved at me and shook hands with everyone in the drunken group. The big clumsy one rubbed his head again, gave me a tough look and went back and joined his buddies. Powell came down to my end with a questioning look.

"What gives Johnny?"

"You've got sloppy friends, Sam."

"Who, Benji? Nah, he's a good guy. What happened, anyway?"

"He tripped over himself."

"Oh yeah?" he said in disbelief. Edward came down and put a red drink in a martini glass in front of Powell without being asked. Powell raised his eyebrows theatrically and said, "Ahhh, behold the Crantini. C'mon, let's sit over by the window."

We went and sat at a table surrounded by leather club chairs that had been angled to look out on the harbour. I saw the kid who had helped me dock *The Saracen* on a 30-foot C & C sloop, winching down and storing the sails.

"Yours?" I asked.

"Yeah," he said, "my little weekend runabout. Boy usually does a good job takin' her down," and he pointed at the kid trying to get the sails down in the stiff offshore breeze. "So, you have any trouble finding the place? You come over on Bob's water taxi or you take the ferry?"

I smiled and resisted the temptation to point out *The Saracen*.

"So last time we saw each other," he said to break the silence. "Sorry if I was a little ..."

"Insensitive?"

"Yeah, listen, it's been hell without Chris. A lot of our accounts, you know, they loved working with him. We've had to really bust our humps to keep 'em happy after he was gone."

"I can't imagine the ways in which the super-rich can be problematic."

"You got no idea," he said shaking his head. "So what's up?"

"I was talking with Chris' brother the other day. He mentioned that your office was responsible for all the possessions after the accident. Who cleaned out the office and the condo?"

"Oh, uh, we had a moving company do the condo. My secretary went through the files at the office and everything pertinent to our accounts, she disbursed them from there. Chris' personal belongings from the office got sent to a storage area somewhere downtown with rest of his stuff. Why?"

"Who inventoried everything?"

"Well, the movers gave me a list of all the stuff from the condo. Jeannie added to it with the office contents that were his. Then she typed it all up and it went into probate. I told the family that when the company cleared everything, that we'd let them know."

"Let them know what?"

"The condo was only part of Chris' holdings. He had a couple of limited companies, one of which held the paper on the condo. He had a few properties around town as income places, as well. He managed his own portfolio through the firm under the limited companies. Corporate tax is a lot lower than personal; it always makes sense to distance yourself from your money. Keep it where the Feds can't get it all, you know what I mean? When everything's figured out, his family's gonna come out of this all right. Believe you me." He glanced over my shoulder and something caught his eye. He stood and smiled and I turned to look as well.

A tall silver-haired man had entered the room and was peering around looking for someone. He saw Powell standing and began to stride over. I stood as he arrived at our table. He was deeply tanned, the kind of tan only possible through careful application of electric sun and lots of moisturizer. He was probably sixty and looked ten years younger. His light blue suit set off his skin colour to advantage and he had about him the aura of power and control.

"Mr. Mugridge, let me introduce Jonathan Birnam. Jon this is Mr. Mugridge, our CEO."

He had a firm, dry handshake and said, "Jonathan, pleasure. May I join you gentlemen?"

Powell nearly fell over himself offering a chair and made excuses to go get Mugridge a drink.

Mugridge settled into the leather chair and smiled. "So Jonathan, are you a new member here?" He probably thought of it as his friendly face but it was like looking at a tanned barracuda.

"No, I'm here as Sam's guest. I don't think I could afford this place."

He laughed and nodded his head imperceptibly as if in confirmation of either what I had said or his own presumptions about me. "I hope I'm not interrupting anything by sitting in?" he said just as Powell returned from the bar.

Before Powell could say anything I replied, "No, not at all. Sam and I were just chatting about his old partner, Christopher Allinson." I saw Powell's eyes widen a little but he was too good to really react.

"Oh yes," he said, sucking at his teeth. "Christopher. That was a terrible, terrible business. Tell me, what is your interest in the matter?"

"Chris was my oldest friend and I don't believe it was an accident."

Mugridge steepled his fingers and regarded me over them for a moment. He didn't even look over at Powell, his entire focus was directed at me.

"And what makes you think it was not an accident?"

I smiled and said, "Well, not enough to mention. For the time being I have little more than my disbelief and my suspicions."

"That's a very serious statement though, don't you think Jonathon? And reckless given you have nothing to support that view."

"Perhaps. But I've never been the careful sort."

Mugridge finally took notice of Powell standing beside him holding his drink. He reached over and took the glass from Powell, who sat again in his own chair and watched the conversation silently.

"I take it you live here in the city?" he said, sipping from his glass.

I wondered where this was going but it isn't hard to find an address so there was no point in subterfuge. "I do. I live down by the water."

"Really?" he said, "And how is that in this climate?"

"Wonderful now," I replied. "We'll see what happens after Thanksgiving though."

He smiled noncommittally and said, "Indeed. Indeed. So getting back to Christopher. I trust the authorities are doing their utmost to investigate?"

"I'm sure they are as well," I said. "But an extra hand never hurts. Besides, I'm a little more motivated than they are."

"Though you have no official standing or capabilities in the matter?"

I smiled at the passive aggressiveness, "Standing no. Capabilities, to be determined. In fact, Sam and I were just discussing what happened after Chris died." I turned my attention to Powell and cut Mugridge out. "So who went through everything after it was stored?"

"What does that mean?" Mugridge asked. Clearly he was someone not used to being cut out of anything he had an interest in. I continued to look at Powell.

"Well, after Chris died and his belongings were inventoried and moved, somebody must have double-checked the list from the movers against what was put in the storage area. Otherwise I'd say your firm missed out on doing its due diligence."

Powell looked nervously at Mugridge and stammered his way through his answer. "Oh, yeah, well no, I mean, I went to the locker to make sure that everything was everything. And the list was complete. We'd never let anything happen to Chris' personal possessions. They belong to his family now."

"And who inventoried the list of belongings from the office?"

"Well, any files or work-related information are the property of the firm. I know that a bunch of extra accounts landed in my lap, and the rest would have been distributed to the others on a merit system."

I pulled the photocopy of the picture out of my breast pocket and unfolded it. He took it from me and looked at it. He gave it the once over then handed it to Mugridge who looked at it as well and then handed it back to me and casually looked out the window.

"Do you know who the people in the picture are?" I asked Mugridge.

He turned back to me, "Obviously Christopher. I don't know the young woman."

"What about you Sam?"

Well, yeah. Chris and some woman. I don't know her. Never seen her before."

"Really?" I said.

"Yeah, don't know her at all."

"Interesting."

"How's that?" he asked.

"Well, you said you and Chris were good friends. I thought maybe you might have been introduced."

"Nope, never."

"Funny thing," I said. "When I went to the storage locker, somebody had been through the personal effects. Had taken some of the photographs. And there was no laptop, no tablet, no cell phone. Know anything about that would you ?"

"No," he said indignantly. "Of course not!"

"Well, somebody does. Somebody has his electronics." I watched as a look of uncertainty crossed his features. "I'm having trouble believing the moving company would do that. That would ruin their reputation and probably play hell with their bond. Why would they go through anything like that? You said you checked that everything that was supposed to be there, was there. So I guess your signature must be on the inventory. That right Sam? Is your signature on the inventory?"

"Sure," he said warily.

"Hmmm," I said, "well, I'll have to go see again. Think you can get me a copy of that inventory, Sam?"

"Well, those things belong to the family now. We're out of it. I don't think I even have a copy anymore, you know?"

"You're right, Sam. I don't know why you'd need to keep a record of that. Besides, I've already got permission from the family. Nick gave me a key the other day to the place, so I'll just have to go and check on that again myself. Actually, I imagine that Nick has a copy of that inventory you signed. I mean, I don't think Chris' family would be too pleased if somebody had removed anything that belonged to him. I also doubt that the police and your insurance company would be happy about it either." I took a final pull from my drink and got up. "Well, thank you for the cocktail, gentlemen. Enjoy the big dinner and dance this weekend.
Mr. Mugridge, pleasure." As I stood to leave, Mugridge looked at Powell and nodded curtly, then stared out the window again.

"Hey, hey," Powell said, laughing and standing with me, "man, you're some kind of hard case, ya know?' He glanced down at Mugridge, who continued to ignore the fact that I was leaving. Powell put a reassuring hand on my shoulder. "All right, all right, listen." He sat down again and looked out the window like his boss to collect his thoughts. When he looked back I was still standing over him with my arms folded across my chest.

"Hey, Jonathan, sit will ya? OK look, Mr. Mugridge I'm sorry, but," he sighed as Mugridge nodded then resumed looking out the window. "The family would be pretty upset if they knew about this, but," He looked around furtively, sowing the seeds of whatever he planned to spin out. I waited.

"Look, I don't mean anything against Chris, but, well you know, there was this girl, the one in the picture. A woman, I mean, and, well she was a ... well she was a pro if you understand my meaning? I mean, anyway, Chris got hooked up with this woman and, well, I mean he even talked about bringing her to a couple of company functions and ..."

Mugridge cut him off. "We wished to ascertain whether there was anything that could potentially embarrass the firm. When we found out what the nature of their relationship was and what the young woman did for a living, we decided we could not take the chance. If there was some kind of impropriety, one of our senior people and... a sex worker."

"And what would lead you to believe it would become common knowledge, let alone interest anyone?"

Powell cleared his throat and said quietly, "Well, you have to understand, Jonathan, our clients are very respectable, very conservative and ..."

Suddenly I was Jonathan, not Johnny. He needed me to listen. And his casual vocabulary was gone as well.

"It could be difficult for us, publicly," Mugridge continued, "if something like that, about that kind of poor judgment on Christopher's part, got out. It would be bad for investor confidence."

"Did he have a personal computer?"

"I'm sure he must have but we would not have touched his personal effects."

"No, no of course not," I said reassuringly. I knew they were lying. There was nothing untoward in the photograph – just two happy people. The first question was why were they taking this line?

"Thank you for being so up front with me, gentlemen," I said. "I appreciate your confidence."

"Yes, well like I said, I don't want you thinking the wrong thing. I mean, me and Chris," Powell held up his forefinger and middle fingers intertwined to indicate how close they had been. "You know, she was a sweetheart. I mean, I could see why, but after his accident…"

"Sure thing," I said, "no need to explain." When I stood this time, Powell and Mugridge did the same. "Well, thank you again for your time, gentlemen. I'm sure I can find my own way out."

"Not at all, Jonathon. Allow me," said Mugridge, extending a guiding hand toward the lobby.

I turned and walked over and slid some money under a bowl of peanuts for the bartender. Mugridge smiled and lead the way back through the club. In the lobby on the way out, we passed the group from the bar. My clumsy friend, whining incoherently, was being helped on both sides by his weaving companions.

As we walked, Mugridge said, "Jonathon, I hope we can rely on your discretion in this matter. Please believe me when I say that we felt it was in everyone's best interest. Our clients, the firm, and of course, Christopher's own reputation."

Once outside, we stood on the gigantic porch looking out at the lake in the shade of oak trees. High up in one of them, a cicada began its song. Mugridge glanced up at the sound and said to me, "It's a sound of summer, isn't it? That noise."

I nodded and didn't reply. He continued, "You know Jonathan, the cicada is a fascinating insect. I was always interested in entomology as a boy. Did you know the cicada takes seventeen years to mature? It spends more than a decade and a half in the dark, underground, feeding on tree roots. Then breaks out of its carapace, emerges and finishes the maturation process in the open. Finally it sends out its mating call. It mates and buries its larvae then dies. Four or five weeks is all it has in the outside world." He smiled and added, "I have always enjoyed the cyclical nature of things. The Chinese thought the cicada was a symbol of rebirth and redemption while other ancient cultures saw it as a harbinger of war." He put his hand on my arm for emphasis. "Like so many things, it all depends on your perspective."

"Why didn't you follow your fascination professionally?"

"Frankly, because there's no money in it," he laughed.

"Mmmmm," I said, smiling, "I remember a story about cicadas from when I was small. A fable actually."

Mugridge looked at me blankly so I continued, "Well, a cicada was singing his summer song high in an oak tree. A passing fox heard the song and searched from tree to tree until he found the cicada. The fox called up into the tree extolling the cicada to teach it such a beautiful song. Now, the cicada knew about foxes and knew they couldn't be trusted. In fact he had seen several of his cicada friends eaten by foxes. The cicada said to the fox that he would never be able to sing exactly like a cicada could, so why should he teach the fox the song? The fox implored the cicada to teach him, so the cicada did. The fox thanked the little cicada and went away singing as best he could. Shortly afterwards the fox returned, claiming he had forgotten the words. He begged the cicada to come closer and teach him again. The cicada dropped down a few branches and taught the fox again and the fox left singing happily under the watchful eye of the cicada. The cicada knew that the fox was up to something so he flew to the ground, picked up a stone and took it back to his perch in the oak tree. The fox returned again and begged the cicada to come closer and teach him again. The cicada agreed and pushed the stone out of the tree. Now, the fox was vicious but not smart. Thinking the cicada was coming closer and fooled by the falling stone, the fox caught it in his mouth and bit down as hard as he could and the stone broke all of his teeth. You see, the fox thought he could fool the little cicada. But the cicada knew that by paying attention to what happens to those around you, one can learn who can be trusted, and who cannot be."

Mugridge regarded me silently and then said slowly in a measured voice, "What a wonderful story. Perhaps I should tell it to my grandson."

"Yes, perhaps you should. It's important to be able to make those kinds of distinctions. Thank you for the drink, Mr. Mugridge."

I stuck out my hand and we shook. He didn't seem pleased anymore though the barracuda smile was back in place. "Thank you for the story, Mr. Birnam."

I turned and walked down to the slip where *The Saracen* was docked. The kid saw me coming and met me at the dock to help untie her. I gave him a few dollars as a thank you and he tossed her lines up onto the deck while I fired up the Chryslers.

I pulled her into reverse and glanced at the club as I backed out and spun the wheel. The bow turned smartly and I eased her forward slowly so as not to create any wash that would disturb the docked vessels. As I came level with the club, I could see Powell and Mugridge standing and talking in the window where we'd had our drinks. They were both staring out across the harbour. As *The Saracen* turned slowly back towards the city, I hit the air horn. I saw Powell jump, startled at the noise, even muffled through the window. They both looked at the cruiser and I grinned at them and shot them with my thumb and forefinger.

# Chapter 23

The hour was early enough that the sun was barely a promising glow with the mist from the night-cooled harbour eddying between the boats. I scrubbed the sleep from my eyes as I padded into the galley. After I made a pot of tea and let the clock creep past 7:00 I phoned Kelly to ask him if they'd found anything at Chris' condo after the car accident. The desk sergeant with the lilting accent took a message for him. Twenty minutes later, Kelly called back.

"You know what time it is, for chrissakes?"

"Yeah, I paid attention in first grade. And you're already at work, you keener you."

"What do you want so goddamn early? Wait a minute." He made sounds like he was mumbling to himself while he read the sergeant's note. "Of course we searched the deceased's condominium, why?"

"What did you find?"

"Nothing interesting. A date book but no cellphone. No computer either. No work files of any kind. What have you been doing?"

"Had a meeting yesterday with Chris's ex-partner and ex-boss. They're being cagey but I don't why. Beyond that, nothing worth telling."

"In other words, this conversation is a waste of time," he said and hung up. I held the phone out and looked at it for a minute. Clearly not a morning person. I went out to the rear deck and gazed across the harbour at the RCYC building out on the Island. The morning light was so low that I couldn't see details but I could pick out the white shape against the dark trees and thought about how everything I learned had the same patina. Dimly seen with not enough light to make out the details. I thought about what Mugridge and Powell had, though falsely, admitted to. But there was no impropriety on Chris' part as far as I knew. Though I'd only met her once, Karolina didn't strike me as a pro, but what did I know? My life experience hadn't taken me to that particular world. So was there some connection between Karolina and the investment firm? But what would the firm have to do with her, whether she was in the trade or not? I couldn't make sense of anything. And I've always thought, when you can't solve something, do something else. If I buried it all in the back room of my mind, some kind of answer would make itself clear eventually.

I went back to the stateroom and got into some shorts and my cross-trainers; then I locked *The Saracen* up and crossed over the bridge to Pier 4. I wandered down to the lake's edge and ambled along the breakwater, stretching occasionally and trying to twist an ache out of my back. Once I was past the bottom of Spadina Avenue I started an easy jog through the small park and past the old concrete silos at the foot of Bathurst.

I picked up the pace a little and ran the path as it wound behind condos and past the sheltered boat basin. There was traffic plying Lakeshore Boulevard to my right, but it was too early for the real morning assault that would come an hour from now. The path headed a little south to run along the lake's edge again. I rounded the corner and began to jog down the access road on the south edge of the Ontario Place parking lot. Heading away from Lakeshore, I could see the bulk of the pods standing awkwardly on their metal stork-legs. I'd come down here as a child with my mother and father and Katherine. Picnic lunches, Children's Village and maybe a concert at the Forum.

Sadly, the Forum and its free concerts were gone now, replaced by the much more modern, acoustically improved, and completely charmless Amphitheatre. Beyond the new venue were the interconnected pods standing high above the water on their fragile looking legs and the geodesic dome of the Cinesphere that formed the main body of the now mothballed summer attraction. I remembered going to IMAX movies in there; the images on the huge screen playing with your sense of balance and sending you out on wobbly legs.

The path became parallel again with Lakeshore Boulevard as it passed between Ontario Place and the Exhibition grounds and I moved my pace up a notch to stretch it out.

My legs felt strong, the muscles moving fluidly. As I ran past the western edge and the lake appeared again, I became aware of a vehicle moving far too slowly in the curb lane of Lakeshore heading west with me. It was a big, silver Mercedes G class. The vehicle for those who feel a Jeep is too down market for them and have a couple hundred grand lying around. I concentrated on my pace and breathing but kept a casual eye on the Mercedes. The path dipped down and stayed with the water's edge as Lakeshore curved up. The Merc rolled on and away as I kept to the path. I had already decided to jog as far as the Bathing Pavilion I'd visited on my first night back, then turn around.

I shook my head to clear away the thoughts that were trying to crowd their way in. As I came up a small hill with a cluster of pines, the path crossed the driveway of the rowing club that was perched above the lake. The Mercedes was parked in the driveway across the running path. As I neared the car, the driver's window slid down with a slight whir. I slowed to a walking pace and then stopped about three feet from the car. Elvis hadn't changed his attire since I'd seen him last, though he had added some jet-black sunglasses.

He tilted his head toward the back to indicate I should get in. I looked at the sparse traffic passing by. At this time in the morning there still wasn't much. The few cars that did pass by showed us no interest. I stood where I was until Elvis poked the muzzle of the Beretta just over the windowsill. I felt my stomach drop. With a sigh and an ache at the back of my throat I got in the back seat, my sweat-soaked shirt sticking to the expensive German leather. A bald guy with a goatee was sitting beside Elvis up front. When the way was clear, Elvis backed the car out of the driveway and we cruised off west along Lakeshore.

We were silent while the car whispered along past the Boulevard Club. They ignored me so I quietly tried to open the door but there was no tension behind the handle. Lakeshore Boulevard crossed over the Humber River and we drove briefly on the elevated portion beside the Expressway before coasting down onto Lakeshore again on the other side of the river. Past the towers of Palace Pier a profusion of lakeside condos had been built, replacing the string of no-tell-motels that had once littered the area. Elvis paid no mind to speed limits or red lights as we sped along and crossed the invisible border into Mimico.

I had read once that the area had been named by bastardizing an old First

Nation's word that meant the "resting place of the wild pigeons." The article said that in the late 1800's, the neighbourhood had begun to be developed and the city's wealthiest families had built grand summer homes at the water's edge. There were only a dozen or so left as most of them had fallen to development after the WWII. The ones that were still intact lined the south side of Lakeshore Boulevard. To the north were much smaller homes, which had sprouted up when the Grand Trunk Railroad had built the Mimico Yard the following century.

The car slowed and turned into the driveway of a magnificent house on the south side. Elvis flipped down the sun visor above him and pressed a button on a keypad affixed to the underside of the visor. Black iron gates at the head of the driveway slid back on tracks and the Merc glided through. I looked back through the rear windshield as the gates rolled shut behind us. The gravel crunched beneath the tires and we pulled up onto the semi-circular drive in front of the house. It was a huge place, built in faux-Tudor with a steeply pitched red-tile roof. The bulk of the house looked like it had been constructed with lake stone, and a series of chimneys at both ends of the roof indicated that fireplaces bookended the house. Carefully trimmed juniper bushes flanked the broad stone steps that led to the wine-red front door. Elvis and Goatee got out and Elvis opened my door for me. I climbed out and he gave me a little shove as they led me up the stairs. Goatee knocked loudly on the door and a moment later a young woman actually dressed in a maid's outfit opened the door. Another push from Elvis and we entered as she closed the door behind us. Large, flat stones were laid in the grand entrance floor, while above my head, a huge crystal chandelier illuminated the front hall. A wide staircase curved around the left wall and out of sight to the landing above. Goatee moved past me through the parlour to my right, disappearing into the recesses of the huge house. Elvis pushed me in the shoulder blade to follow.

I turned around and he smirked at me. "Do that again," I said, "and I will hurt you."

"*Bazdmeg*," said Elvis.

"That is enough, I think," said a voice above and behind me. I turned to see a man in his late sixties coming down the curving staircase. He was deeply tanned with a broad face and spatulate features, dressed in olive-coloured pants, a light blue shirt and ox-blood loafers. The shirt sported French cuffs with silver links.

Above his fleshy nose, his eyes were amused. The hand skimming the banister held a cigar that trailed smoke behind him. When he reached the bottom of the stairs he opened his arms expansively.

"Please, please, Mr. Birnam. I am sorry for the rudeness of my associate. Liev, you should not speak to our guest that way," he admonished.

"Liev?" I said to Elvis, "Gee, I only missed by an 's'."

"Please, Mr. Birnam," said my gregarious host, smiling and holding out an arm pointing beyond the parlour.

The three of us wandered through the parlour to the back of the house. We went down a few steps into a solarium filled with plants that ran the width of the house. Beyond the doors of the solarium a broad terraced flagstone patio with a glass-topped patio set overlooked the terrific view. The city followed the edge of the lake and disappeared in the early morning haze. I could just see the Islands in the near distance and thought longingly about *The Saracen*. The tall buildings of the financial district were framed by the almost colourless sky. The lake was calm, with a light breeze that had brought out some early sailing folk.

"You are confused about the time, I think?" the man said. He laughed and sat in a wicker chair with a large curved back. "I am always the early riser. You catch the worms that way, yes?"

He motioned me to sit across from him. When we were both seated, the girl from the front door in the maid's outfit appeared carrying a tray. There were two glasses in ornate silver holders with a steaming amber liquid in them. She set them out on the table between us along with a silver dish with misshapen cubes of brown sugar and a pair of silver tongs.

"Do you take the sugar?" he inquired.

"No, thank you."

He took two cubes and dropped them in his tea, then stirred meditatively. "I think the Russians did many things badly. But I think I love the formal tea like the Russians. It is very civilized," he said. "Please, please. You should be tired after your running. Have some tea, you will feel better."

As I reached for the curlicued silver handle, Elvis and Goatee came back into the room and sat at another table at the far end of the solarium.

"Mr. Birnam," the man began, "I call you Jonathan, yes? Jonathan, I wanted us to have a little talk. How is your tea? It is good? Excellent. So, as I say, I wanted to meet with you and talk with you a little bit.

"Ahhh, but you must be wondering, who am I?" He put his tea down on the table, clasped his hands together and leaned forward on his knees. "I had a teacher once. A very stern man. But a very good teacher also. He would say 'What is in a name?' Do you have this expression?"

I nodded. "Yes, I know the expression."

He laughed. "Good, good. You are an educated man, I think. You know this expression. Then you know that my name is not important right now. What is important is that we say hello, we drink some tea together, and we talk, yes?"

"Fine."

"Good, I think you are going to like me, then." He stretched his arm out and thumped his fist on my knee. "I wanted to meet you Jonathan. You are very interesting man to me."

"Why is that?"

"Well, you are loyal. This is an excellent quality. I admire this. You seem very determined. I like this also. I would have you work for me. You are very capable man."

"Is this a job interview?"

He threw his head back and laughter boomed from his chest. "And the sense of humour as well. Very good! I like this." He thumped my knee again. "No Jonathan. Not job interview." He chuckled, "No, no. It is talk over tea. Why, are you searching for job?" He laughed at his own joke and looked at me expectantly.

His personality was infectious and I smiled despite myself. "No."

"It is too bad. Yes, I would have you work for me. You know, when I came to your Canada I was young. Younger than you are now. My boys," he paused and smiled at the two sitting at the other table, "they were very small. My wife and I, we came to ask for the asylum, it is called. Have you been to Hungary, Jonathan?"

I shook my head.

"No? It can be a beautiful country. My city, Budapest, very pretty." He pronounced the word 'Boodapesht'. "The two cities together, did you know this? Yes, Buda and Pest, across the river from each other, together yet separate. Buda is like the country, very hilly. And Pest, Pest is on eastern side of the Danube. Very flat.

That is the side I come from. It was not so nice as in Buda. I grow up in part of city called Angy-Alföld. In English, you would call this Angel Land. But not so much of the heaven, I think. It is rough part of Pest. Poor, very poor people. My wife and I, we want to make better life for our sons. Many people living together in old houses. Small houses. Very poor. It is better now that the Communists are gone. Though I tell you, when the Communists are there, there is no unemployment. Everybody get an education. But business? No good for business, for building a future for one's family. I tell you something, the living in Angel Land during hard communism, very difficult to make a good life. I decide, I will make a better life somewhere else. I study at Business Science University. The Közgazdaságtodományi. Under the Communists, everybody get an education. It is good. Maybe one good thing. So some years later, I come to your Canada. And it is very nice. Very clean. Very big. No Communists. I like this!" He laughed again as the girl returned with two fresh teas, which she put down in front of us and then left with the empty glasses.

"We have a samovar. You know this? Samovar? Yes, we keep samovar making tea all day. I drink so much tea, my insides are tanned like the boot leather!" He chuckled at the age-old joke. "So, Jonathan, I come to your Canada to make good life for myself." He swept his arm around the room and took in the panorama as well. "And I have made a good life, yes?"

"Can't beat the view."

"Ha! You see! You are right! You cannot have better view. My wife, she did not live to see this house." He glanced at a black and white photo in a silver frame of a severe looking woman sitting with her hands in her lap. He smiled and his tone shifted down a notch. "Now Jonathan, I want to tell you something." He leaned forward again and put a fatherly hand on my arm. "You are disturbed, you are troubled, I think. No, no, I can see in your eyes. You are troubled man. And I tell you something. I think you must not be troubled. You should be happy. You are young man." He patted my arm in a fatherly way and sat back in his chair.

I sat for a moment trying to collect myself. "I don't know what to say," I started. "You're right. I should not be troubled. But," I leaned forward and motioned him closer. He leaned in and cocked his head to listen. "This morning, I was jogging along, and these two men came and kidnapped me at gun point."

He inhaled sharply and wore an expression of mock surprise.

"No," I said, "it's true. And these two men, they took me to this beautiful house." He nodded his head, feigning rapt attention. "And this nice Hungarian man gave me tea and told me his life story." He looked down demurely. "And as nice as this man was, I couldn't help but worry about what he really wanted. You see he never actually came to the point."

He nodded his head sagely. "Yes," he said, "I can see now, why you are troubled. I tell you this. I would very much like to sit with you and tell you stories of Budapest. I think you would enjoy them. But I know that you must have many things to do. You must care for your beautiful boat, no? So I tell you, you should go and enjoy your life. You should be happy and live long. Perhaps you will have a house with a magnificent view someday as well. But for now, you should go. I hope that someday we will be able to talk again. But not of the past. I think it is good to let the past alone. Do you not think? Yes, I think it is better to live now, in this time. Do not trouble yourself with the past, Jonathan." And he gave my knee a final pat.

He stood and I realized I was being dismissed, so I stood as well. "Liev will be happy to drive you back to your boat, Jonathan."

"No thank you," I said. "I'll make my own way home." Elvis had walked over from the other side of the solarium and was standing right behind me. I had my right hand at my side. I turned my body slightly to get the aim right and casually crossed my left arm across my waist and held my right wrist. Then I began to strain my right arm backwards, pulling against being held by my left. "By the way," I said, "what does that word - 'Bazdmeg' - mean?"

The old man tut-tutted. "It is not very nice word. It means 'fuck you' in the English."

"Ah," I said. I let go with my left and my right fist flew backward and hit Elvis in the groin. With a surprised grunt he doubled over and fell on the tile floor holding himself and coughing. The old man was shocked at first, and I suddenly remembered I had just hit one of his sons, but then he burst into laughter. Goatee jumped up but the old man waved him off. He shook my hand vigorously.

"Yes, yes," he said through his laughter "If this was interview, you would have job!" The girl came back in the room and stopped short when she saw Elvis writhing on the floor. The older man said something in Hungarian to the girl and then switched to English for my benefit. "My young friend, it has been pleasure to meet you. And I hope you will take what I say to your heart. You must listen to me, do not dwell in the past. You will be happy and, very important," he looked at me hard for emphasis, "I will be also if you do this. Goodbye Jonathan."

The girl led me back through the house to the front door. I glanced back and saw Goatee helping Elvis to his feet. I was pleased to see his eyes watering in pain. The old man put a finger under Elvis' chin and tilted his head up. Then leaned in and spoke quietly and sharply to him. When he let go, Elvis visibly sagged against Goatee. The old man looked up and saw me watching and waved good-naturedly.

I took a cab back to the marina and made him wait while I went to the boat for money since I'd left both my wallet and phone when I went for my run. After the cab was paid and had pulled away, I wandered down to the concrete edge of the pier as the sounds of the awakening city began to amplify behind me.

I still felt the sick rush of what had happened. Someone I had never met was before knew who I was, where I lived and was quietly threatening me. I had no idea what to do now. Everywhere I turned, people wanted me to drop Chris and Paul. I was beginning to feel like my strings were being pulled constantly. And did that make the old Hungarian the master puppeteer? The more I thought about it, the more I didn't like it. Whoever he was, he might or might not be the epicentre of everything that had happened. Clearly Elvis searching my boat was supposed to scare me off, and when that hadn't worked, the old man had taken matters into his own hands. But scare me off of what, exactly? Whatever it was, my being brought to his house and meeting him face to face did not concern him. The obvious presumption was that I wouldn't do anything further for fear of reprisal. And veiled threats notwithstanding, there probably wasn't much else that they would do that didn't involve being lethal. Jesus Christ. What the hell was I into?

I called Kelly and left him a message to call me as soon as he could. After I'd had a shower to sluice off the sweat from my run, I went to the galley and scrambled some eggs with scallions and goat cheese. I took my breakfast out to the rear deck and sat and forced it down as other people's days were still beginning, without being threatened by Hungarian criminals quoting Shakespeare. When I was finished, I cleaned up and grabbed my cell and the numbers Laura had given me. I stared at the third number for a time, my mind flitting from memory to memory. Then, without quite knowing why, I called it again.

"Hey, this' Chris. Sorry I'm not here right now. You know what to do."

I tilted my head back and stared at the ceiling in the salon. Sighing, I let the silence hang between the voice and me. I went up the stairs to the fly bridge and sat in the captain's chair.

"Tell me man," I said finally into the phone. "Tell me what to do."

# Chapter 24

"Awright!' Ron said, smiling and brandishing the deck. "Comin' out," and he began to flip over the first three cards in front of him. "Cowboy spade, nine spade, two of hearts…"

We'd started the game with six of us — Mack, Jason, Ron, me and two guys from Jason's office. The office boys were knocked out first and had left around eleven claiming impending grief from their wives if they didn't make it home soon. Jason's family was up at their cottage for two weeks with Ron's wife and kids. Now it was just we four; the old hardcore group minus some original members.

When the cards were flipped, I tilted my hole cards and had another look. A diamond ten and Jack of spades returned the look. Ron left his cards down while a little tip of his tongue showed at the corner of his mouth as looks of concern passed over his face. Beside him, Jason had looked at his cards once, then put them down in front of him and was calmly watching everybody else. Across from him, Mack was holding his hole cards fanned in front of him.

It was a very comfortable place. There were framed original oil paintings on the wall. The furniture was new and looked very expensive. There were two floral upholstered wingbacks with a low cherrywood table between them facing the fireplace. The tall marble mantle had a huge gilt mirror hanging above it, tilted down from the top so you could see yourself in it though it was eight feet off the floor. Dark brown, gleaming hardwood ran throughout the living and dining rooms with the furniture areas described by antique oriental rugs. We were set up at a card table in the living room. Jason had lit the fire for ambiance and then turned up the central air to compensate. The firelight reflected off the gumwood paneling, which ran around the entire room. The big bay window at one end of the room was curtained with sheers and looked out on the quiet street, front yard and driveway where my bike squatted beside Mack's Lexus, Ron's Land Rover and Jason's Porsche.

Jason opened the betting with ten and everybody followed with no raises. Ron flipped the fourth card and the ten of spades appeared. Ron looked again at his hole cards and set about rearranging them, the crease between his eyebrows deepening a little.

"OK then," I said. "Ten to stay." Mack saw my bet, as did Ron. Jason saw my bet and raised me another ten. I called and Mack, with a moment's hesitation, called as well. Ron huffed and then grinned.

"Ah, why not! Only money, right?" he said and tossed his money in.

I felt nothing but hope from Ron and Mack so Jason was the one to worry about. He was either sitting with two pair and waiting for another to complete the full house, or looking for the fifth spade to fill a flush. A Queen of anything would fill my straight and the lady spade would cap it. The odds were split between us with Jason a little better off. Mack checked the bet as did Ron. Jason went twenty to clean away any deadwood players. I called but that was enough for Mack and Ron who pushed their cards in disgustedly. Ron turned the last card over and the lady spade smiled up at me benevolently. I bet twenty, which Jason raised by twenty again. I hesitated briefly and then raised him again. Jason saw the raise and smirking, flipped his cards showing a non-sequential flush to the ace.

"Straight flush to the cowboy," I said, turning my hole cards.

Jason tilted his head and smiled at me. "Straight flush? You filled it? Christ, I knew you were reckless, but …"

I grinned at him. "You filled yours on the last card as well, mate." I said. I reached over and plucked my winnings out of the middle of the table. I stacked the chips in front of me. "And you think *I'm* reckless?"

"OK, who's empty?" I asked, holding up my empty beer bottle. "Winner buys."

"Me," said Jason.

Mack, with his hands laced behind his head, said no.

"Ron?"

"No man, I'm good," he said, passing the deck over to Mack for shuffling.

"I'll come with you," said Jason. We got up from the table and headed to the back of the house where the kitchen was.

The kitchen was dimly lit by small halogens mounted inside the glass cupboards with larger versions set into the ceiling. An antique butcher's block sat on the tiled floor in the middle of the kitchen with large serving platters set on the gallery shelf below it. Jason reached into the fridge and grabbed two more longneck beers and handed one to me. He hopped up onto the butcher's block and sat in the small depression worn in the wood by a century of knife-work.

We clinked the necks together and I took a long pull from the bottle.

"You've changed your tell, buddy," said Jason.

"What do you mean?" I replied.

"When we used to play cards in high school — when you thought you were golden, you'd whistle quietly. Now, you fold your arms. New tell."

I smiled at him and tilted the bottle in salute. "Nice life, Jason" I said, waving the bottle generally around the room. I turned and looked out the kitchen window and saw the terraced decks and English-style garden that ran to the edge of the property. Through the night gloom, I could make out the solid shapes of pines and maples reaching up at the end of the garden and towering over the house.

"Livin' the dream, pal," he said, raising the bottle to his own good fortune. He pointed out the window at the terraces. "We built all that last year. Terri tried forever to make a big garden but you know, the trees make it really tough. Not enough sun and they just suck the ground dry. But she's got all that space at the lake now, so she's got what she wants. Makes her happy."

"That's great, I'm glad for you two."

"Thanks buddy. So, what's with you? Mack says you got a boat. What are you, crazy?"

I laughed. "Mack's already given me the winter speech. I know all of that."

"So you're here to stay then?"

I nodded. "It feels good to be back. Good to see you guys again. It feels comfortable, you know?"

"So Mack said you're looking into what happened to Paul and Chris and everything."

"Yeah, I wanted to talk to you guys about it," I said. "Let's go back in." We returned to the living room and sat down with Mack and Ron again. Mack picked up the cards and shuffled three times and snapped the deck onto the table for me to cut, which I did then he began dealing out. When we all had our hole cards and the five communal cards were face down, the game started.

Ron opened the betting ten dollars and we all called. Before Mack could turn the first three cards, I began. "Jason and I were just talking, and I wanted to talk to you all about Chris and Paul. About what I know so far."

Everyone nodded and I started in. "OK, Chris' accident is still under investigation and there's no movement on it as far as I know. I've talked to a Detective downtown and he's filled me in on a couple of things." It was hard to say it out loud to the others. Saying the words made it permanent, made it real. But there was nothing I could change about that. It already was permanent and real.

"Paul did not drown. He was killed. And whoever did it tossed his body into the harbour. Kelly, that's the cop, said he's keeping that news from Laura for now and he wants it to stay that way, until the investigation wraps up. I talked to Nick. Everybody remember Nick?" There were nods all around the table. "He wasn't much help. But he did tell me that Chris started paying more attention to his family a short time before the accident."

"Anyway, Chris came around to see his mother and brother more often. I met with Chris' ex partner at the firm. Sam. One of the pallbearers. Last meeting included his boss. Seems everything was normal at their office, no problems. The CEO was toeing the same line that nothing involving Chris was out of the ordinary except for some tap dance about Chris dating a sex worker. It made no sense, especially because ... wait a minute, let me back up. A couple of days ago, I went down to where all of Chris' stuff is in storage. I got the key from Nick. I went through everything and found some pictures missing from frames. When I spoke to the guy from the office he said he hadn't taken them. It doesn't play for me though. That or I'm looking too hard."

Mack flipped the first three cards, five of diamonds, seven of diamonds, Ace of clubs. I checked my hole cards for the first time and I had a pair of Aces back that made my poker heart sing.

"As far as I can tell the police seem to be following the deaths as if they're connected, and there's two detectives working in concert. Paul was murdered so there's an investigation underway. Chris' accident is being viewed as a suspicious death but there's not much to go on. I'm getting the feeling that unless something breaks, they're just going to file these. So that's all so far. You guys got any ideas about any of this?"

Jason spoke up. "Listen, I can't speak for everybody. I mean, Chris and Paul were our buddies forever. Y'know for all of us. And, I don't know, I think maybe we should just let them rest, y'know? I don't know what good it's gonna do to stir all the shit up."

As Jason spoke Ron nodded his head. Mack was staring out the living room window, his hands again laced behind his head. "I mean, you weren't here Jon. No offense, but when Chris died, I mean if something was up, the police would've arrested somebody by now. And Paul, aw shit, I'm as pissed as anyone, but you should let the cops handle it," Jason finished.

"Wait a minute," I said, leaning forward and resting my elbows on the card one hand in a closed fist, the other pointing at them. "You told me that when Chris died, you all thought it didn't make any sense. That there was no way it could have been an accident. Why are you changing your mind all of a sudden?"

"Hey, hey, be cool, Jon," said Jason. "We just … I just think it would be better if the cops took care of it, that's all."

"Jesus! This is getting repetitive. You're the fourth person in two days to tell me to forget about it," I said, shaking my head.

Ron spoke up. "Who else you been talkin' to Jon?"

"There was this …" but something in Ron's tone stopped me. I looked at him and he stared back at me. "Who cares who I've been talking to?" I sat back in my chair, suddenly under the impression the game was over.

"Who you been talkin' to Jon?" Ron repeated.

I calmed myself down and spoke in as even a voice as I could. "I don't think I'm going to tell you."

"Tell us Jon."

"No," I said flatly.

"Fuckin' tell us, goddammit!" he yelled.

I stood and Ron stood with me. Both Jason and Mack instinctively pushed their chairs back and watched us. Ron and I faced each other across the card table and I was stunned as I found myself wondering if I could take him. He had at least three inches and fifty pounds on me. I didn't think I was going to be on the winning end of this one.

"So much for old friends getting together over some cards," I said. I looked at Mack. "You know this was coming?"

Mack turned his gaze from the window and looked at me. Then he looked down at the table and didn't speak. I shook my head sadly.

"Are you idiots involved in this? Is that what's going on? You want me to drop this because you're in it? You all still together? A little gang all grown up?"

"Fuck you Jon," Ron growled.

"The hell with you," I said. "You're dead wrong if ... if you idiots got into something and two of our friends are dead because of it, and you're just going to roll over because why? Don't want it all to come out?" I looked from one to the other. "Or are you responsible somehow? Is that it?" I turned back to Ron. "Are you to blame?"

Ron lunged forward across the table and grabbed me by my shirtfront. I didn't know what he was prepared to do, so I went with the pull, offering no resistance. The table got caught between us and Ron yanked harder and the table squeezed out between us and flew off to one side, scattering cards and chips everywhere. When he had pulled me close enough, I brought my forearm up and drove it into the front of his throat. Ron let go of me and staggered back, both hands around his neck; his eyes bulged in surprise. Jason jumped up from his chair and grabbed my right arm above the elbow and spun me around. I twisted his hand over with my left and dug my fingertips into the soft veined area below his palm. He yelled in pain, letting go, and with both hands I pushed him up and backwards, putting my entire weight behind the shove. He went sailing over his chair and landed against the table beside the couch, knocking over the lamp and some family bric-a-brac.

"Enough!" bellowed Mack. "Jon! Cut it the fuck out!" He was standing now and waiting a careful distance from me, holding out one hand.

I was breathing hard, not from exertion, but from anger. I could feel my body trembling slightly from the awful, sickening adrenaline rush. I stood in the middle of the room, watching the three of them, feeling a little like a kid surrounded in a schoolyard waiting for the tar to get beaten out of him. I wiped my hand across my mouth and straightened my shirt collar.

"Let it go, Jon. Please," Jason said from the floor.

Ron straightened up from the far wall, still massaging his neck. He was angry but the forearm swipe had chastened him. When he spoke, his voice rasped out of his throat.

"Listen." He coughed twice, trying to clear his voice. "We didn't have anything to do with Chris and Paul. But we're asking you to drop it, Jon. C'mon man."

It didn't feel right, hitting my friends, despite whatever little ambush they had set up for me. But I wasn't going to let it go.

"Are you going to tell me what the hell is going on?" I asked. Jason had stood by now and was righting the lamp and the bits and pieces on the table again. He and Ron looked at each other, some tacit communication passing between them.

"Mack? You got anything to tell me?"

Mack looked at me, then looked away and said, "There's nothing I can tell you, old friend."

"Then we're done here," I said. I turned and brushed past Jason and opened the front door. When I looked back, the three of them were still frozen in a tableau. Jason beside the table, Ron massaging his throat and Mack staring at the floor.

"If you're in whatever this is, then shake yourselves loose. Do it now. 'Cause I'm gonna pull this thread until whatever it is unravels. And if you're connected ..." I left the threat hanging in the air. I opened the front door and walked out into the cool of midnight and fired up the bike. I was shivering, my legs vibrating slightly against the metal of the gas tank as I did the thousand-yard stare at the tachometer, waiting for the idle to drop. Then I slammed the bike down into first and headed home.

# Chapter 25

My cell rang while I was in the bilge replacing the throttle cable connections on the twin Chryslers. I pulled the rag out of my back pocket and wiped the white grease residue off my hands. Popping my head out of the compartment hatch, I grabbed it from where I'd left it lying beside the opening.

"It's me," said Kelly.

"Hey," I said, cradling the phone in the crook of my shoulder while I finished wiping my hands.

"Got some news. We got lucky. I used to work vice, so I called an old friend there and sent him the picture of the Magyar woman and he remembered her."

"Vice? Ah no... he remembered her?"

"Yeah," he said tonelessly.

I sighed. "So what did he say?"

"Said he knew her from a year back. Remembered her 'cause of how scared she was. She got picked up in a raid on a private party. Said she burst into tears when she got grabbed up. Some guy came down and made her bail."

"Who was the guy?"

There was silence as Kelly paused, then he said, "Chris Allinson."

It was my turn to be quiet. Then I said, "Jesus, so it's true." Mugridge and Powell had been telling the truth. She was in the business. And that gave credence to their explanation they felt justified their actions. "What else did your friend say?"

"Well, she wasn't in the system. She gave a false name and by the time she got bailed out by your buddy, nobody had done the background on her. It doesn't matter anyway, as a first-timer she would have been cut loose."

"How's that?"

"You have to remember, the act itself isn't illegal in this country. People can only be charged with solicitation and living off the avails. And solicitation rarely sticks. Most cases are built so we can nail the pimps and then the real organizers. Mob, bikers, whoever's on top. But it's tough to make it that high. Open up the daily rags and they're filled with ads for companions and massage parlours. And the parlours are nothing but a front for whatever you're willing to pay extra for. When I worked vice we'd go after the recruiters and hustlers downtown and the bus terminal and Union Station. There are a lot of hacks that moonlight in the trade as well. Perfect for them 'cause they can provide transportation and make sure the cut comes back to where they want it to. But the higher-ups are impossible to get to. Either they're invisible or so removed that we can't make a case against them."

"You sound bitter."

"You're goddamned right. Worse part is, a lot of the women who do this for a living are only doing it 'cause they can't make enough money stripping or massaging. They pay so much of the wages back to the handlers that they end up offering more to customers just to make a living. Lot of domestic strippers draw the line at anything else, so the extras fall to foreign dancers. That may explain the accent. She could have come here to dance and then got forced into more. Vice is a cesspool and every day is more depressing than the last."

"And nothing can be done?"

"Let me give you a little history lesson. Years ago, the Feds actually created a program to fast-track dancers into the country. I know it sounds insane but there were a lot of misplaced programs to help immigration back then. Now this was about the same time that the Supreme Court made lap-dancing illegal. So now, there were all these foreign dancers whose other avenues for earning were cut off. Then, they changed the rules and exotic dancing was no longer a skilled employment field with insufficient home-grown workers."

"You're kidding me."

"No, I'm not. Your Federal dollars at work. So when they changed the employment evaluation, suddenly you had all these foreign born dancers who had even less protection and less opportunities to earn. It meant that a lot of them had no choice but to work the back rooms. It made them vulnerable to their handlers because they were outside the program now. Just before I transferred out of Vice, I was part of a huge sweep of the clubs around the city. A lot of the women who got netted could avoid getting a record by attending a special training and awareness program. Problem was the girls and the club owners had to sign up for the program together, which still left all the power in the hands of the owners. The skim on the extra work is usually more than seventy percent, which is a powerful incentive not to let the women off the leash. And despite everything we tried to do, the Feds were doing nothing. They helped create the problem and then walked. Why I transferred to homicide, couldn't seem to get anywhere."

"Christ, I had no idea."

"Most people don't."

"So, anything else to brighten my day?"

"Yeah, there's something else. I got to thinking, it didn't make sense to me when you said the numbers on Amber Road didn't go high enough for that cell phone address. I had a cruiser do a drive that way and I was right. Seems a year or so ago, somebody developed the area the next block over from your skatepark. There were some houses that had laneway access in the back for their cars. The developer knocked it all down. Took out the older houses and the garages and threw up a bunch of townhomes. They continued the addressing as Amber Road. 257 is in the circle of places on a cul-de-sac."

"Did you send somebody around?"

"Got no reason to. I don't know who lives there. I don't want to have to explain rousting the wrong person to the higher-ups."

"OK. I got it. Mind if I take a look?"

"Operating as a private citizen, I would say that you would not be contravening any municipal or provincial statutes by knocking on the wrong door by accident," he said and hung up.

I went back below and finished tightening the new cables into their housings and thinking about what Kelly had told me. Then I went above and checked the tension behind both sets of controls. Keeping her in neutral I turned her over and gave the throttles a workout. The engines roared and the exhaust pumped out as the power plants revved under no load. By the time I had finished testing my work, cleaned up and showered, it was dusk. I picked up my gear, locked up and went to out to the bike.

I went north and rolled on in the light traffic uptown. When I got above Lawrence I turned up a side street and wound my way to Amber Road. I circled St. Mary's and the pavement changed perceptibly from old to new. I found the cul-de-sac Kelly had told me about. It looked like four houses had been taken out to create eight tall, thin townhouses. They all had that faux-Victorian frontage popular with developers. Each house had a little Juliet balcony off the second-floor master and I was suddenly struck by the memory of my dream. The owners were all using different paint choices in a futile attempt to appear unique. There were single car garages set into the below-ground level of each house with ten or twelve steps leading up to the front doors. Number 257 had a glass door with beveled-edge frosted panes for privacy. I pushed the bell and heard the bing-bong chime inside. Nobody came to find out who I was. I went back down the stairs and tried the garage door but it was locked. There was a narrow path beside the garage leading to the back of the house. I tried to look like I'd been there before, in case of curious neighbours. It wasn't dark enough yet and I didn't want anyone thinking I was skulking around. At the end of the path was a tall wooden gate with lattice at the top. I knocked loudly on the wooden door, but nobody, not even a dog, answered.

I wandered back down the path to the front again to where the bike was parked in the driveway. I started it up and drove a couple of blocks away and parked it between two cars at the curb. After locking my helmet and jacket to the bike, I went back on foot. A few people were sitting on their front porches enjoying the evening, and I nodded to them as I walked past. By the time I got back to the cul-de-sac, the dark was full on. I went back down the side path at 257. When I got to the gate, I stood on tiptoes and reached around the four-by-four post. I felt the latch and pulled it up and the gate swung open. There were dim lights lining the flagstone path that led to a low deck off the back door. The garden itself was in darkness. I could see the silhouettes of tall plantings at the back of the garden. There were only a few lights on in the house but they threw no illumination on the garden. Checking the neighbours on either side to make sure nobody was watching, I moved quietly to the back of the garden and found an aluminum shed in one corner. Behind the shed was another gate that let onto an alleyway behind the townhomes. I unlatched the gate and stuck my head out. Behind each garden fence were waist-high wooden boxes that people must have used for garbage and recycling bins. I left the gate open and unlatched in case I had to leave suddenly. There were some plastic lawn chairs stacked inside the shed. I was about to make myself comfortable for the wait but was interrupted by the sound of heels clicking quickly down the sidewalk out front. I went around the back of the shed again and moved behind the edge, watching the house. I heard the thump of the front door closing. The indistinct shape of a person came into the back of the house. Keys rattled onto a countertop and then whoever it was slid open the glass door that let onto the back deck.

Then came the blue glow of a cell phone waking up. Whoever it was must have had their messages on speakerphone because the next voice I heard was my own.

"Tell me man," I heard myself say, "tell me what to do."

I moved around from beside the shed and crept up to the kitchen window, rolling my weight slowly from heel to toe to keep the noise down. When I got to the window, I saw the figure in the darkness of the kitchen with one hand on the fridge door, head hanging down, chin on chest. There was the sound of the phone being turned off, and then the fridge door was yanked open, spilling its harsh light into the kitchen. Karolina bent over and pulled a plastic bottle of water from one of the shelves. She turned and saw me standing by the window. With a yelp of fright, she dropped the bottle, which bounced heavily and rolled into a corner. I moved quickly away from the window and onto the deck. She rushed to the screen door separating us and began to hurriedly close the glass door.

"Karolina!"

"No! No!" she yelled.

"Karolina, listen to me. I need to talk to you." I slid the screen open and put my foot up onto the jamb before she slid the glass door completely closed. It banged painfully against my riding boot.

"No. I do not want to talk with you! I will phone the police!"

"No you won't."

"And why should I not?" she said imperiously.

"Because you won't, given your past."

She stopped bashing my foot with the door and narrowed her eyes at me.

"What do you mean. I have done nothing wrong."

"I know, Karolina. I know that you were arrested. And I know why, now let me in."

She regarded me furiously, but resignation crept into her face. She gave up pushing the door closed and moved back, letting the pressure off my foot. I pushed the sliding door open on its track, and then closed the screen door behind me, leaving the glass door open. The house was stifling with trapped summer heat. I bent over and picked up the fallen water bottle and handed it to her. She sat down in the booth of the little eating alcove that was built into a corner of the kitchen. As I stood watching her with my arms folded across my chest, she drank from the bottle, keeping her eyes downcast. Finally she looked up at me, her eyes brimming with tears. Her blond hair was unkempt from her effort at the door. I sighed and sat down across from her.

"Karolina," I said, "I spoke with a policeman today. He told me what happened to you, that you were working a private party." While I talked, she slowly swung her head back and forth in tired denial of everything I said. "I know that Chris was the one who helped you then. Did he know about what you did before that?"

"Why did you call and leave such a message?" she asked. "How did you get this number?"

"I didn't realize it was your phone. I got the number from the wife of my friend who died last week. She said Paul had the number listed for Chris. This morning, well, I had a disturbing morning and I don't know why I called the number, I just did. The message wasn't for you. It was for Chris."

"I don't understand. Christopher is dead."

I shook my head in annoyance. "Jesus, I know it doesn't make any sense. I just felt confused and I thought about calling my old friend to talk to him about it. I guess I wasn't thinking."

"You miss your friend."

"Yes, I do."

Karolina began to cry full out now. "I miss him too," she sobbed.

I reached across the table and she took my hands in hers and squeezed them tightly while her body was racked by sobs. I felt her tears on the backs of my hands as she lay her forehead down and let the grief consume her. After a time, she began to calm down, little whimpers and hiccups replacing the sobbing. When she was quiet again I asked, "Can you tell me about it? Karolina? Karolina!"

She started and lifted her head off my hands. Then she nodded in resignation, let go of me and wiped her face with the back of a hand. She got up from the table and disappeared into the next room. When she came back, she had a small bottle with a tan liquid in it and two pony glasses. She poured us each a glass and sat down again. She sipped her drink and then closed her eyes, savouring the taste.

"This is Tokaji," she said. "Do you know Tokaji?"

I shook my head and took a sip. It was slightly sweet and cloying.

"Tokaji Aszú. It is a wine from Hungary. Christopher found this and bought it for me in the first week we were together. It is hard to find outside of Hungary. It is a taste of home for me."

I nodded but stayed quiet, not wanting to stop her now that she had begun.

"I was in school, at the Müszaki. I was studying to be a water engineer — for the safety of the water for the cities. It was the spring and my school was finished for year. I need to find work for summer. I went one day to the employment office at the university. There was a piece of paper; it was very official. It said that they would help you to find work as a," she stopped and searched for the word, "a helper, with children ..."

"A nanny," I said.

"Yes. Yes, a nanny. It said there were families in Canada who want the nanny for summer. It said the families would pay for the airplane tickets and pay for you to work. It seemed like a very nice thing to come to Canada for the summer. My mother was very nervous. I go for the interview to an office in Budapest. I meet with this woman. She said that I would be an excellent nanny and that they would like to hire me. She ask me many questions about my family and where they live. I tell her it is just my mother and myself. My father died many years ago, when I was a child. I was very innocent, very trusting. I should not have told this woman about my mother. I should have not trusted this smiling woman."

"So I fly here to Canada. I go to the Halifax city. I take another airplane on the next day to Toronto. A man meets me at the airport and he say I will meet the family with the baby. I go with this man to meet the family but we do not go there. He drive me to place, a bar with women dancing. It is very crowded and dirty. I don't want to go but he forces me. He take away my passport and my visa.

I don't know what to do. I do not know anyone in Canada. I have little money. I live in small apartment near the airport with many other women from Hungary, from Romania, from Poland. We are very scared. At night, the men come and take us to the bars where we must dance on the stage. I know of these places in Hungary. But I never go there before. They tell me I owe them money for the airplane. I say I will not do what they ask." She paused, the tears beginning again. "They say to me my address in Budapest. They say they will hurt my mother if I do not do what they ask. So I dance in the club. Soon, they tell me I must work in private rooms. I say no and they beat me. One night, the man who came to the airport is in private room. He tells me I must dance for him. I do and then he, then he ..." She sobbed and the tears spilled down her cheeks. I put my hands across the table but she moved back from me.

"This man rapes me!" she screamed. Her crying got worse as she fought for control. Her breathing rasped in and out of her throat and her chest was heaving. It took her some time to calm down and then she sighed and continued. "I cannot do anything. I cannot tell. I do not know who to tell to. No one will help me. Soon, I am not in the bar. I am working at night, going to parties with men who are strangers to me."

"An escort service."

"Yes, escort. And these men are, sometimes they hit me. Sometimes they want me to hit them. I run away at this time but the man from the airport, he finds me. He is Hungarian, like me. He tells me I will work on street if I cannot be … be … behave? Is that the word?"

I nodded.

"So I tell him I do not want to work on the street as *kurva*. As prostitute. I promise him I will behave. He takes me back to apartment and he beats me. But he does not hit my face. He tells me I must look beautiful for the men. He hits me in my, in my," without looking at me, she waved her hands across her breasts and then pointed below the table edge.

"What did this man look like?" I asked, my anger boiling an acid pit in my stomach.

"He is tall, like you," she said. "He has black hair and here …" she pointed at her own jaw hinge, "he has the …"

"Sideburns," I finished.

"Yes, sideburns," she said, trying out the new word.

"What happened after that?" I asked.

"Now it is the winter. One night, three women and I are taken to party. A Christmas party. It is in a very tall building. Many people are there. Important people, I think. We are told to go to this party and to work. We are told that we have been given money already and we are to go with any man who ask us. We are told we must not go only with one man. After, we must come back to party to find other men. That is the night I meet Christopher."

With the mention of his name, her face softened and she smiled for the first time. It was only a small smile, but it was a start.

"He was so shy. I see him when I come in. He is standing and talking to some other men. He sees me come and ... oh, he had such a sweet smile. Very gentle. I go to him right away. He is very embarrassed. I ask him if he would like to dance. Christopher was a very bad dancer." She laughed a little then, self-consciously hiding it behind her hand. "I ask him if he would like to go with me. To leave party and go somewhere. He says yes. He does not take me to hotel. He takes me to a restaurant. It is very high up. The view is wonderful. There is snow falling and there is a man playing the piano. We sit and we talk. Christopher was very kind. Since I come to Canada, no one is kind to me except Christopher. We talk until the restaurant is closed. He asks me about Hungary, and I tell him stories about my family. About my studies. He listens to me. He was a very good listener, Christopher. He make me feel young, like a girl. He make me feel clean."

"Soon it is very late. The restaurant is closed. I ask him if he wants to go to hotel and he say no. No, but he say he would like to see me again. I remember, my face felt so hot. He say I am ... blushing? Yes blushing. I did not know this word before in English, but Christopher say I look very pretty. He gives me card with his telephone number on it." She was crying again, but they were silent tears. I wasn't even sure she was aware of them.

"When I get back to apartment I am so happy. I am thinking maybe ... I don't know. But they know I am only with one person for night. The man is very angry. He tells me I am going to work on street. I say no! I was brave because of Christopher, I think. The man with the sideburns takes away the good clothes. He puts me in the car and we go into the city again. I am put in new apartment with two women. We have one bedroom for all of us. He tells me I must earn 1000 dollars every week. I must work every night or I will be sold to other men. On the first night, I am arrested by the police. I don't know what to do. So I call the only person who is kind to me. I call Christopher and he comes to the police station and he pays the money so I can leave. He takes me to his apartment. It was very beautiful. He tells me he want to help me. I cannot believe this man. He is so sweet and he is shy. He tells me I should stay with him. I think he wants to have sex with me. But he says I should rest. He takes me to a bedroom and there I lie down and go to sleep."

"So what happened after that?"

"After that day, Christopher says that I never do that again. Never have to dance in the bar or be escort again. I stay with Christopher and soon we become ..." She looked down and began to cry again, her hands twisting in her lap.

"Christopher and I, we were very happy. I think we are in love. I begin to go to school again. Christopher says I do not have to work. He was very successful, Christopher. So I go back to school and begin my studies on the computer. And Christopher, he buys this house for us. He do so much for me. He says he help me to become citizen in Canada. And then, he is seeing his family again. He says that the next week he will introduce me to his family. On Sundays, after his family, he always stay at apartment downtown. He say it is easier for going to work on Monday. So I am waiting for him to call me at night. He does not call me so I telephone his apartment but there is no answer. He does not call me from his office in the morning like always. I go to school and I telephone him in the afternoon. A lady asks me who I am and I say a friend and she, she says ..."

I put my hand out and this time she didn't recoil. She took my hand and squeezed it tightly in hers as the memory slammed into her. The tears streamed down her face and she began to wail and cry to herself in a quiet voice. She was rocking back and forth rhythmically and I realized she was praying. Eventually, the rocking slowed until she was finally just whispering to herself. Then she made the sign of the cross on her chest.

After a moment I asked, "Karolina, why didn't you go to the police? They could have helped you."

She stirred and shook her head. "No. I cannot speak to the police. The man from Hungary will hurt my mother in Budapest if I say anything to the police. I know this."

I thought of the threats that had been leveled at me that morning by the friendly old man. I knew how she felt. I sat back a little in the booth and tried to think of a way out for her. She was going to have problems staying here. She had no visible means of support. She was without a passport and I didn't know how far Chris had gotten with her citizenship. And if he had acted as her sponsor, his death would have truncated any further proceedings.

"Karolina, can you go home, to Budapest?" I asked gently.

"No. If I go back to Budapest they will find me again. It would be worse than staying in here in Canada. They ..."

"What Karolina? They what?"

"The man from the airport. One day I am coming out of a building and he is standing in front. I was ... I did not know what to do. He takes me in his car and we drive away. He," she looked at me uncertainly. "He tell me that there is a man. I tell him no. No more. He say no, I will do this thing they ask or my mother ..." She paused and looked everywhere around the room except at me. "I must speak to this man only. I must tell him to go away. I must tell to stop what he is doing. If I do this, they will let me live. They will let my mother live. Oh, oh!" And she buried her face in her hands. "Jonathan, I am sorry. I do not know what to do."

"It's all right," I said. "I'm not angry. That's how you found me? They told you where I lived, about my boat."

She nodded her head, her face still hidden in her hands. "Yes. They tell me that I must speak with you. That I must take you away from your boat."

I blew the air out of my lungs in frustration, angry for being manipulated. It didn't matter that I had no idea that others were moving me around the board. But it offended my sense of self that I could be so easily shuffled around. I reached across the table with a tentative hand and put it on her shoulder.

"Karolina?" She kept her face hidden so I squeezed her shoulder in reassurance. "Karolina, it's OK. Really. Do they know about this house? Do they know where you live?"

She came out of her embarrassment and misery and took her hands away from her face. "I do not think so. Christopher, when he bought our house. He told me the house is in ... trust? Is that the proper word?"

"I don't know, Karolina. Maybe he knew a way to keep both his and your name off the title. But have the other men, the men from Hungary, have they ever been here?"

"No! No, never!"

"Good, OK. I just want to make sure you're safe here."

"Yes, I am safe, I think. But, I have very little money. I cannot work because I am afraid they will come for me. Soon there will be things that I must have money for." She waved her hand around the room to indicate the house. "And they know that I am studying. But every day I am careful. So they do not find this house. They tell me they will leave me alone if you stop asking about Christopher. Jonathan, I do not know what to do!"

"Karolina, listen to me. It's not your fault. The man from Budapest had already come to my boat. The day before we met, I caught the man from the airport on my boat. He ran away when I chased him."

"I do not understand," she said.

"I'm not sure I do either, but don't worry." Regardless of my words of comfort for her, a sinking worry settled in my own stomach. They had already been to the boat once. Why did they need me away from it again? "For now, let's just make sure that you're safe. Can you miss a couple of days of school?"

She nodded. "I do not want to, but yes, I can."

"Then I think you should stay here for the next few days. Don't go out. Do you need food or anything else for a couple of days? Prescriptions, anything at all?"

She shook her head, "No, I have food. And I," she paused and thought. "No there is nothing else to need."

"All right. Then you stay here. If you need to get a hold of me, call me day or night. Here." I reached over the table for a pencil and paper and wrote Kelly's name and number on the pad along with my cell. "If you can't find me then call this number. This man is a police Detective. He knows about you, but he doesn't know about the men from Budapest. I haven't told him and I'm not going to. And I don't want you to tell him either."

"But what will you do?"

"I don't know yet. I need to find out what happened to Chris and my other friend. When I have enough information, then we'll talk about what to do. OK?"

Karolina nodded and said, "Yes, I will wait."

I got up from the bench and she followed me to the front door.

As we got to the door, a thought occurred to me. "Karolina, when Chris died, did you go to his apartment? Did you go through his belongings, clothes, photos, any of that stuff? Do you have his computer?"

Karolina shook her head sadly. "No," she began to tear up again, "the only picture I have of Christopher is the picture on beach that I show to you. Why? He gave me my own computer. Why do you ask about these things?"

"I don't know. Look, stay here and don't worry."

"Thank you," she said. "But you will not tell this man?" She waved the paper with Kelly's name and number.

"No I won't. I won't tell him. You stay here and I'll be in touch."

She nodded slowly and I left and went to shake down someone who used to be a friend.

# Chapter 26

I collected the bike from down the street and drove to Jason's house. I checked my watch and it was almost midnight by the time I pulled up at his place. The house was dark but I could see the flicker of a fire throwing orange and dirty yellow splashes of light into the living room.

As I came up onto the front porch I saw a figure slumped in a chair through the big window, legs straight out in front, pointed at the fire. I knew the family was still away so I hammered on the front door with my fist. The figure in the chair stirred slightly and a glass fell onto the floor, spilling its contents, but the figure didn't move any further. I tried the door but it was locked, so I stole around the back of the house and up onto the wide deck in the nightshade of the tall trees. There was a paned window in the kitchen in front of the sink. I drove my elbow through one of the panes and glass clattered down into the sink. After reaching in and unlatching the window I swung it open and prayed that no silent alarm was going off. I scrambled through the window, careful to avoid the broken glass. The house was dark but I could make out the shapes of things enough not to bang into them.

When I got to the living room, I was blasted by a wall of heat built up from the fire. It was eighty degrees outside and must have been a hundred and ten in the house. Jason was slumped in the wingback chair, head lolling against one of the wings. There was a bottle of rye whiskey on the floor, almost empty, and he reeked of stale alcohol and sweat. I swung the glass doors mounted below the marble mantle closed and the radiating heat lessened a little, then I closed the blinds on the main window and brought a nearby table lamp over and set it on the floor.

After unscrewing the retaining cap, I pulled off the shade and turned the light on. The lamp threw everything in the room into sharp relief. Jason closed his eyes tighter at the bright light and whined, turning his head to avoid the harsh glare.

"Jason!" I said sharply.

He whined some more and tried again to turn away from the light. I shook him on the shoulder and he mumbled incoherently.

"Frummmph, frumpph ... whassisit ..."

With one hand I turned his chin back to the light and slapped him lightly with the other. His eyes flew open at the slap and then squinted shut again from the glare of the bare bulb.

"Jason!"

He swiveled his head away from the glare and tried to go back to sleep, muttering.

"Istthmmmmph ... whasttimessss?"

"Midnight, Jason."

"Issst Jon?" He opened one eye but squinted against the light. He looked at me for a second, blurry and drunken sleepy. "Godammnyoujonsttt ... god ... screwedevything ... evythinghup!" The last word ended with a hiccup and he settled back against the chair wing again.

"Jason, wake up, you need to answer some..."

"Awww ... hellwithyoushunofabitch," he yelled at me, eyes still closed, spittle flying from his mouth. His breath was foul. I was getting tired of people who couldn't look after themselves. I tried to think of a way to get what I needed. Feeling pitiable and with not a little self-loathing, I reached down, picked up the table lamp and touched the hot, naked bulb to his cheek. His body convulsed with the singe; he jerked his head away and settled again, one hand absent-mindedly rubbing the cheek.

I pushed his hand out of the way and this time held the bulb against his face. His eyes opened wide at the pain as he tried to pull his head away. He tried to bury his face against the wing of the chair so I mashed the bulb into the nape of his neck. Involuntarily, he whipped his head down towards the new sensation of pain and the bulb exploded when it was trapped against his shoulder. Hot glass showered his chest and my hand. He jumped up from the chair, holding his shirt away from his skin and trying to clear the shards from underneath the material.

When he looked up again, taking in me and his circumstances, his eyes narrowed and he took a long telegraphed swing at me. I ducked easily. His own momentum carried him around and he toppled over his chair. Jason let out a long, animal cry of frustration and pounded the carpet with his fists.

I put the ruined lamp back on the table and let him scream it out while I went to the kitchen and put on the kettle. I felt terrible. It is the small violences that sicken us the most. We watch television and movie characters pound each other without regard and without realistic damage, but when it visits us personally, when we physically hurt someone, the effect is grotesque. Actually hit someone who's reasonably defenseless and aside from probably breaking your hand, you feel nothing but an embarrassed self-disgust. I could feel the revulsion squatting in my stomach like a grinning toad. I glanced up at my reflection in the kitchen window over the sink and shook my head at my sorry image. By the time I returned to the living room, Jason was half standing, leaning against the overturned chair and trying to get all the way up. I helped him make it and saw that I had left two healthy burn welts on his cheek and neck. Like any good drunk, his short-term memory wasn't the best. He looked at me as if I had only just arrived.

"Oh ... yeah ... thanksh Jon ... yeah ... helpmetothebathroom ... yeah ... goodbuddy ... thankshjon."

We stumbled comically across the living room and down the basement stairs. In the far corner of the family room I saw the door for the bathroom so we negotiated the minefield of kid's toys, pillows from the sofa and piles of clothes. It was a small three-piece bathroom and I let Jason go in by himself. I stood outside leaning against the wall with my arms folded across my chest and felt sorry for both of us. After a minute when he didn't come out I banged on the door but got no response.

When I opened it I found him collapsed on the floor beside the toilet, snoring quietly. Grabbing him by his collar and belt, I muscled him into the shower stall and turned the cold water on full. He jolted awake and struggled up into a sitting position. Jason tried to crawl out of the shower so I jammed my foot against his midsection and pinned him to the wall. He whipped his head from side to side and kept trying to grab my calf to get loose. I turned the water to scalding hot to make the point, then shut the shower off and let him catch his breath. He heaved in big gulps of air and when he looked at me again there was hatred behind his eyes, but I knew he wasn't going to try anything else.

We went back upstairs and Jason leaned heavily on the butcher's block like he had the last time we'd been in his kitchen. I found some instant coffee and made a big mug of it with plenty of sugar. He took it from me but didn't start drinking it so — hating myself and everything else at that moment — I gave him a flick of the hand on the welt on his cheek. He cowered like a head-shy pet hit too many times and began sipping the hot coffee.

"We're going to have a little chat you and I," I said. "A little chat about Chris and Paul and everything you idiots have been up to lately."

Jason shook his head stubbornly, so another tap of the hand across his cheek. It was getting easier to hit him and I wondered what that said about me. I felt sour inside. He winced, spilling some of the coffee on his leg and nodded his head this time. Jason pulled a face at the strength of the coffee and made to put it down.

"Uh-uh," I said. "Finish it, Jason."

"It's awful. Too strong," he complained.

"I don't care, finish it. And then you're going to have as many as it takes until you're straight enough to talk to me."

"You're a bastard," he muttered.

"Yes I am. Now do what you're told." His brief show of spirit was heartening. He didn't have it in him to go up against me, but if I tipped him the right way, maybe I could pry the truth out of him. Maybe he thought he could still rationalize his actions and that would make him spill it all. Sometimes when we don't have much to prop us up, we grab whatever it is that can make us feel better about ourselves. Even if we know deep down that our crutch is fragile and rotten.

"Tell me about it. All of it."

I was leaning against the counter, arms across my chest, with my back to the window I had broken to get in. Jason looked at me for a moment, then past me, out the window at his terraced yard.

"Why couldn't you leave it the fuck alone?" he said finally.

"Because it got Chris and Paul killed."

"We didn't ... we didn't think it would ... goddamn Chris. Shit."

"Well spoken. Very erudite."

Jason glared at me but didn't hold it. When he looked away he sighed resignedly.

"How did it all start Jason?"

He shook his head slowly and finally said, "Chris."

"Chris what?"

"It was Chris. All of it. Paul's law specialty was immigration. Chris had this client. Guy was occasionally bringing in refugees from the Eastern Bloc — Romania, Hungary, Slovenia. It was a sideline. Small firm. I mean, I deal with transpo from that part of the world all the time. I know stuff. I hear stuff. Chris had an idea to push the business in a different direction. Chris needs to set up a special kind of agency. Says he needs some good people to help with certain things. So Chris and Paul get together and set up a much more detailed operation. Chris saw the bigger picture. Saw what it could be and what it could mean financially. Paul said our biggest problem was gonna be the work visas. So we figured out this loophole that made it easier."

"What kind of loophole?"

"It was Ron's idea. He said in his business, if the movie people need a certain actor or whatever, they gotta file for a temporary work visa. And the easiest category to get a visa for is like entertainers, actors, magicians, dancers, people like that. Busker visas they call them." His animation was building a little as he told me his story.

"So anyway, Paul does the legal end, I've got transport sewn up, and Ron's got his security contacts. So we all help this client set up an agency to, you know, help new immigrants and stuff. And this agency starts doing a lot of things. Like dealing with foreign investment and business expansion here and in the U.S. They'd help foreign athletes and actors and people like that to come here. It was pretty wide-ranging."

"Why do you think they came to you?"

"Well, I told you, Chris and Paul first bring it to me and tell me about this thing they need set up and how they need some advice on transport. Inter and intra-country shipping transfers, brokerages, filing procedures, all the things I do. So I say we should bring Ron and Mack in. Room for all of us. Paul said yeah, I should talk to Ron. He'd talk to Mack, yeah, so we work out all the details. And when the bills come due, well, there was more money than we thought there was gonna be. I mean more than good, it's like, spectacular. The deal was that the client was gonna pay us on a commission basis, you know. So we billed it through this shell corporation that Chris set up. Then this client says he needs ongoing advice, so he starts paying more dividends into our company. We got a percentage of everything the agency did."

"So if it was all so innocent, what went wrong?"

Jason looked less sure of himself suddenly. His skin became noticeably ashen and his hands started to shake.

"Nothing. Nothing, man. Everything was sweet."

"Bullshit, Jason. It went bad and two of our friends are dead because of it."

"Jon, no."

"Here's what I think," I said. "Maybe by chance, maybe not, but this 'client' picked Chris. I think these people don't leave anything to chance. I think they picked Chris 'cause he was ripe. I think they saw somebody they could use. They found out what they needed and told Chris to get all his talented friends involved. And they knew they'd hit the jackpot when they saw you falling all over yourselves to set this thing up. You solved the problem of the visas, you set up routes and paperwork, provided security. Don't tell me you didn't think something was wrong. Where did you think the money was coming from?"

"I told you already," Jason blurted out. "There were foreign investments and ...'"

"Jesus, are you stupid as well as greedy? It was a front! You fools created a way, a legal way, to import women and girls from overseas."

"Man, it wasn't all girls."

"Fine, whatever, so they did some legitimate business to hide behind. And it was perfect Jason, and you had Chris laundering the money."

"No." Jason shook his head sadly. "It wasn't laundering, it was legit. Chris did the investing on behalf of the corporation."

"And you were bringing over people, girls and women, under this bogus employment category?"

"Hey, nothing bogus about it. It was all perfectly legit. And we weren't bringing that many in. Maybe a hundred, hundred and twenty a month. Through Michigan, across the St. Clair into Sarnia; down the St. Lawrence through Montreal; East Coast — Halifax, Moncton, whatever, wherever."

"*Whom*ever. These are human beings, you piece of garbage. A hundred women a month?!"

"Yeah sure." Pride began to seep into his voice. "What they're gonna do here has gotta be better than what they're coming from."

"How philanthropic of you."

"Hey, fuck you Jon. It's true."

"So what did you think? Do you think these women stayed dancers for long? When all this money started flowing, where did it all go?"

"I told you already, that was Chris' part. Chris was in all the way, even though we didn't really need him, except for the money side. Paul thought Chris was the weak link, so Paul told him just what he needed to know, cause we had to have a way to ..."

"To launder the money."

Jason tried his best to look innocent. "Chris took care of the investments," he said belligerently.

"Without caring where the money was coming from?"

"We didn't get that much. We just had our little piece of the pie."

"How little?"

"Fuck you. That's between me and ..."

Before I could stop to think about it I levered myself from leaning against the counter and gave Jason a backhand slap across his face. The coffee mug flew across the room and shattered against a baseboard. Jason screamed and rolled away from the butcher's block onto the floor. I reached down and hauled him up by his shirtfront, took two paces and slammed him against the wall. He brought his hands up and tried to flail punches at my head. He was weak with fatigue and alcohol but one of them smacked my ear. I rolled my shoulder into his flailing and pulled him back and slammed him into the wall again. I heard the inside of the cupboard beside us give way and a river of crockery came pouring out through the doors.

I pulled him away from the wall and slammed him into it one more time. He stopped trying to hit me and let his arms fall to his side, whimpering. When I let go of him, he dropped in a heap, mindless of the broken plates that littered the tile floor. I stood over Jason while he started to cry. I was breathing hard from effort and anger.

"What the hell did you think you were doing?" I yelled at him. "Are you that self-deluded that you thought you were helping these women?"

Jason shook his head back and forth in denial. "No, no that's not what we ..." he tried.

"Shut up Jason! Your little game made you all rich but Chris and Paul got killed because of it. Who did it? Who killed them?"

"I don't know!" he cried, "I don't know, I don't know."

"Who's in charge now that Paul's gone?"

"I don't ... they said we better... that they couldn't trust us anymore. It... they said that you better stop or they'd... shit, Jon, we got families and ..."

I crouched down and grabbed Jason by his hair, forcing his head back against the wall. Tears streamed down his face and spittle soaked his chin.

"Let me be clear about this, Jason. I. Don't. Care. I don't care about your problems. I don't care about Ron's problems. It's your own goddamned fault that this happened. You put your family in harm's way, not me. If you're so worried, why not go to the cops?"

"The cops?" he cried. "What are they gonna do? These guys are serious. They... they already did Chris and Paul. Jesus, Jon when they found out you were back and askin' questions, they told us we better shut you down. Besides, we go to the cops an' what's gonna happen to us?"

"When did they find out about me? Who the hell told them who I was?"

"I don't know. I hate dealing with them. They scare the hell out of me."

The lot of them had managed to back themselves into a corner and had no idea how to get out. And they were indirectly responsible for two deaths. I was tempted to walk away from it all and let them face the consequences.

"Jason, you're going to give them a message."

"Uh-uh, I'm not tellin' them anything."

I reached down, grabbed a handful of hair and banged his head against the wall to get his attention.

"Yes. You. Will." I banged his head on each word and felt sick at myself for doing it. "You tell them I got scared. You tell them that after the meeting at the old man's house I finally decided to leave everything alone. The night I came to play poker here, I told all of you that I knew I was out of my depth and I'm going to drop it."

"Too late. Too late."

"What's too late?"

"We were supposed to call and tell them that. Ron told them you wouldn't back off."

So that explained why I got picked up so quickly the other morning. Nice to know the people I had grown up with were willing to sell me to save themselves. Sometimes you realize that shared history isn't a good enough reason for lasting friendship.

"I don't care whether you want to or not, Jason. Tell them after the old man talked to me I'm terrified. That I told you last night when we were all here. That I don't know what's really going on, but that I'm out." I banged his head again for emphasis, "You're going to do it."

He held his hands up to protect himself and whimpered, "OK, OK, God, I'll talk to them. Please stop. Oh God."

"Where's your office?"

"Wha…? My office?"

"Here at the house. Where is it?"

"Upstairs. Spare bedroom. Why?"

I dragged him standing again and pushed him ahead of me. "Move," I said.

Jason stumbled along and led the way upstairs, gripping the banister with both hands and leaning heavily against it trying to keep on a straight track.

He led the way into a sizable room lined with bookshelves and a desk up against the window looking out into the night of the garden below. There was a laptop connected to a larger monitor and two external hard drives.

"Which one?" I asked, pointing to the hard drives.

Jason wouldn't look up. "No Jon, don't. Please."

"Which one? I don't care. Fine. I'll take it all." I began to pull the cables out.

"Jesus don't! My entire business is here! Please Jon!"

I spun and hit him in the solar plexus with my elbow. His chest caved in and he stumbled back against one of the bookshelves and collapsed on the floor. "Give me what I need," I said.

"The red one," he said defeated and pointed up to a portable drive in a hard nylon case with red badging.

"Is it encrypted?"

"No man, plug and play."

"After you give them the message, keep your goddamned head down. And tell the others to do the same. Any of you come near me and I'll blow this thing wide open."

"What are you gonna do?"

I moved towards the door and Jason cowered like I was going to hit him again. I crouched in front of him and put a closed fist on his forehead.

"Do what you're told, Jason. Do it and stay invisible." I got up from my crouch and looked down at him. He looked shrunken and misshapen, still sitting against the bookshelf, legs out in front of him, office supplies and books littered around the floor.

"Don't screw around on this, Jason. You call first thing and tell them I don't know enough to be a problem and that I'm leaving it alone."

He was pathetic but he was beyond pity. He was a fool whose life didn't provide him with enough sensation; the ordinary comforts and successes weren't enough for his callused and cauterized soul. So he and the others had found a way to add some excitement and the spice of danger to their little lives. Not to mention lining their pockets. And to their minds, the women they had helped bring over were nothing more than ciphers. In their quest for excitement, they'd managed to conveniently forget about what was right and what was wrong. I turned away. I went back down to the main floor to the ruined kitchen, undid the latch on the sliding glass doors, walked out onto the deck and went back to the gentle reassurance of *The Saracen*.

# Chapter 27

I slept for only a few hours and was up before dawn. The day was a greasy smudge in the east as I got dressed in the dark of the master stateroom. I realized I couldn't let my outrage cloud my thinking. I was going to have to move quickly and with clarity if I was going to dig out from under this. The first thing to do was make sure both my lady and the one Chris had left behind were on safe ground. I didn't know what or who I could trust anymore. I replaced the contents of the small locked compartment under the seat with Jason's hard drive. When I was ready, I gunned the bike north towards Tara's house. A few minutes away from her place, I stopped at a darkened gas station and pulled out my cell.

"My, my," she said, laughing. "We're up rather early today."

Her voice and playfulness were the best things I'd heard lately. I felt some of the knotted tension in my shoulders and stomach release.

"Mmmmm, so we are," I replied. "And what makes you so cheery this morning? You got your spare boyfriend over there? If he's still there in two minutes, I shall be as a *Deus ex Machina* upon him. Tell that callow youth to be on his way. Your man is coming over."

"I'll have you know that I have been up for some time now. I have exercised, I have breakfasted and I am ready for you, big boy."

I laughed and said, "Then I am on my way. But I have a little favour to ask. How would you feel about a roommate for a couple of days."

"Oh goody! Are you moving in? Or are you taking me somewhere romantic?"

"I'll see you in a few."

"Whoopee!" she said and hung up.

Then I called Chris' third number. Before the message kicked in I hung up. I redialed and hung up again before the phone kicked over to messages. I repeated the operation twice more, hoping that the repeated ringing would awaken Karolina and get her to pick up. On the fifth go I let the phone go to messages and after the greeting had played I said, "Karolina, it's Jon. Pick up the phone. Karolina? C'mon Karolina, it's me. Pick up the bloody…!"

"Yes, yes. Jonathan.." came the out-of-breath reply.

"Karolina. I'm sorry to call so early. I just wanted to make sure you're OK. Is everything all right?"

Fear resonated though her voice. "Why Jonathan? Jonathan, what is wrong?"

"I can't go into details right now. You said that you trusted me. Chris said you could trust me? I need you to just stay at home. I'm not going to be at my boat like I said and I don't want you to worry if you can't reach me. I'm going to give you another number. Do you have a pen?"

There was the sound of her digging in a nearby drawer and then she said, "Yes, I have a pen."

"OK," I said and I reeled off Tara's number. "If you need me, I'll be at this number. If a woman answers, it's OK. She's my friend and she'll know where to find me if I'm not there. Karolina, it's going to be OK. If you need me, if something happens, call me, right? Will you do this for me?"

Her reply was uncertain and filled with unasked questions but she said, "Yes. I can do this."

"Good. I'm going to be at that number for a couple of days. If you need to find me and can't, my friend will know where I am."

"I … I understand."

"Don't be worried, Karolina. Everything's going to work out." It sounded weak, but I wanted her to stay at home and not venture out.

I hung up and restarted the bike and drove to Tara's parent's place. Now her place. The other houses on her street were just beginning to show signs of life. The occasional neighbour jogging past or walking dogs. Tara's was the last house on the street that ended at the edge of the park. A small slope led to a shallow creek bed that wound for two hundred yards until it spilled into the larger Sherwood Park. The same park where Chris and I had cemented our friendship all those years ago.

I snapped down the sidestand and as I did so, Tara opened the front door and smiled at me. Looking at her, framed by the light behind, I felt falsely unencumbered and content. I smiled back at her and walked up the flagstone path and into her arms. We hugged and I moved her inside and eased the door shut behind me. She was still dressed in workout gear, sweatpants and a purple sweat-soaked workout top. Behind her was a suitcase on the living room floor that looked like it was big enough to be the overnight bag for an invading army.

"What's that?" I asked laughing.

"It's my overnight bag for our romantic getaway."

"That's not an overnight bag, It's an overyear bag."

"Shows what you know," she said, whacking me in the chest. "That's the smallest suitcase I own. It may not be big enough even."

"I guess we're not taking the bike."

She looked at me askance. "We weren't taking the bike anyway."

I laughed and said, "Really? You are not entranced by my preferred mode of transportation? Man, some people's kids. C'mere a second," and I walked her back into the kitchen. Once there, she started to make tea for me and a coffee for herself. I began to tell her what I knew.

"Chris had a girlfriend. She's from Hungary. She came under the assumption she was going to be an au pair for some Toronto family. When she got here, the group that brought her over took away her passport and her visa and made her work as a dancer, then an escort, always threatening to make her life worse. The business operated on a system set up by Paul, Ron, Jason and Mack. And Chris laundered the funds. It seems the head of the operation had done business with Chris before and the legal means to bring them into the country began to dry up, when they needed to find another avenue for bringing in women, they arranged everything through Paul and the others. This woman, Chris met her by accident when she got sent to some party he was at. When she got picked up later by the cops, she called him and he bailed her out."

"So, is that what happened to Chris? Did the men who brought, what's her name?"

"Karolina."

"Karolina. Do you think they murdered Chris?"

"Yes, that or they had it done. Yesterday I got grabbed by the men who ransacked *The Saracen* and taken to see the head of the operation, a friendly old man who tried to scare the hell out of me. He's who Jason was talking about; he hired Chris and Paul to set up an employment and immigration agency for people from the Eastern Bloc. They also did legitimate business here and in the U.S. But I'm sure that's a mildly profitable front, the money is in the women. Paul brought Jason and Ron and Mack in to look after different aspects of the business. They got Chris to handle the proceeds through a shell corporation. So he invested it on their behalf. Then circumstances conspired to allow him to meet Karolina and maybe something changed for him. Something she said, maybe his conscience caught up to him. This whole thing is wound so tight that a couple of paths had to get crossed somewhere. And I think maybe Chris decided he'd had enough and threatened to expose everybody and that's why he was killed."

Tara shook her head in disbelief. "Jon, you've known them all your life. Why would they ...?"

"You know when I first met them we hated each other. They were like a feral pack. The friendships came later and when I think of it now, I can't remember any good reason why things changed, they just did. I was never really part of their group, I always felt like an outsider. Mack was different and I'm disappointed to know that he's mixed up in all of this. But the others, I don't know, maybe I'm not that surprised. It would be nice to think Chris began to redeem himself when he met Karolina. But in the end, it was just greed. They all got rich off of this. Paul and Jason and Ron and Chris have not been living small. I don't know what Mack's end is on this yet. And I don't know whether they were all blind or whether they just acted blind. I don't know which is worse. I hope to God they didn't know what was really going on. If they did then there's no saving them – they're beyond redemption. After Chris was killed, it must have been a warning shot across the bow. I think when Paul went in the water, everybody who was left over got petrified. And with good goddamn reason. Right after the thing on the Island, we all met at Mack's bar, friendly as could be, and the three of them tried gently to put me off. They had the girl try to convince me to go away. And when I made it clear I wasn't going to drop it, the old man summoned me for a chat. When I kept at it, they all invited me for a poker game and they tried again. So whether they're just trying to dig out from under, or whether the man in charge just wanted them to stop me, it doesn't matter. I told Jason to tell them I was giving up."

"But you're not going to, are you?"

I looked at Tara and saw a thousand questions behind her eyes.

"No, I'm not."

"What are you ... you'll go to the police, won't you?"

"No I can't, not yet." I said shaking my head. "I made a promise to Karolina. If I get Kelly involved right away, then her life becomes hell. If she stays here, she's got nothing. If she gets sent home, then the people in Budapest know where she and her mother are. Either way she has no options. And as much as Jason and the others may deserve it, I turn this over to Kelly and their families are going to get hurt. So I need to figure something else out."

"Jon, please talk to the police. Tell them everything you know," she implored.

"Tara, I can't. I'm not ... I don't want to hand it over to them. It'll all go wrong. There's got to be something else I can do."

"Like what?"

"I don't know for sure but I have an idea. Kelly warned me how the system works here. Probably the same way it works everywhere else. The girls will suffer and the ones in control will walk away. So I'm going to find a way to take the old man out."

"What?"

"It's not all there yet. It's just an idea. But first I have to buy some breathing room from the old man."

"Why should he listen to you?"

"I don't know, maybe he won't. But for some reason, the old man likes me. He's evil but there's little point in giving into the fear. If I thought going to the cops would help I would, but this thing seems too entrenched. And if the police are brought in... they'll follow procedure and subtlety won't factor in too strongly. And who knows if they'll reach the top of the food chain — likely small fish who run the day to day. It'd be a temporary fix and who knows what the fallout would be. If the old man who runs this believes Jason then I've got the breathing room I need. If I can swing it, then maybe I can help Karolina get free from all of this."

"And Jason and the others?"

I looked at her and saw the girl I had fallen in love with behind the eyes of the woman I loved now.

"It's so easy to fall into the trap of thinking of those close to you as just satellites revolving around you," I said. "You forget that they have their own lives, distinct and separate. Jason and the others made that mistake. They became so focused on their quest they didn't see the women whose lives they were helping to ruin as people. I honestly don't care what happens to them."

"Are you sharpening up your sword? Getting ready to storm the castle?" she asked, a sad smile playing on her lips.

"I want you to do me a favour," I said. "I can't trust anyone but you. I think Jason's so panicked he'd sell his sister to save himself."

"But you told him to give them the message."

"Yeah, and maybe the only person he'll convince is himself. My boat isn't safe anymore. Can I stay with you for a couple of days? I can't stay there and I may have sell it. At the very least I'm going to have to move it somewhere else. But even then, I think getting off it is good idea."

"Why do this, Jon? Why not just let somebody else do this?"

"Because no one else is doing anything about it. I just need the old man to go for it. Besides he's Hungarian. The land of Rubik's Cube, should be easy…"

Tara laughed a little and took my face in both hands and looked at me hard. I tried to smile back as confidently as I could. Tara nodded and kissed her fingers then touched them to my mouth.

"Of course you can stay, you stupid man. But gourmet dinners and sexual slavery is the price. Non-negotiable."

I laughed and leaned over and kissed her. "Hard bargain. OK, I've got to go." I stood to leave. "By week's end, this will all be solved. I'm going to spend tonight on the boat, pack a few things and get a couple of things in motion. But I'll call you in the morning and see you tomorrow night."

Tara reached over and rifled through a drawer, coming up with a small ring of identical keys. She worked one off and handed it to me and as I took it from her she held onto it a moment.

"Jon …" she said.

We looked at one another and I felt something deep inside chunk into place. I smiled and took the key and kissed her, then I went out the back kitchen door and around the side of the house.

I checked my watch and it was just past eight. The day was coming full on now and it brought no promise with it. I pointed the bike south and went back to my boat.

# Chapter 28

There was still no message from Jason. I had no idea whether he had told them I was backing off. So now the question was if he had, would they believe him? And if they didn't, what were they going to do about it? It was impossible to know. All I could do was be prepared for what they might do.

I parked the bike in an underground parking lot out of sight. I prepped the boat from top to bottom, topping off the fresh-water tanks and making sure the batteries were fully charged. I called Bluffer's and booked a slip for a week. She was already full of fuel, so I disconnected the water and electrical hook-ups. Then I fired her up and cast off the lines while the engines settled into a steady rhythm and when she was ready, I pulled away from the slip and out into the harbour. I saw a tanker trundling through the harbour on its way to the docklands. It was riding high in the water so it had yet to fill up on sugar, grain or containers and take its cargo somewhere across the latitudes. I headed toward where it had come in through the Eastern Gap as I had that night with Tara in what seemed like a lifetime ago.

I took it slow and it was lunchtime by the time I arrived at the marina in the shadow of the magnificent sand cliffs. It was a view I could get used to if I had to. I checked in with the manager, who assigned me a slip, and paid for it in advance. Once she was docked and tied up, I called a cab and went back for the bike then went and rented a car from the same place I had for Paul's funeral. This time I got myself a very comfortable, ubiquitous sport utility with a nice stereo, climate control and leather seats. Then I drove to Mimico in automotive splendour and parked on one of the side streets that T-junctioned at Lakeshore. I pointed the car at the house and sat and drank a large take-out tea. Nothing happened at the house all day that was worth watching. Even with the sunroof open, I baked slowly in the August sun. Around five the girl who'd served us tea came out through the iron gates and walked a medium-sized tan-coloured dog. When she returned from the walk she was inside the house for twenty minutes then came out again and got in a car. Shift over. I had little frame of reference but I was beginning to realize that a stake-out was maybe the most boring thing in the world. And to think I walked away from the chance to do it professionally. Blessedly as the sun dropped lower, sitting inside my steel and leather greenhouse got easier to bear.

Around six-thirty, the big silver Merc rolled down the driveway and the gates opened on command. I started up the truck and followed the Merc from a safe distance as it cruised along Lakeshore Boulevard. It turned up the on-ramp and picked up the Gardiner Expressway going downtown. I dialed around on the radio until I found an all-jazz station that was doing a Dinah Washington tribute. So while Dinah growled through her songbook, I tailed the silver Mercedes up onto the Expressway and into the core. We both took the Jarvis offramp and went north past the Market. When we got to midtown, the Merc slowed and turned down a side street and parked in front of a disheveled four-story low-rise. I pulled on ahead and up to the top of a ramp that led down into an underground garage. I had unpacked my digital camera back on the boat and took reflected shots with the side mirror of Elvis getting out of the Merc and entering the building. It might have been where he lived for all I knew, but I doubted it.

He stayed in the building for only fifteen minutes and when he came out he had a woman with him. She was dressed for work with a hip-hugging mini skirt, knee-high boots and short leather jacket. He put her in the back seat and then drove away from the curb. I had re-parked well behind the Merc while he was inside, so I pulled away and resumed following him and his charge. They turned south and fifteen minutes of downtown traffic later, stopped at another rundown place. Elvis went in and came out a few minutes later with another woman who looked like she shopped, or was shopped for, in the same place as the other woman in the Mercedes.

After she was packed into the car as well, Elvis guided the car north through the traffic up to the highway. Once on the highway, we headed west for fifteen minutes and then up the Allen. After a while we turned west again and soon pulled into the parking lot of a tacky strip mall. Elvis parked by a long low building with a half-circle awning that said Elite Gentleman's Club — a perfectly antithetical name. The front windows were painted black with silhouettes of lithe women painted in pink in the centre of each frame. Elvis got out and opened the back door of the sedan to let the girls out. When the three of them opened the door and entered the bar, I could feel the low throb of the music through the closed windows of the truck. The bar shared the mall with a donut shop, a convenience store and a burger joint. The other three businesses looked empty, yet the parking lot was almost full. I sat in the truck for over an hour and the boredom crept up on me again. Three overweight men in T-shirts and riding chaps came out of the bar and walked over to three choppers sitting in the shade of the building. All three opened up the large containers affixed to the back of their bikes and shrugged on leather vests. All bore a flaming skull insignia with The Ragged written in Gothic script around the crest. I had worked door as a bouncer at a club during college and bikers knew we wouldn't let them in wearing colours. Guess the rule was still in place. They sat astride their machines, fired up with a unified bellow and roared off along Finch. And an idea began.

Eventually Elvis came out, this time with a different woman who, like the others, got hustled into the back of the sedan. The two of them drove off to the west. I didn't need to see inside the dance bar, I already felt grimy enough just tailing Elvis. I pulled out of the lot and followed the Merc to another bar, also called Elite Gentlemen's Club, near the airport. There was a small clutch of Harleys sitting in the parking lot of this one as well. Elvis dropped off the woman and then took two more girls to another Elite Club in Brampton that advertised Hot Europeans on the marquee over the awning. By the time he'd finished his rounds, eight places in all, I'd noted Harleys at all but one, taken a lot of photographs, and eaten a couple of drive-through burgers that sat like a stone in the bottom of my stomach.

I headed back to the rental agency and ditched the car and got my bike back. Then I went back to *The Saracen* and took a cleansing shower.

I eschewed dinner as my stomach still felt lousy so I took a glass of red out onto the back deck and called Tara as boats with lights strung on their mast lines bobbed in the small bay.

"I'm sitting here, with a nice Corbières, watching evening sloops drift on small waves and thinking of you," I said when she answered the phone.

"Are you really?" she said. I could practically hear her smile through the line. "I have Raoul my cabaña boy here, pouring me a margarita and waving a palm frond over me."

"No kidding?"

"Yes," she said through her laughter, "the two of us are having a wonderful time and I don't miss you at all. In fact, I don't think I've thought about you for at least two minutes now."

"Well, that's more like it," I replied. The silence that followed was full and connected us more than banter could. "How are you, really," I finally said.

"Much better than I was a few minutes ago," she said, sighing. "Are you all right?"

"Yeah, yeah. No, really I'm fine. I've just spent the evening driving from strip club to strip club. I need a little more information for leverage. That and I've always been curious about 'Hot Europeans'."

"I know a hot Canadian ..."

"Mmmm ... so do I. Are we thinking of the same person though?"

"We better be," she laughed into the phone.

"Anyway, I tailed Elvis all night in a rental. Looks like they own and operate a chain of dance clubs. I've been to a number of them and there's probably more."

"Have you called that detective yet?"

"Mmmm-mmm. Things are starting to come together, I have an idea. I'm going to try and leverage Mack and Jason and Ron out of it and have him leave Karolina alone."

"What are you going to use?"

"Now that I know about the clubs and the fact that they're bringing women into the country under false pretenses and forcing them into servitude, I'm going to talk to the cops. Maybe now Kelly will have enough to shut this thing down without needing Karolina and Jason, Ron and Mack can offer evidence and get out from under."

"When are you going to do this?"

"Tomorrow. I'll go and see Kelly. See if I can sweet-talk him into squeezing Karolina and the others out. If not, then I have another idea."

"Well, I can't think of anybody else who's better at it than you."

"Why, because I sweet talk you so well?"

"You do many things to me well."

"Very true."

We fell into silence, neither of us knowing quite where to go from there. I wanted to tell her not to worry. I wanted to promise her everything would be all right. But the words would have been more for me to assuage my guilt for making her worry, for making her wonder if everything was going to be all right. I stayed quiet and listened to her breathing. When I spoke again, my voice was thready.

"OK, are you all right?"

"Aside from constantly worrying about you? I pulled out some of the old yearbooks and went for a stroll down memory lane. I'd forgotten how dorky you were in high school," she said, laughing.

"Nice."

"But dorky or not, maybe you can prove how un-dorky you've become when you come to stay here."

"No."

"No? What do you mean no?"

"I was thinking I could un-dork myself in maybe Paris. Or Vienna? Or Florence?"

"I know a lovely café near the Duomo."

"I bet you do."

She paused for a second, her playfulness suddenly gone. "Jon, these people ..."

"Tomorrow, babe. I'll have finished my backgrounding, then I'll put things in motion, I'll stay with you while the fallout happens and it'll all be over. Karolina will have her life back. She'll have her freedom. And Mack and Jason and Ron and their families will be out of it as well. That's the plan anyway."

"God, Jon. Please be ... you'll be careful, won't you?"

"What, risk pissing you off? I do that and you'll kill me."

Tara laughed and said, "Damn right I'll kill you, if somebody else doesn't." Her laugh choked off and her breath hitched in her throat.

"Hey." I said. "Hey. You and me. Right? You and me."

She was silent, then I heard her sigh quietly and she seemed to have it under control again. "Yes," she said. "Me and you."

"OK then, I'll call you tomorrow and everything will be over."

"Goodnight Jon," Tara said and I listened while she ended the call. Then I went up to the fly bridge. It was an overcast night and if there were stars out, I couldn't see them.

# Chapter 29

In the shadow of Casa Loma lay the city archives. A building built of ancient brick from the Don Valley works, it is the repository, like all archives, of the beginnings of all things. In my case, it held what I needed, the property rolls for every building in the city dating from as recently as a few days ago right back to the founding of the town. The woman at the front desk was delightful, the registration form easy, and the records a combination of microfiche, photocopied original records and computerized searches. It was as fascinating to pore over the copies of old hand-lettered rolls as it was clinical and dull to type words into search fields.

The inevitable outcomes of revolution; the cold calculations of progress; the desire for ease of life — all have created a process that feeds itself by forcing old ways and values to the wayside. So the old-fashioned and lovely pleasures of reading for entertainment or edification have been replaced by the soul-destroying glow of incandescent computer screens. The required effort to attain knowledge through research has been fundamentally undermined by ready electronic access to glib and shallow worldwide sources.

And the requirements of the new technologies are such that subjugation has overflowed into the human arena. We've all been forced to pare down our thoughts and interests because the onslaught of the potential input is overwhelming. We complain so about being pigeonholed but we've done it to ourselves. The ancient intricacies of discovery and meaning and interconnection have been replaced by the necessitated simplicity of typing a keyword into the field with the flashing cursor and hitting enter. And the funneling of thought and the speed with which access can be granted has driven us to simplify other areas of our lives. These are new religions and they are the religions of utter faith and devotion to exclusionary practice. The days of the renaissance individual are over because maybe in the end, we're all afraid to venture away into the potential discomfort of multi-mania. Embracing the alien is no longer interesting to us and that xenophobia may well be the tolling of the bell.

I hadn't known how far back to go, so I started with the property records for the nineteen-sixties. Each entry detailed the size of the lot, the year the structure was built, most recent survey dates and a list of the history of ownership dating back to the first occupant. It took the better part of a very pleasant and low-tech two hours to find everything I was looking for.

The elegant stone house on Lakeshore Boulevard had been owned by someone called Melanny until '61. A corporation bought it for six figures and the company had kept it until '92, probably as an executive residence. The house got bought and flipped for profit three times during the real estate boom in the mid-nineties, bringing its price to just under a two and a half million in '99. Up to that point there didn't seem to be anything out of the ordinary. Then in the late spring of that year, the Federal government bought the house. The view of the lake, the relative privacy and the ready access to downtown made it ideal to be a government holding.

But there were others who had felt the same way. In the fall of 2010 the house was purchased under an agreement between governments and became a consulate. There were notations detailing the paperwork that had been filed to designate the property as sovereign for an indefinite term. But it was only used as a Consulate for a couple of years. It was sold to someone named Lazar Tardos. It appeared that Mr. Tardos had bought the house for a steal, picking it up for less than half of what the consular government had paid for it. Perhaps he was a government official who had been granted a discount by his employer. Perhaps he had impressed them with his classical education. Might have been the minor real estate drop of 2009. Or perhaps he was able to provide a service outside that of the usual real estate transaction. I took the volume from the eighties and nineties and photocopied the appropriate pages detailing the transfers, surveys and lien searches.

Then I settled into a computer station and did some research on the Elite

Gentlemen's Club locations, going through ownership records and compiling lists of all the locations. I checked as well on the apartment building I'd followed Elvis to, the day he shuttled the women around. The same corporation that owned all the clubs owned the building. It was likely that the entire apartment block was full of working girls. Then I plugged Jason's hard drive in and scoured it. Records for all the transportation arrangements were there: ports of entry, passenger manifests and visa applications along with detailed financial accounts of the laundering.

I sat back and laced my hands behind my head. Kelly had said that all kinds of groups were involved with the exotic dance clubs and prostitution business, everyone from the Mob to small business to the bikers. That the Feds had helped create the problem was not surprising but that they were nothing more than a hindrance in cleaning up the mess was even less of a surprise. If I was going to get everyone out of this, I needed a back-up plan in case Kelly was unwilling or unable to close it down and keep Karolina and the others out of it at the same time. So who else could I sell the information to that would do something with it? Who would take on the old man without needing to go through legal channels? I could think of only one possibility.

After I had packed up and returned the books, I used the computer to sort through past newspaper accounts and magazine sources and carefully made a list. It took a while to sort through the conjecture and gossip to establish just the information I wanted. I needed a local group, preferably with national affiliations so they would seriously consider the offer. When I was through sorting and had rejected the bigger, more dangerous fish, there were two groups that had potential. I noted the addresses and whatever names were mentioned in the articles in case I couldn't get past the doors. The group of individuals I'd seen outside the strip clubs had an interesting history. According to the news accounts, the Raggeds had started out in the west, an off-shoot of a US outlaw gang. They had done well in the usual drugs and guns and had begun to swell their ranks until a crackdown had cleaned out the upper echelon and had closed all of their clubhouses. They were new but they had learned that it was the new recruits who should do the wet work and leave the leaders to enjoy deniability. The articles conjectured that after the western crackdown the Raggeds would move east and would set up shop in central territory where they wouldn't stand out so much. It also suggested the

Raggeds were probably angling to be picked up and absorbed into the Angels, as almost all other small gangs in the province had been, if they could only prove their worth. So the question became, were the bikers I'd seen at the clubs there as patrons, or were they doing reconnaissance? I was betting on the latter. I printed everything and made more copies. Then I plugged Jason's hard drive in and copied its contents onto two spare drives.

I realized from the grumbling in my stomach that I had skipped lunch and, according to my watch, I was now moving out of the dinner hour. I went down to the ground floor and out to the motorcycle and went southeast to where my home was hopefully still floating.

I went in the door off the side deck and down into the master stateroom. After ditching my packages and changing into frayed shorts and cotton shirt, I went forward and popped the small hatch in the foredeck to let in a little fresh air. The sun was extinguishing itself in the west and throwing the cliffs into starkly shadowed relief, like jagged teeth in a rotting mouth. Water birds circled high above and occasionally came to rest in the scraggly trees that lined the shore. It was stale and stifling below decks so I turned the air conditioning on low. In the galley I opened the fridge and surveyed the possibilities. I was hungry as hell, but didn't feel like going to a lot of trouble. There was a thawed striploin wrapped in cellophane on a plate and in the crisper I found some baby spinach. Good enough. I pulled out the steak, threw it in a bowl and poured some wine and dried rosemary on it. As night settled in, I took a glass onto the rear deck and dropped into one of the cushioned chairs. I snapped a wooden match alight and lit a cigarette. The light from the salon behind me poured through the sliding glass doors and washed the rear deck in a pale yellow. I wanted dark, so I got up to turn out the lights. As I stood, a glint at the scupper edge of the rear deck caught my eye. I had to half bend again to see it a second time. When I was sitting or standing, the light didn't hit it quite right.

I put down my glass and bent down to see what it was that had caught my eye. I felt around with my hand flat on the rear deck. Suddenly there was a stabbing pain in my palm. I jerked my hand back and embedded in the centre of my hand was a tiny aluminum shard. After plucking it out, I grabbed another wooden match and lit it with the glowing tip of my cigarette. When the flaring of the match had settled I found a brother to the piece that had stuck me. The metal was very thin and pliable. I stood and ran my hand over and around the brightwork railing. The railing was too heavy for these little pieces. I surveyed the rear deck, trying to figure out where they could have come from. My eyes came to rest on the propane barbecue that was attached to the rear railing. I crushed out my cigarette and bent down and looked underneath the sooty black body of the unit. I couldn't see anything obvious so I stood and ran my fingertips around the underside.

The body of the barbecue was cast iron and seemed solid. I traced the path of the venturi pipes that ran from the gas feeder assembly into the burners inside the bottom of the barbecue. When I was halfway along the left pipe, I caught the pad of my index finger on a jag. I bent down to look and saw a series of drill holes. When I checked the right pipe there were drill holes at roughly the same place facing the rubber flex hose that ran to the propane tank. Despite how dry my mouth was I worked up some spit and smeared it around the area on the hose adjacent to the drill holes thinking of the old Scottish man of my childhood who had taught me how to find holes in bicycle inner tubes. I turned the tank on and watched as the escaping gas made little bubbles in the saliva around minute incisions in the tube. As soon as the barbecue had been fired up, the flames would have worked their way out of the holes in the venturi tubes and ignited the leaking propane. The tank would have exploded and because the fuel tanks for *The Saracen* were directly below this area of the deck, the whole craft would have gone up with me.

I was frozen, smelling the leaking propane that was supposed to blow me to kingdom come, my eyes defocused. I brought myself back to reality and shut off the gas, then I disconnected the tank from the feed assembly. I sat down heavily on the rear deck and stared at the blood seeping from my hand. When I came out my fugue and looked at my watch again, minutes had passed and I couldn't remember them. The time was a little past eight and my appetite was gone. Dear Christ. I'd moved the boat and they'd come and found her again. They wanted me gone. Jason hadn't convinced them of anything.

I went back my stateroom and looked at three piles of information sitting on my chart table. I'd needed tonight to be sure I knew what I was doing to set up everything with Kelly and Walsh. But now everything had changed. Things were moving faster than I wanted them to but if somebody else was playing, then I was going to have to keep time. I went and got three manila envelopes out of my desk and put one set of copies in each one. I put the camera disk with the photos in the one for Kelly. I tore a page out of one of my map books and wrote a letter on the other side. When it was finished I didn't sign it. Then I put in it Kelly's envelope and labeled and addressed it, the other two envelopes I left blank. Then I locked up my still-floating refuge and went up to the main building to call a cab. A black and orange cab happened to be in the parking lot and when I waved, he heaved out of the parking space and pulled up. I motioned and he dropped the passenger side window down.

"Need a person-to-person delivery here," I said. He looked at the address then back at me. Before he could reply I handed him a fifty-dollar bill and continued, "Don't get stopped. You get it to him or her and you put it their hands. Done?"

The cabbie nodded and said yeah and the window went up. I held my hand on the roof of the cab for an extra second before it pulled away then left for my first meeting of the night.

# Chapter 30

Half an hour later, when I pulled up at the cinderblock building, I drove the bike onto the sidewalk and maneuvered around the multiple steel posts set into the concrete. The cameras mounted on the front of the building stared at me with a seeming indifference that would be antithetical to those watching the screens inside. Heavy fencing surrounded the sides and back and was topped with razor wire. The entrance was built like a bunker, in an L-shape, again out of cinderblock. I left the helmet sitting atop the tank and walked over and banged on the steel door with my fist. A logo in rusty iron of two wings spreading out from a smoking tire was welded to the door. There was no answer so I banged again. This time the door swung open on oiled hinges and a guy who was beyond burly stood in the doorway. With muttonchops and square, rimless sunglasses perched on the end of his nose, he looked like a massive hippie. He was wearing the same kind of uniform I'd seen outside the strip clubs, jeans and white T-shirt with his colours emblazoned across the back of a black leather vest. We stared at each other silently for half a minute while he made up his mind about me. Then he stood aside and let me squeeze in. I had to squeeze because even stepping to one side he still filled the doorway.

"Yeah?" he said closing the door behind us.

"Who's in charge of new business development?"

He guffawed and said, "Why? You from the Chamber of Commerce?"

I smiled back. "No. But I have an excellent opportunity for expansion. Wanted to see if anybody had an ear."

He looked me over from head to toe again. "Take off the jacket and turn around," he said. I did what I was told. He patted me down while I held my jacket and the envelope out. Then he went to take the envelope. I pulled it away from him.

"Nope. Not for you. Top of the food chain." I shrugged.

"Wait."

At the end of the corridor he knocked on a door and went in. The place was permeated with the smell of hydraulic fluid, solvents and gasoline. Through a doorway to my right I heard the clang of a dropped tool ringing off concrete. I glanced through the opening and saw two men working on the clutch assembly of an engine mounted on a bench. The empty frame of a big Harley Panhead sat in a corner with electrical harnesses dangling in the open space of the engine mounts.

A moment later the doorway at the end opened and the Sasquatch motioned me to come and I walked down the corridor. Just before the doorway there were two shoulder-high plastic and metal stands on either side. It took me a second then I realized they were metal detectors. I stepped through and when the door closed behind me I took a look around. There were small television screens on one side giving a view of the circumference of the building as well as the roof. The floor was cracked linoleum scuffed with boot marks and dragged furniture. There were no windows at all, the light was provided by humming fluorescents hanging in boxes from the ceiling. On the other side of the room were three men sitting around a table playing cards. They looked at me with a combination of mistrust and amusement. What the hell was I doing here? They probably wondered the same thing.

One of them stood and came over to me. He smiled quietly and looked over at the video screens, squinting his eyes myopically at the images.

"That your kraut burner?" he asked.

"Yeah."

"What is it?

"BMW, GT1200"

One of the men sitting at the table said "Fuckin' German crap. Kinda like dating a fat broad, man. Maybe fun to ride until one 'a your friends sees ya." And everybody but me laughed.

"What year?"

I told him.

"Over-priced piece 'a shit. You should be drivin' domestic brother," said the heckler again.

The man who had gotten up from the table laughed at his buddy and grinned hard at me. "Who're you?" he asked.

"Doesn't matter," I replied, shrugging my shoulders. "Got something for you."

He turned and cocked at his head at the men at the table then turned back to me. The movement washed his smell at me — cigarette, stale sweat and malice. "Depends," he said, with a mocking smile.

I opened my jacket, slowly mind you, reached in and brought out one of the folded manila envelopes and handed it to him. "You gentlemen are interested in some clubs, I think. This might be of help. Have a look. If you don't want it, I'll take it somewhere else."

He raised an eyebrow at me and opened the top of the envelope, peering in. Then he went back to the table, pushed a pile of money out of the way and dumped the contents onto the card table. Each of the men at the table went through the pile of printouts slowly while I stood and waited.

"Who do you think you are, man?"

"Somebody with information"

"What's the deal?" another of them said. "Why you bringin' this to us?"

"No deal. Papers say the cops think that you run girls in the East End. It's not against the law, so everything's everything. And if it's true then maybe you probably have a desire for some central and west turf. That," I nodded toward the papers askew on the card table, "represents the control of a lot of west and central business. Not only that, you have details of supply out of Europe by legal means and you have some nice ideas about how to clean the income. A foothold like that means the beginning of a monopoly. And the beginning of a monopoly always brings both respect and further opportunity. Don't get me wrong gentlemen, think of me as a Good Samaritan looking out for your financial well-being. You don't want it?"

"Didn't say that."

"OK, then."

"What d'you want?"

"Nothing but for you to take this and do something with it. You'd have to take one or two people out. And that part is not for me. I help you, maybe you end up doing something for me. You don't need to know why."

The man in charge snorted again and said, "Help us? You believe this guy? You jobbin'? I don't like this…"

"Yeah, you do. It's all there, routes, business locations which you already know about as I've seen your boys there. And now you have detailed information on the system in place, how to keep it legal, the supply chain and the money laundering. It's all on the hard drive. You didn't have that piece of the puzzle before. Now you do. Your recon didn't tell you how to make the whole thing work. Everything you need to take over immediately and without complication. Well, one complication… you're gonna have to earn it a little is all. Change of command is gonna mean resistance. And the resistance is your problem. You have the address on Lakeshore in question. So you have to earn it a little is all. You and I both know the payoff is worth the effort. So am I going elsewhere?"

"Like where else?"

"Where the bigger fish swim. I did a little research on you. This is prime and now you're even further prepped. My guess is you've been interested in this before I came along. Now you have all the backgrounding you need to take it over. So, you want it or do I talk to someone else?"

"No, no, man, this works. Yeah, we're interested. We'll see what we see. You wanna finder's fee? Couple a points maybe?" he said laughing.

I shook my head. "It's all yours. I have no interest in this. If this works out for you, you'll be solving a problem for me. I got another place to be. And right now. So I would suggest you should keep tabs on me tonight. Then you'll see I'm serious and that this is for real."

He stroked his chin and nodded. "We gotta have a discussion here first, you dig? Where do we find you when it's done?"

"I'm going to the address on Lakeshore. So make it fast. Other than that, you don't find me. You probably want to run my plate. It's Florida, so don't waste your time. You take this over and watch tonight and that's enough. Other than that we're done. I'm going there now," I said and pointed at the top sheet on the card table that showed Tardos' house. "If you don't, then maybe I change my play and you miss the opportunity. That's it, that's all."

"You got some fuckin' stones, bro'," he said, looking back at his friends. "You sure you gotta book? You wanna stick around for a little cards? Do your thing another night? We can talk this out more? Three-way poker sucks."

I smiled and said, "No thanks. I gotta do this tonight. You're right. Three-way poker does suck. So come and watch."

He grinned back at me. "Suit yourself." He held up the envelope and shook it a little. "We'll see what we see." I turned to leave and he added, "Hey! I wanna be crystal on this. You know, we're gonna have a problem if…"

"Relax. I'm not on the job and this isn't a set-up. I need it done. And you want it. Motivation for you to do it is all there. You've got questions, come along for the ride."

He nodded again and said, "Yeah, maybe. Awright. Lennie, take him back. Hey!"

I turned and waited.

"You got a name?"

"Yup."

We smiled at each other and said nothing. Then he nodded and waved his hand. "Cool." The giant saw me back down the hallway and out through the solid door. I walked out and stood beside the bike and stared up at the few stars I could see that weren't dimmed out by the night-glow of the city. The knowledge that maybe everything would have been better if I'd never come back in the first place was a sharp reminder in my gut. I felt like I needed to purge some kind of emotional nausea. This time last year I had been living in paradise. Working somebody else's boat on open water. My responsibilities were immediate, my pleasures simple, and my future didn't involve trying to stay alive. But now the blinders were off and I was sickened by what I saw. Whatever occurred from here would happen because I put it in play. I waited another fifteen minutes outside. Nobody came out. I wondered if I was going to make it alone.

# Chapter 31

I pulled up at the heavy black gates and pressed the intercom button on the unit attached to the brick pillar. When there was no answer I pressed the button down and held it. I could see the big Merc parked nose-in at the garage attached to the side of the house. After I held the buzzer for more than a minute, the front door was yanked open and I saw Goatee silhouetted in the doorway. I let go of the button and we stared at each across the expanse of the drive for a moment, then he put his hand to the inside wall and the gates vibrated and rolled themselves open. I drove the bike across the gravel drive and parked it on the leading edge of a flagstone path that seemed to go around the other side of the house. I made sure to back it in so that it was pointing at the gate and killed the engine. After balancing my helmet on one of the rear-view mirrors I walked over to the front door and smiled at Goatee as I brushed past him.

He closed the door behind us and walked away without a word, disappearing into the house. The chandelier above had been dimmed so that the light was quietly even in the entryway. After a few minutes Goatee came back into the front hall.

"Come back other time. The gentleman not home tonight," he said in heavily accented English.

I smiled and said, "Tell Mr. Tardos that I only need a few minutes of his time."

Goatee looked uncertain when I said the old man's name then shook his head firmly. "No," he said. "It would be better if you came back."

Preferably on the wind in little pieces blown across the lake, I thought. Holding my other hand in abeyance I reached into the inside pocket of my jacket and pulled out my cell. I scrolled through the extra photos I'd taken and settled for one that showed Elvis pushing a woman into the Merc. The Elite Club neon sign was clearly visible over his shoulder.

"Here," I said, holding up my phone, "see if this helps with his availability."

Goatee peered at the screen, glared at me, then went back into the bowels of the house. A moment later he returned and motioned for me to follow him. We wandered through the parlour as we had the last time I was here but instead of going on into the solarium, Goatee led me into a large study. The walls were paneled floor to ceiling in deep oak with ornately carved timbers arcing across the ceiling. Tall lead-paned windows looked out on the lake; the evening harbour lights made a lovely picture that tugged at my stomach. To my right was a large stone hearth with a low fire burning. In front of the fire were two brown leather club chairs and a dark wood drum table with ornate silver candelabra perched on top. To my left, bookshelves ran along the entire wall with a rolling ladder on casters to reach the upper shelves. A beautifully detailed cherry-wood desk faced the fire in front of the banks of books.

Goatee told me to wait and left the room. I ambled over to the shelves and scanned the titles. Most of the books were handsome leather-bound volumes and seemed to cover all the literary high points of the last four centuries; Rousseau, Marlowe, Pepys, Jonson, the Brontés, Chekov, Strindberg, Ruskin, Tennyson, Fitzgerald, Sartre — the greatest hits of western literature.

A noise behind me made me turn and I watched as the old man strode across the room and sat in one of the club chairs. He gave me an angry look. "We shall not spend a large expanse of time," he quoted.

"Which would be planted newly with the time, as calling home our exiled friends abroad, that fled the snares of watchful tyranny. Act 5…" I finished.

The old man's face relaxed a little at the recitation and he grimaced sadly. "Jonathan. Jonathan," he said, shaking his head. "Jonathan, why do you come here? Why do you not do what I ask? You are a stubborn man."

"If we forget the past, how are we to learn from it?"

"Do you know what Shakespeare called the last act?"

"The last act is named Catastophe. And yes I am stubborn and yet, resourceful. Be of good cheer, Lazar. I'm here to propose a solution to our problem."

"Jonathan," he said, leaning forward, "you know my name. Do you think you know anything else? Do we have a problem, as you say?"

"Yes, we do." I reached inside my jacket and brought out the other envelope and laid it on the drum table between us. The old man glanced at it casually, then back at me.

"What I want is very simple," I said. "Some people we both know are in business with you. They are not going to be able to continue to work for you. These men who helped you with your ... with services you provide, are no longer available. There was a young woman who once worked for you. You asked her to speak with me. She's out of it as well. And I want assurances her family back in Hungary will remain unmolested. What happens after I leave your house should be immaterial to you. I have no intention of our seeing each other again. I know everything. How you bring the women in on false visas. How the profits are laundered. Everything. More than enough to have the authorities scoop you up and toss the key. To be clear, much as what you do offends me, I have no interest in stopping you, that's not what I care about. And despite how charming our talks have been, I'm a realist, Lazar. I understood your message last time I was here. But the people involved with you want to get out."

I leaned back in my chair while the old man regarded me. The girl in the maid's uniform came in and he beckoned her closer and spoke in whispered Hungarian. She left and came back with two snifters on a silver tray followed by Elvis and Goatee who leaned on either side of the broad doorway. When the girl had put the drinks down and exited, the old man picked up his glass and stared at the fire. I took a sniff of mine, but didn't drink. It was the same kind of wine that Karolina had given me the other night.

"Who are these people you think work for me?" he said.

"They were once my friends. Long ago. They have helped you with your business and to launder the proceeds. Again, I don't care about that. But I want them cut loose. Completely. The woman too. And one more thing. I want whoever's responsible for the deaths of my two friends."

There was a snort of derision from the doorway, but I kept my eyes on the old man. He smiled for the first time and said, "Really, Jonathan? Who do you think is responsible for the deaths of your friends? Do you think I am?"

"I think you had someone do it," and nodded my head at the two standing in the doorway.

"Jonathan, do you not think your friends are responsible for what happened to them?"

"Indirectly yes, of course they are. But I'm not interested in debating the morality of choice with you. Because my friends were murdered, I want whoever did it."

"Of course you do, Jonathan. Of course you do. It is natural to want to avenge the death of a friend. But you must take my word, it is not as you think. Now, as for what you ask. Jonathan, why do you think I should do this? You have some pictures of my son helping women into a car. I do not think this should mean anything to me."

I held out my hand with the snifter and clinked our glasses but still didn't drink. They made a beautiful crystal tone. "Well, Lazar, here's what I think. You said you emigrated here some time ago. It doesn't matter what happened in the intervening years but in the last decade, but you and your fabulous children here began your little operation. I think you managed to become a purveyor for somebody within this house when it was the Hungarian Consulate. Extortion is the gift that keeps on giving, isn't it? And with the help of this consular officer you brought more women in from the Eastern Bloc. Women who had dreams of a better life than the one they ended up with when they came here. Or maybe they knew what they were getting into, but coming here was better than what they were leaving. In any event, your business was so successful that you were able to diversify into legitimate arenas. It gave you the patina of respectability."

I continued. "You grabbed this house for a song. I think whatever you had on them made you sacrosanct from their prosecution. They probably even helped you out with any problems from our government. We have a bad habit in this country of being lenient with foreign malcontents."

The old man held up a hand to stop me but I plowed on. "When your contact within the Consulate dried up and the laws changed, you needed another avenue. Your lawyer, Paul Hobbs, said something to you. Or you planted the seed in his head, it doesn't matter. Paul and the others worked out a solution to help you continue to bring in women from Eastern Europe. And with the help of Christopher Allinson and his partner at the investment firm, the proceeds were washed as clean as Sunday's linen. Chris had a knack for keeping your investments growing without sending up any flags. You set up the Elite Gentlemen's Club providing an environment for the women as exotic dancers. The girls would dance the clubs as well as working as escorts. And if they got out of line, I have no doubt you used creative punishments."

"And everything rolled along until Chris changed his mind about where the money was coming from. And that was your fault. He met the girl at a company Christmas party. That was stupid. I've heard it said that even dogs won't defile a fresh water source. But you did. You sent women to the Christmas party of the company that laundered your money. So when Chris realized the human cost of what was going on he probably spoke to the firm and then went to Paul and the others and they all came to you. You took care of both Chris and Paul to stem the tide and put the fear of God into the ones left."

"Unfortunately, I came back and stirred up the bottom. You dispatched Elvis over there to check me out and scare me off. You told Karolina Magyar to talk me out of pursuing what happened to Chris. When she couldn't, you had my old friends try to take a run at me. And when all else failed, you had me brought here for morning tea and threats."

The old man had been looking reflectively into the fire while I spoke. He stirred finally and said, "Jonathan, yes. Yes, I should have you work for me. You are passionate and I admire this about you. So why should I not deal with you as you think I have done with your friends?"

"Because I know enough to be very bothersome to you. And you have nothing to hold over me. I'm not in your pocket and I'm not afraid of going to the cops. They're close but they don't know what I do. Not yet anyway. I have copies of everything that I've shown you and this package will go to them if you do anything other than agree to this. You don't want me to have to do that do you? It makes more sense to meet me halfway than do anything else. If that package goes to the cops, it will ruin the lives of everybody else I'm trying to protect while it brings you down. If you come after me, then everything I know becomes public knowledge and it won't matter to me what happens. There are already those who know I'm kicking around this who could make your life much more difficult than I could."

"I'm not asking for much," I said. "I merely want your word that if certain people walk away, that you'll leave them alone. As a businessman, I think you'll take the path of least resistance."

"Why should you trust me, Jonathan?" he said. "If I am the man you say I am, why should you not worry?"

I thought about the explosive little surprise they had left for me on the boat. Cold anger roiled in me but I kept on as if I hadn't found it yet. As if I hadn't already sent the package to Kelly and Walsh. "Because I believe in the handshake, Lazar. We will agree, we will shake hands and we will never see or hear from each other ever again."

Laughter bubbled up from the old man and he shook his head in disbelief. "Ah, Jonathan. You are interesting man to me. You come to my home with these wild stories to tell to me. You say you must try to save your friends and hope to tell me what I should do."

"Lazar," I said, "don't misunderstand me. In the end you'll do whatever you want to do, I know that. But if we don't come to terms, then I'll have no choice but to keep annoying the hell out of you and your people."

The old man laughed again and said, "Jonathan, what makes you think you are annoying to me?"

"I'm sitting here, aren't I?"

"No Jonathan, no. I enjoy your company and I hope you ..."

I put down the untasted snifter on the table and stood and looked down at him. "Lazar," I said, "I've come to say what I had to say. I expect I'll have your answer soon enough. Think about what I've said. I have enough information to make your life very difficult. You know what I want and you know what I'm willing to do about getting it."

On the far side of the room, Elvis lifted himself out his slouch and glanced at his brother. He looked at me and then looked at the old man with an eyebrow raised. Tardos looked at Elvis and then at me sadly. Fear blossomed in me but there was nothing to do about that.

"Perhaps, Jonathan, if you must look for answers, then you should look somewhere else," the old man said.

"And, where would I look?"

"Where you won't want to," said a voice behind me.

I turned and standing in the doorway was an old friend returned from the other side, and while he was smiling at me, the smile didn't reach his eyes.

"Hello, Jon."

There was white noise in my head as I looked at Chris standing in the doorway flanked by Elvis and Goatee. My stomach dropped at the sight of him.

"Doesn't matter, really, does it? Here we are a decade on and both alive." He walked towards me with his hand outstretched, but when I merely stood there, he turned the motion into a theatrical gesture and went past me. As he crossed the room, I watched him, dumbfounded, until he came to rest behind the old man's chair. "You know, when Lazar and I decided I should disappear and open new territories, I figured nobody would care. Nick maybe. My mother doesn't have much memory of me left. Then you came back, and I gotta tell you, I was touched. No, really, it meant a lot that you came back and started digging into everything. Now, you shouldn't have; I mean, we wouldn't be here now if you'd left it alone. But somehow, I knew you wouldn't. When I heard you were back I told Lazar you'd probably shake the tree, and you didn't let me down. Did you know, there have been a couple of times I almost came by your boat to see you? I wanted to, truly. And maybe, maybe if I had, you wouldn't have been such a pain in the ass about this."

"Who was in the car?" I asked quietly.

"Oh, well, that was tragic," Chris said with mock seriousness, tugging at his chin. "One of our associates recognized my new assistant as undercover. And when he, after only a month or so, said he needed some time off, well, what can you do. We just aren't a union shop." He smiled and continued. "So we already knew who he was. Files were disappearing or being copied. Quiet questions were being asked. It all lead back to him." He nodded his head at the old man. "We discussed it and Lazar decided it was necessary. My position within the organization had been compromised by his meddling, so after dinner at my mother's, I left in a cab. Around two in the morning I called my assistant and told him I was too drunk to drive and had left my car, full of files, and would he pick it up for me asap. Naturally, he jumped at it."

"Forensics would have eventually shown he wasn't you."

"Mmmmm. true, but the fire slowed things down enough. Gave us the time to sort out enough for us to move on. I hear he was a family man. Shame..."

"Move to where?"

"New markets. This business travels well, you know. Like funerals, everyone needs our service eventually."

"Not everyone."

"Yeah, everyone, maybe except you, so upright and uptight. Tell me something buddy," Chris said, "is there really a difference between the justification of perceived immorality and the simple act of explaining away a position in conflict with that of others?"

"Your phrasing alone gives away the answer," I said.

Chris laughed and shook his head, "It's good to see you again, Jon. It's been a long time and I've missed talking to you. Same old. We never did agree on anything, did we?"

"Hardly ever. Makes me wonder how we became friends in the first place."

"People like us, we don't have to agree. We're the same anyway — so sure, so committed to what we think is right. And as for friendship, you remember how we started out? We weren't friends. Man, me and the others, we gave you a helluva ride back in the day. But we were friends finally, weren't we? You know, I was talking to Karolina a few weeks before I died and damned if I didn't start tearing up, telling her about how it was in the old days, when you and me used to hang out. But things change, don't they? Things get complicated."

"Is Karolina a 'complication'?"

"No, Karolina is sweet and delightful. And temporary." As I watched his hardened face for any sign of the friend I thought I used to know, he continued. "She's innocent. Like we used to be."

"Don't speak for me."

"Then don't moralize, Jon, not to me. I've known you too long."

"So what about Karolina then?"

"What do you mean, what happens to her now? She's got options. She's back at school with her tuition paid for. She doesn't know it yet, but the house on Amber Road is hers. When everything clears probate, she'll find out then. Jon. Leaving her behind is easy. I picked her out that night and," he shrugged, "decided to keep her for a bit."

"Jesus Christ."

"What happens from here? That's up to you, Jon. Or, maybe not. Personally, I had hoped to see you understand all of this. The others did. And they've made out quite well. But I suspect you won't, especially as we kept asking so nicely." As Chris spoke, I heard Elvis coming up behind me.

"What happened to Paul?

"Paul?" Chris shrugged and looked at Elvis over my shoulder. "Paul wasn't as tough as he thought he was. He thought he could play the short game when he grew a latent conscience. Paul was the genesis of this. I don't know what changed for him. Doesn't matter. Took me aside and said he wanted out. That we didn't need him anymore anyway. Well, he was certainly right about that part," Chris shrugged. "Things were getting too complicated by then. So his timing was actually propitious. We had been infiltrated; competitors sniffing around; founding partner got a sudden case of morals. Easiest thing in the world is to disappear. Hell, you of all people know that. You did. I just did it with more flair."

He spread his hands fatalistically. "What do you want to happen Jon? Don't know? Well, I'll tell you what I wish could happen. I wish you could forget what you know." He nodded at the envelope and its contents on the table between us. "You've done well here. Shaking down Jason gave you the hard goods, the rest was available knowledge. But getting Jason's files opens the whole thing up to scrutiny. I wish you had walked away and forgotten. Everything. What you think you know. And what you don't know. This version of the business is over. It was over the day I died. If you'd walked away then nothing would happen to you, or Karolina, or anyone else you care about."

The threat brought things into sharper focus. Chris said. "But you know what? You can't stop. Your code would be violated by that wouldn't it? It's why you quit the cops. That night in Scarborough all those years ago. What you saw that night. What you were pressured not to see. Just didn't sit right did it? So you left. Like you should have left this." He looked down at the old man who nodded his grey head and made a trifling gesture with his hand.

"What will you do, Jonathan?" asked the old man. "You are foolish boy. I have protections. Do you think you can so easily come to my house and make demands? Leave now. Christopher has asked me to let you alone and I don't agree, but you may go. However first, my son has asked me a favour."

I turned and Elvis grinned and brought down a very fast high right fist aimed at the side of my neck. I got my left up in time to block his wrist and flat-palmed him hard in the chin. His head snapped back and I put two fast blows into his stomach and then a kick to the groin. He doubled over but I saw him reach inside his jacket. I pulled his head up by the hair and grabbed his arm with my left hand, pinning it inside his coat. We struggled that way for a moment, neither of us getting anywhere. I screwed my heels down into the floor, and drove my right fist into him, into the nerve center just below the sternum. I didn't pull the blow. I tried to punch right through to the other side, as if I was trying to finish the movement a couple of feet behind him. Elvis lifted off the carpet with the blow, then he steadied himself and smashed his forehead down against mine. I saw stars and dust motes dancing in front of my eyes. The pain in my head was searing but I didn't let go of the arm inside the coat.

I had twenty or so pounds on Elvis and I was able to shove him back hard against the mantle. I didn't think of anything else, not Chris or Goatee or the old man. Everything collapsed and coalesced. Nothing existed except trying to stop Elvis' hand from exiting his coat. I put my right forearm under his chin and began pressing backward hearing his neck creak with the strain. I pushed with everything I had and his head bent slowly back, knocking over an ugly china figurine, which shattered on the floor. While Elvis struggled to get his pinned arm free, he hammered at my kidney with his other fist. I turned slightly to take away the target and drove my knee into his groin. He faltered and I ran my hand inside the coat down his arm until I felt his own hand on the gun butt still in the holster. I got hold of two of his fingers and yanked them backward.

Elvis growled deep in his chest and his eyes opened wide in rage and pain. He smashed our foreheads together again. I tried to clear my head and gave a sudden heavy pull on his bent fingers because if he hit me in the head again I was afraid I was going to go down. I felt and heard them break, the small snapping sound of the bones satisfying. He screamed and I felt his arm tense with the pain. I undid the clasp on the leather holster and pulled out the weapon, stomping on the side his knee at the same time. Elvis collapsed on the floor. Then there was a deafening crunch as the back of my head exploded in hurt. I staggered back, away from Elvis, my arms spinning, the gun in one hand, trying to keep my balance. I bent over at the waist, one forearm across both knees, doing my best not to collapse onto the beautifully patterned carpet. Tardos rumbled something at Goatee through gritted teeth.

"*Menj a picsäba, csepp a fegyver,*" Goatee said.

I stood up straight, lights dancing in front of my eyes, which watered from the pain. Goatee rushed at me again knocking the Glock out of my hand. He grabbed me by my shirt but I spun right, smashing my right arm down on both of his. Then I knifed my left palm into his throat and kicked his legs out from under him. I followed him as he fell and slammed his head down into the floor before he fell all the way. He grunted and his head lolled sideways, his eyes squinting in pain. I grabbed the Glock off the floor and stood. I looked at the four of them, through my blurred and uncertain vision. There was silence as I backed out of the room, Elvis' gun still at my side, my head searing. Chris smiling and the old man glowering; his two sons getting to their knees.

"Jon?" Chris said. "What makes you go away? Who do you think we take out next?"

I didn't say anything but my stomach dropped. I needed to get to her first. Somehow I found the front door and pressed the button to open the iron gates, then stumbled out into the arms of the night.

# Chapter 32

I stopped at the same gas station near Tara's place I had on that early morning that now felt like years ago. It was well after closing time and the building was dark and empty. I left the bike idling on its centre stand, with my helmet sitting on the tank, the low rpms causing the chain to turn the suspended back wheel slowly. The arc-sodium lights above the single set of pumps made a low humming sound as they cast a perfect circle of light around the gas island. I dug the card out of my jeans along with my cell. Kelly then Tara. Tara's voice was the panacea I needed and I was the warning she needed.

As the other end was picked up, the light just above my head exploded in a shower of sparks. I ducked instinctively and a second bullet slammed into the side of the pole where my head had been a microsecond earlier. I turned and ran to the bike and leapt onto it, my weight forcing the machine off the centre stand. My helmet fell off the tank and bounced away on the tarmac.

With a guttural roar, the big silver Mercedes bounded up off the road and suddenly a hole appeared in the middle of my windscreen. I yanked on the throttle and dumped the clutch. The bike's wide back tire screamed for traction and I threw myself down onto the gas tank to make sure she didn't pop her front wheel off the ground. The bike surged forward and roared away from the gas station with the Mercedes right behind. I swerved around the oncoming traffic and took off north as the Mercedes sideswiped a minivan and followed, the horns of other cars bleating in anger.

Big splats of rain began to fall and made odd-shaped explosions against the plastic windscreen. Without my helmet, the ones that hit me in the head stung my forehead and cheeks. I looked over my shoulder and saw that the silver sedan had pulled around the traffic and was accelerating hard up the lane. I smacked the gear lever down and banged her into second. When I let go of the clutch the back wheel locked up and began to slide. I counterbalanced my weight, throwing my hips and upper body to one side to correct and then yanked the bike over and swept into a low turn onto Sherwood Avenue that scraped the outside edge of the foot peg on the asphalt. I goosed the throttle and up-shifted to unlock the back wheel. Out of the corner of my eye, I saw the Mercedes cut off another car as it swept from the left lane and turned after me.

The brick pillared gates at the entrance to the park flashed by and I began to descend the curving roadway that led into the ravine. The hill and the rain, which had made the pavement slick, weren't helping. I could hear the Glock rattling around inside the tank bag and with one hand on the throttle I tried to feel around for it.

Suddenly the end of the roadway loomed at the base of the hill where there was a short, wide bridge spanning the tributary that ran through the ravine. It allowed city maintenance vehicles to access both sides of the park and was made of concrete with dark green iron railings on either side. The walking trails through the park were defined with wood chips and the surface of the bridge was littered with them.

I pulled my hand back from rummaging in the bag and pulled the clutch and down shifted. The bike bounced onto the bridge and lost all traction on the slippery, rain-soaked wood chips. Panicked, I braked too hard with my foot and locked up the back wheel. The bike went down hard with a crunch of fibreglass and slid across the bridge on its side. I'd fallen enough in the past to know how not to get trapped underneath, but stupidly, I held onto the handlebars and was dragged along behind as my machine banged and skidded. When it finally slid to a stop, I tumbled into it gracelessly. Shaken, I clambered over the damaged bike, the back wheel spinning helplessly while the engine gasped for breath. I fumbled the Glock out of the tank bag and looked up at the roar of acceleration. The Mercedes was bearing down me, rainwater glinting off the hood. I rolled to one side and threw myself to the railing of the bridge as the Mercedes smashed into my prostrate motorcycle and ran over it. The protective plastic spoiler under the front bumper of the ungainly sedan tore off and the Mercedes bounded over the bike, crushing the panels, gas tank and gauges. The upturned handlebars got caught in the undercarriage and the back of the sedan fishtailed, sweeping in a wide arc while the front of the car stayed stuck on top of the bike. When the SUV ground to a halt, it was canted at an angle, pointing back up the hill.

I vaulted over the railing and landed on a protective iron gate designed to stop leaves and branches from clogging the drainage system. It knocked the wind out of me, but I kept rolling and came up on my feet in the two-foot-deep water. In this part of the winding park system, the river had been forced into a broad concrete culvert with steeply poured walls with the water running fifteen feet below grade. I moved up one wall as best I could, wet and out of breath. When I got to the top of the embankment I crouched low and looked back at the ruined vehicles. The headlamps were still alight on the Mercedes. The interior light went on and I saw Goatee clamber out of the passenger side. He yelled and pointed at me, squatting on the top of the culvert. We were deep into Sherwood Park here. On one side, the park rose for two hundred feet with deep woods separating us from the houses at the top. Across the tributary was a wading pool and playground. Beyond the were a few small Parks and Recreation Department buildings, then more woods with trails that meandered all the way to Bayview Avenue and the beginning of the Sunnybrook section of the ravine system. Somewhere to the north was Tara's house. These were the woods that I had played capture the flag in, the river acting as the dividing line between the two teams. I'd known them like the back of my hand when I was a kid. There were no trails on my side of the river, just the steep wooded hill. I would be too exposed trying to climb the slope. All they'd have to do would be to sit at the bottom and wait for the right moment to pick me off. But the other side had trails that criss-crossed through the forest and led north towards Tara's place. I needed to get across and lose them in the woods on the other side.

The cold weight in my hand reminded me I was still holding Elvis' weapon. After pulling the slide back and chambering a round, I held the gun in the standard two-handed grip, the left hand underneath to steady the right. Holding the gun brought back a flood of tactile memories of being in the reserves and on the job. I tried to think about what I had been taught. Breathe. Hold. Fire. The rain was coming stronger now and making it harder to see. I squinted into the downpour, tried to make out details and couldn't, but the headlights still showed me where the car was. I needed to get across with cover fire. I put three rounds into the side of the car and heard two of the slugs whumping through the metal. The third caromed off an edge of the car with a whine. The Glock jumped with every trigger-pull.

Hoping they had kept their heads down from the barrage, I tried to bolt down the embankment but lost my footing and ended up sliding down painfully, the rough concrete abrading the palms of my hands. I stumbled into the water again and made my way up the other side. Through the rain I could see the bulk of the playground. I made for it and looked back and saw muzzle flash. I dove to the ground and rolled but not fast enough. It felt like somebody smacked me with a baseball bat as the bullet tore into the back of my left shoulder. The point of entry and my left arm went dead. I came up out of the roll and stumbled on. When I got to the edge of the largest of the colourful plastic and painted steel structures I ducked around the edge heard the solid chunk of another bullet slam into the hard plastic wall I had just cleared.

I crouched down and tried to bring my breathing under control. Peering through climbing holes molded into the plastic, I saw two moving shapes outside the Mercedes. There were no details in the rain so I brought the automatic up and sighted on the shape to the left. I aimed for the middle, dead centre. It was the biggest target and you were more likely to hit something than not. I squeezed slowly, trying not to anticipate the recoil and grip the gun too tightly. The Glock boomed and the shape on the left grunted and dropped to its knees. The shape on the right flattened on the ground as whomever I had hit toppled sideways into the mud.

I was sure they had seen the muzzle flash, so I rolled over and over until I was twenty feet from where I'd shot the first one. The place I had been crouching suddenly began to jump as bits of wood and mud began to fly with bullet hits and slugs whanged off molded plastic and steel. I wanted to take my jacket off because the leather was so tight it was restrictive. But I couldn't feel my left arm, so taking it off would have been comically impossible. Besides, it was black and afforded me some measure of invisibility. I squirmed on my stomach, mud and leaves smearing my shirt through the open front of the jacket. I didn't have enough cover and eventually I would be picked off. I wormed back into the trees until I felt the beginning of one of the stepped paths that mazed through the forest. I got into a half crouch and worked my way up the steps into the dark woods. I turned and watched through a gap in the trees as the figure on the right jumped up and ran across open ground to where I had been lying. I heard a groan of effort and I saw my other pursuer crawling back towards the Mercedes.

The hiss of the rain was everywhere and the drumming of it on the leaves and the playground shapes and the muddy ground was a constant white hiss that drowned out all other sound. I knew there was a road only a hundred yards away but I couldn't hear any traffic. I hoped that somebody living nearby had heard the gun shots and called it in.

I got up on one knee slowly and watched for my other attacker. Past the edge of the path railing I could see him hiding behind a bright green plastic slide, so I stood slowly and crept backward deeper into the relative safety of the woods. The edge of the forest was only twenty or so feet beyond the edge of playground but there was enough light where he was. There were light standards at opposing corners of the sandpit where the fort squatted in the middle but they both flickered dully, showing that the bulbs needed replacing but it was enough to see him.

Still walking backwards I moved into the trees until I was enveloped by leafy branches. I stood in the blackness of the forest canopy and watched the playground. The strain of concentrating was giving me a headache. Finally I saw some movement as the figure peered around the edge of the structure. In the dimness of the light I could see it was Elvis. There was a white gauze bandage around his right hand and he was holding the weapon in his left. He bolted from his hiding place, firing repeatedly at the other tower. When he ran behind the next set of structures closer to the woods and me I lost sight of him but I heard him cursing in Hungarian. Slowly, he peered around the edge of the climbing wall and scanned the distance between us.

I needed to melt into the forest and get the hell out of there and get to Tara. I could feel myself getting weaker and looked down and saw blood dripping darkly from the fingers of my left hand. I realized that, without thinking, I had brought the automatic to shoulder height and was pointing it at the fort. It was reflexive I told myself. It wasn't really my hand that had lifted the weapon. Then I suddenly saw that my forearm and the gun were caught in a shaft of light reflected from the playground.

Elvis ducked out from behind the climbing wall and looked quizzically at the gun and my arm gleaming dully from the forest. I saw the flash and suddenly my left side was on fire again, then I heard the crack of the shot. I fired as well and fell backwards, ending up in a half-crouch against a tree. I fired blindly again at playground and then stumbled further into the depth of woods. There was movement and noise behind me but I kept lurching my way into the forest, not looking back. When I happened onto a forking path I could see down its broad expanse out to the bridge. Goatee was lying with his back against the side of the Mercedes, his head down and arms limp at his sides.

Suddenly the area of the bridge was awash in headlights as another car came down the hill. It began to skid at the base of the road and then ground to a stop, hitting the Mercedes and knocking aside Goatee, who was clearly dead. I stumbled down the forking path toward the other vehicle, with the sound of the rain in the trees filling my ears. When I cleared the edge of the woods I looked back and saw Elvis burst down the river path. I kept on until I was out completely of the trees and ran as best I could towards the car on the bridge.

I heard Elvis running and turned to look. As he passed under a light by the edge of the path, I dropped to my knees and fired. I saw him duck instinctively and he fired two shots back at me, one missed and smashed into the windscreen of the Mercedes. The other caught me high on my left chest and I struggled to stop from falling over with the impact. I steadied and ran towards the bridge and as I turned, the pathway lamps picked Elvis again out of the wet blackness. I saw his weapon come up and I dropped and fired at his running figure. Elvis' head snapped to the side and he dropped his weapon and clutched the side of his throat. A noise behind me made me turn and the driver's window dropped and the figure inside fired. I heard the high whine as the bullet just missed my head. I rolled and rolled, came up and emptied the Glock into the driver's side door as it flew open. Then silence descended and it was just the rain filling my senses.

I struggled to my feet and staggered towards the car. I tripped over the edge of something and went sprawling across the hood of the second car. I rolled slowly over the fender and landed hard on the concrete. The interior light cast heavy shadows across Chris' body, which lay sprawled half out of the car. One of my shots had caught him under the ear below the shelf of jaw. Pink aerated blood bubbled out from the wound. His face was pulled back in a rictus of pain. He looked at me for a moment without comprehension and then his eyes went dim. He fell completely onto the pavement and his dead eyes began to fill with rainwater. I stumbled away, fell to my knees and threw up into the grass.

When my stomach was empty and the heaves had abated, I realized I was still on my knees with my forehead against the wet ground. I tried to pick myself up and the effort of doing that simple task took away any energy I had left. I put my head down again and closed my eyes. It would be so nice just to stay like this. Just a little rest. Just rest my eyes.

A stab of pain in my side snapped me awake and made me sit back on my heels. I gingerly peeled back my jacket and shirt and saw a dime-sized hole about an inch or two above my waist and an inch in from my side. Blood oozed from the wounds in my side, chest, and shoulder and was washed away by the rain.

My world tilted and toppled me over onto the ground. What was supposed to be up didn't make sense anymore. My head was the size of a tennis ball and my body had ballooned to gargantuan proportions. It would be so nice to just stay here. It was a nice park and the rain was very nice. I wasn't nice. I had not-nicely killed 4 not-nice people. Person. People. How many? They weren't nice. They had tried to hurt me. They started it. I chuckled a little. It sure was nice to feel the rain on my face. Would it be nice to move? No, it would not. I thought about it for a few years and decided that it made sense. I should move. No rest for the not nice.

I rolled over onto my stomach and pushed myself up awkwardly. One of my arms didn't work. I managed to stagger to my feet and looked back to the cars, trying hard to focus. Bodies lying awkwardly on wood chips. Lots of wood chips. An ocean of wood chips. I remember these wood chips! We're not in Kansas anymore, Toto, so follow the wood chip road. I looked up the wood chip road and saw lights dancing about fifty feet away. Some of them were blue, no red, no blue, no ... oh I see, they're both! I sank to my knees and then fell onto my back. I craned my neck and watched as smaller upside-down white lights danced closer.

Somebody stood over me and took something out of my hand.

"Hi!" I said. Friendly.

"Jesus," a voice said.

"The rain is nice," I muttered.

There were shouts all around and people kept running past. Somebody was leaning over me. It was a woman.

"Did you know," I said. "I used to play here when I was a little kid?"

"Don't talk," the woman said.

"No really, I did. You know this is a great place. I used to come here all the time. I came here ..."

"Shhhh," she said, and I felt her pull open my shirt. I thought about telling her I already had a girlfriend. Was that funny? While I wondered whether it was funny, a roaring sound slowly filled my ears. Then my vision telescoped and everything receded as I fell down a long well.

# Chapter 33

It was daylight when I woke up the first time. There was sun streaming in through the blinds and I could see an azure sky with wispy tendrils of cloud floating high.

It was nighttime when I woke up again and a driving rain was hammering my window. I tried to roll over on my side away from the sound but pain erupted from just above my waist. One arm had a tube running out of it and the other was pinned to my chest by a sling. Both of my hands had dressings on them. I tilted my head off the pillow as best I could and peered down. Everything seemed to still be there. That was a relief. There was a drain coming out my side and running out of sight underneath the bed. The effort of lifting my head made my vision swim and I passed out.

It was twilight and there were voices. Somebody made a clucking sound in their throat and said something about being lucky. Another voice muttered that it was time to change my bandages. I felt a pinprick in the arm that was across my chest and darkness swallowed me again.

I felt warmth across my body and kept my eyes closed, enjoying it. When I did open them a crack there was the last glow of the setting sun stretching from the window and angling across my body. I opened them wide to clear the mists and turned my head. Tara was asleep in the chair beside the bed with a book lying on her stomach. Her chest lifted and fell rhythmically and she made small mewling sounds in her sleep.

When I opened my mouth to say something it felt like it was filled with cotton. I managed two syllables that sounded very much like 'Hewwdo.' Tara stirred slightly and rolled her head from one side to the other. She sleepily opened one eye and when she saw I was awake she jumped up as if on a spring.

"Oh God, oh dear God," she said in a rush.

"Hedo." I was having trouble with some consonants.

"Oh God," she said again. She reached over and smoothed my hair back from my forehead and laid her cheek against mine.

"Ow oo eye ook?" I asked. "Ettie secky, uh?"

She laughed and nodded and blinked away tears. "Pretty sexy," she agreed.

I swallowed hard and said, "You too." What do you know, I had my consonants back.

"I'll get the doctor," she said. "Wait here."

"OK, I'll just stay here," I croaked as she ran out the door. A couple of minutes later she came back in with a woman in a white coat who looked impossibly young and a nurse in blue scrubs in tow.

She took out a thermometer and jammed it under my tongue, then took my wrist and peered at her watch. "Well, how are we feeling?" she asked.

"I think I was shot a couple of times," I replied around the thermometer. "How are you feeling?"

"I wasn't shot," she said, removing it and glancing at the temperature.

"Ahhh, that explains why I'm lying here and you're not."

Tara said, "Jon, for God's sake, shut up."

"How old are you anyway?" I asked.

"I'm older than I look, twenty-nine," she said laying my arm back down again and writing on a chart.

"Jesus," I said, "Tara, go and find somebody who was born in the same decade as me."

"Don't worry," she said, "I had a real doctor watching while I took the bullets out of you and sewed you back together again. And a guy, just in case you're a chauvinist..." She smiled and reached into her lab coat and brought out a little plastic container and shook it. Two shapes rattled inside. "Wanna see?"

I grimaced and shook my head. "No thanks," I said, "from me to you."

She grinned at me. "I'm Doctor Hatcher. Do you know what day this is?"

I shook my head and replied, "I seem to remember waking up a couple of times.

Maybe two days?"

"You've been out for four days."

"Four days?" I looked at Tara and she nodded her head in agreement.

"The bullet in your shoulder was the main worry. It was impacted in your shoulder blade. Your leather jacket slowed it down. The one in your chest did a lot of tissue and nerve damage. Worried you'd lose mobility in your left arm."

I tried not to strain too hard, but lifted it a little off my chest and flexed all the fingers. Hatcher watched and nodded in approval.

"The other bullet was a through and through," she said. "If it had been a little higher it would have done serious damage. As it was, it nicked your liver on the way past before coming out your lower back."

"As if my liver didn't have enough problems ..."

"Yes, well we can talk about that another time. After we got the bullet out of your shoulder, there was some infection around your liver to deal with. We kept you under because we wanted your body to be able to fight. You're pretty tough. Three shots, one lodged in your back, one in your chest and the other through your gut."

I lifted my good arm and gave her a thumbs-up.

She ignored me and continued. "Regardless, you seem to be on the mend. Your vital signs are good and that drain can come out tomorrow. We'll give you some painkillers and the sling has to stay on for another two weeks. The nurse will show you how to change the dressings. Your hands were badly cut so leave those bandages on until they scab over properly. You should recover completely if you can manage not to get shot for another few weeks."

"Hadn't planned on it..."

"Good. In the morning we'll take out the tubes and you should be on your way by shortly after lunch, all right? Good. Then I'll see you tomorrow."

Hatcher left and the nurse checked the lines running in and out of me, smiled and left us alone. There was silence while I stared at Tara, drinking her in.

"So?" I said finally.

"So ..." Tara said, worry passing over her features.

"Is Karolina OK?"

Tara nodded and said, "Yes. She called the same night you were shot. She's been here every day. She's been so upset and she feels completely responsible for what happened to you."

"Not her fault."

"That's true, but she feels terrible anyway."

I nodded my head and couldn't think of anything to say to that.

"And what about you? Are you OK?" I asked.

Tara held my hand but looked past me, out the window.

"My God."

I squeezed her hand as best I could and shook my head. "Everybody was backed into a corner, from Karolina to Jason and Ron and Mack."

"He's been here every day as well."

"Has he? I haven't talked to him since that night at Jason's but, by trying to find out what happened to Chris, I guess he was part of it. I didn't see that. They tried to blow up my boat, T. The night it all went down, before I went to see the old man, I found a surprise rigged for me. They were tired of me stirring things up."

Tara shook her head, "I don't understand. Jon slow down."

"After I went to the house, they came after me. I was coming to you but they followed me. Something ..." I could feel the edges of a memory and then I saw Elvis staring into the cold rain. "I shot one of them. Then took off, then I shot another, but there was somebody else there... a blue car."

"I don't understand. Tell me what you remember."

Before I had a chance to speak again, the door opened and Walsh came in.

"Tara, this is Detective Walsh. She was working with Detective Kelly."

"We've already met," said Walsh. "Ms. Kerr, would you mind giving me a moment alone with Mr. Birnam?"

Tara loosened her grip on my hand but I held on and said, "I'd mind." A memory coalesced and I said to her, "You were at the park, weren't you?"

Walsh nodded and Tara said, "The Detective told me she was first on the scene. She probably saved your life, Jon. Detective Walsh kept pressure on your wounds until the ambulance got there."

I nodded to Walsh and said "Thank you. So, how much trouble am I in?"

"Let's hear your version of the events in the park." She pulled a cellphone out of her purse, set it up and pressed the record button and said, "DS Walsh interviewing Jonathan Birnam." She glanced at her watch and reeled off the time and date then set it down on the hospital tray in front of me.

I told her everything I could remember, including the Mercedes destroying my bike and the second car. "Where is my bike anyway?"

"In a couple of weeks, I'm sure bits of it will show up in iron planters all over the province."

"Oh. Anyway they chased me into the park and wrecked my bike. I got away but they kept coming and shooting at me. I shot one of them as I ran. The other chased me into the woods. I shot him too. My memory is a little shaky right now. There was another car there too, and somebody was inside I think... I don't know... I'm having a problem with details right now."

"And the weapon?"

"Took it off one of them."

Walsh shook her head and sighed at the same time. "We assumed as much. The prints on the gun matched your records and one of the men you shot. Ballistics is having a field day with that gun. Seems we can clear a number of un-solveds with the same weapon. Were these men involved in what we told you stay away from?"

"Yes, they were. But that's really all I remember."

She looked at me with pursed lips and a look that told me she didn't believe a word of what I saying. But she couldn't prove it and we both knew it. "Planning on going anywhere anytime soon?" she asked.

I looked down the length of myself and held up my sling, "Doubt it," I said.

"Then I'd say the worst of your troubles happened while you were passed out. The Crown will not be prosecuting you for the incident in the park despite the desire by some to do so. But scene reconstruction makes it pretty obvious what happened. And there were several motorists who came forward and told us about the shooting at the gas station and how you were chased. Self-defense. The Crown Prosecutor's got some questions for you and there'll be paperwork to sign off on. Other than that, you're pretty much in the clear on the park."

Tara squeezed my hand in reassurance and I smiled up at her.

"Not so fast. There are still some outstanding problems. One, you called Kelly from your cell. That's how we found you in the park. He scrambled me. I had them do a triangulation and then ten minutes later reports of gunfire in the same vicinity came in. That's how I got there with the first wave. Two, I received a package that same night you were wounded. A cab driver was very insistent that it get to me personally."

"Really?"

"Yes, really. You probably wouldn't know anything about that would you?"

"I might."

"There was a portable hard drive full of financial records, visa applications and business structure. Along with a lot of surveillance photographs of strip clubs. And of a big house on Lakeshore. There were incorporation documents and property titles. Photocopies of articles concerning a local motorcycle gang. And there was a note explaining that bikers might be involved in taking over the clubs."

"And?"

"I'm in homicide. Gangs fall under the purview of the Intelligence Squad. I passed it on to them and they promised to let my superiors know about the inter-departmental co-operation."

"Congratulations. But why would you think I would know anything about that?"

"Just a hunch."

"Mmmmmm…"

Walsh regarded me for a moment when a nurse poked her head in and told us visiting hours were over.

"We'll talk more about this, Mr. Birnam," Walsh said.

"I have no doubt," I replied.

She extended a hand to Tara and said, "Ms. Kerr, nice to see you again." Then she nodded curtly to me, but with a small smile. "Mr. Birnam." Then she left and the door closed quietly behind her.

Tara regarded me silently for a moment and then asked, "What was she talking about, Jon?"

I blew the air in my lungs out very slowly. Then I said, "I didn't know what to do. That last night. I got back to the boat. I was going to give it all to the cops. Maybe if I'd dropped it. Well, it wouldn't have come to that. I didn't know if I'd be able to make the deal with them. I got back and they'd rigged her to explode. It changed everything. And if they could get to me, they could get to you. This all started because I wanted to know what happened to Chris. I thought I owed him that much. I never thought… Anyway, I had a back-up plan and if it wasn't that night, they would have found another time and another place. But I got to the house and Chris was there. He wasn't dead, it was his assistant in the car. They told me to drop the whole thing and leave. But I'd already found the trap on the boat. They weren't going to stop there, they wanted me gone. So I needed to finish it. And I couldn't have them coming after anyone else." I squeezed her hand.

She squeezed back. "Jesus, Jon. Chris was alive?"

"Yeah. Seems he orchestrated the whole thing after Paul set up the initial meets. Chris and Tardos were partners."

Tara said, "I know you Jon. And I know where your sense of right and wrong lie. But did you do everything she said? If you did, then, despite whatever reasons you had, what you did was …"

"Uh-uh," I said, cutting her off, "When I went to the house I knew what might happen. I was just trying to buy some time, but I never thought that Chris was involved. I didn't want this. I'm not going to start second-guessing what I did. Down the road I might have some trouble with all of it or I might not. But they wanted me dead. So to be honest, love, I'm just glad to be alive."

"Jon. This… what you did… I don't know if…"

Tara looked at me and I watched as something changed behind her eyes. She bent over and kissed me on the forehead. Then she put her cheek against mine and I whispered to her. "You are why I do everything. You always have been. I couldn't lose you again." She laughed a very little and when she stood up again, tears were glistening and threatened to spill over.

"See you in the morning? I need to know babe…" I asked.

Tara nodded her head and put her hand over mine on my chest. "I know you do," she whispered back. Then she picked up her bag and walked across the room. Tara opened the door and stood looking back at me, framed in silhouette against the bright light of the corridor. Then she was gone.

Some hours later the pain in my side brought me up out of sleep. When I opened my eyes there was a figure standing at the end of the bed. I felt around for the switch above my head and the soft light over the bed flickered on.

Kelly sighed heavily and folded his arms across his chest. I reached over and, using the electric controller, winched the bed higher so that I was sitting up. We regarded each other silently.

"So?" I said finally.

"You think you're a real tough guy, don't you?" he said, walking around the bed slowly.

"Yup."

Kelly looked at me and said, "You set those guys up, didn't you?"

I shook my head and said, "Uh-uh, you did."

He stopped pacing and looked at me. "What the hell does that mean?"

"You know, ever since I came to see you that very first day I've been annoying as hell."

"Your waking state."

"And yet you've done nothing but be semi-helpful. By the time I came along, you must have suspected that it wasn't Chris in the car wreck. It was his assistant. Forensics couldn't have been long in proving that."

"Maybe I wasn't motivated as much as you. Wasn't my friends who got chilled."

"Maybe. But like I said, I've been wondering why you never shut me down. A couple of calls and I would have been up to my neck in obstruction and interference charges. Walsh was ready to nail my feet to the floor that day in your office. She didn't want me to have anything to do with the investigation. But every time I talked to you, you helped. Sort of."

"Yeah, so?"

"So I was back in town less than a week before I bought *The Saracen*. And a day after I bought her, the guy that got killed in the park was searching my boat."

"The guy you killed," Kelly interrupted.

"Fine, the one I killed. There were only a couple of people who knew I'd bought her and I refuse to believe the other guy would sell me out. I came to the precinct to register my complaint and you let me know right then and there that you knew about my boat. You gave me the girl's address but wouldn't check her out yourself. I kept waiting for you to step up and you never did."

Kelly started pacing again but didn't say anything so I continued. "The night of the shooting I went to the old man and threatened to expose him. And then it turned out Chris was still alive. He and the others had a lucrative practice going.

The cart was tipping, though. The old man said that he had 'protections'. Maybe the old man decided that it was easier to shut me up like he had Paul instead of invoking his 'protections,' so he had Elvis and Goatee try to take me out. You knew it would have occurred to me that I had access to the same information that you did. Chris' brother, the girl, the firm where Chris worked; it was a mistake to have the women at that company Christmas party. Maybe it was a way to send a message to the powers that be that the firm was in Tardos' pocket. They were all getting rich and the source of the money made them beholden to the syndicate. As it turns out, Chris wasn't who I thought he was. He wasn't outraged when he found out where the money was coming from after he met Karolina. He started it all. His company, his client, his old pals. Chris controlled all of it with the old man. They had the assistant killed to forestall an investigation and Paul was the postscript on the message."

"And you knew before you threatened Tardos with exposure that he wasn't going to bend. Even before you went to see him that night?"

"If I'd stopped to think about what I was doing maybe I would have played it smarter. But they set up an explosion on my boat. I had no choice but to back myself up. When I went, I wasn't just trying for time. I was setting another solution in motion.. I thought he'd already killed Chris and Paul and God knows how many others. Nobody gets to where he was by knuckling under."

"But Chris wasn't dead."

I sat silently for a moment, surprised that I felt so little. The final memory from the shoot-out coalesced. The driver of the blue car... "Is now."

"So I was right about you."

"I want to be pissed at you," I said. "But I went into this for my own reasons, not yours. And I wouldn't have got nearly close enough to the truth without your help. So are you going to tell me what I did for you?"

Kelly shook his head and a small, unhappy smile crept over his face. "We've met before. You don't remember do you?"

I shook my head.

"Scarborough. Almost eleven years ago. We were both there that night. I was still a Constable 4$^{th}$ class. You were 1$^{st}$ class but you were about to get bounced up the chain. The night the girl was shot in the back by the undercover detective...

her name was Parsons. Krista Parsons."

I thought back through the mist of time. "The gang tussle at the strip mall." I said nodding. "Undercover said there was a knife but it was never recovered. 'Cause it was never there. All the interview notes and audio interviews of the witnesses disappeared out the back of the cruiser."

"You were on scene."

"Yeah. My partner and I were first. We got it settled down and people were already dispersing. We'd called for backup already, but we had it handled."

"And…?"

"The undercover never identified himself. He pulled up in an unmarked van. He got there before anyone else. Got in the middle of it when we had it quieted. Guess he figured a couple of uniforms couldn't handle it but we had the whole thing sorted out. He tried to grab the girl and she shrugged him off. He shot her three times in the back. She was walking away 'cause he never identified himself and she just thought he was a civilian. She died in the parking lot before EMS could get there."

"There was no knife, was there?"

"No. There wasn't. And he never identified himself. She mouthed off at him and he killed her."

"SIU buttoned it and cleared the UC. But it stank and everyone knew it. Your partner backed the official line. You didn't. And it made you unpopular. Didn't help when you punched the UC's lights out. No charges, but you got demoted. So you quit."

I looked at him and shrugged. My shoulder reminded me that it had been shot and I grimaced.

"You remember I said I transferred out of Vice? I told you we couldn't get high enough through procedure. I left a good partner behind when I transferred. He was green but he was my partner and my friend. We kept in touch after I transferred out. He'd done a degree in finance and when he made detective, his first assignment was undercover at the firm where Allinson worked. He was one of the leads on an investigation into organized crime ties in the financial sector. I heard about the car accident and kept an ear out because of who was supposed to be in the vehicle. A few days later, I caught the case of the murder on the Island. Next day the forensics came back on the real victim of the car wreck and I knew they were connected. My superiors put Walsh on it as well. And then you turn up and make no bones about the fact you were gonna chew on it no matter what."

"You used me."

"We used each other. I couldn't do to them what I knew you would. I don't have the freedom you do. My old partner had a wife and two little ones. Prison wasn't enough. And I'm saying that because I know it stays here. You proved who you were that night in Scarborough. I figured you'd do what needed doing. You want to know what's been happening while you've been napping?" I nodded my head and he continued. "Same night of your park fireworks, there was a four-alarm fire out in Mimico. Big place overlooking the bay burned flat. Took the trucks seven hours to put it out. When they finally got in they found a body burned beyond recognition on the main floor. There was only one person home and so far it looks like the body was at the epicentre of the blaze. The Fire Marshall is still investigating but they've already detected the presence of accelerants. Somebody set the owner of the house on fire and the whole thing burned down around him."

"Seems mean."

"Two days later, Vice lets it be known that there's been this line of strip bars that's been taken over. That we should all be watchful 'cause these things never go easy. Vice figured a little turf war was going to erupt. But the war didn't start. It was actually a very quiet flip. And I got a buddy in Intelligence." he said.

"Really?"

"Yeah."

"And what does your friend in Intelligence tell you?" I asked.

"Cabbie delivered a package to Walsh. She passed it to me and then it went up the chain. Seems the new owners of these clubs are a local bunch who are expanding. They popped up last year in connection with Operation Snowdrift up north. OPP finished up a big cocaine crackdown in Simcoe County and a couple of their people got shaken loose. They were just a fringe group then, looking to make a name. Call themselves The Raggeds. They've been under the radar for a while because they're not affiliated with anybody big yet but we have a guy on the inside. Seems The Raggeds are the new owners of the peeler bars. They took them over quietly with a minimum of fuss. Very quiet and very professional. Inside guy says there were a couple of imports from an affiliated gang in the States. But now they're gone. Intelligence can't find them now. Two men were seen fleeing in a speedboat by a neighbour just before the house went up. The thinking is they headed down the lake and probably crossed into upstate New York on the other side. Boat's probably collecting zebra mussels on the bottom as we speak."

"So..."

"So the problem has always been we couldn't get enough. Vice tries to nail a group and they only end up with smaller fish. The surface pimps, managers, you know... Vice, Homicide and Intelligence are putting together a new joint operation. We do it right, we can bring it all down and take The Raggeds off the board."

I smiled and said nothing.

"My friend also passed me a report on a wiretap. Apparently, somebody met with The Raggeds the same night. They couldn't identify the voice, said they'd never heard him before. No names were used and this guy, whoever he was, was in and out of there in twenty minutes. But after this individual left, there was a fast discussion — timing, manpower, seed money and whether they could trust the information they'd just been given. Then the two US guys left the clubhouse."

"Interesting."

"I thought you'd find it fascinating."

"Sounds like a lot has happened lately."

"Yes, doesn't it though."

We stared at each other, both waiting to see who was going to commit themselves. And neither of us was.

"So when all is said and done, it looks like everybody is out from under."

"So it does," replied Kelly, smiling. Then he turned and walked across the room. When he reached the door I said, "A stone for the fox."

Kelly turned and looked at me. "What does that mean?"

"It means sometimes you've got to make people believe one thing to get them to do another. And sometimes that takes special bait."

"And?"

"And if you can't tell who the bait is, then it's probably you."

He stared at me and finally said, "Could be."

"Maybe we'll see each other around."

"You can make book on it," and he stepped through without turning back.

# Chapter 34

The next morning a nurse came in and removed the drain from my side while Tara looked on silently. An attending was left to patch me up and then Hatcher came in to give me a final going over. After probing my wounds, she declared me fit to go home and left us alone.

Tara had brought some fresh clothes from the boat and had watched until the medical proceedings were finished. Once they had all cleared out, Tara sat at the edge of the bed and took my bandaged hand in hers. She stared down at our intertwined fingers and said nothing. I could feel the worry in my stomach and my eyes began to sting a little.

"Jon," she said, "I've been thinking about what you've done. I know you. I know that what you said last night to Detective Walsh wasn't the whole truth. I know you need to be careful with her."

"I need to be careful with you too."

"Why? Why do you say that?"

"Because I'm afraid of how you're going to feel."

"How do you feel?"

"Conflicted. I trained for some of what happened but I never knew how visceral it would be in reality. But, there was little else I could do."

"Tell me."

"When I knew enough about what I thought had happened to Chris, I realized that there was no way I could make it all go away. But I didn't know how to fix it all. For a while, I thought Kelly was dirty. He never shut me down when he should have. He read me well enough to know if he fed me enough, I'd go after them. I don't know how much he knew and how much I discovered for myself but in the end, I could pull strings and do things he couldn't. He knew why I quit the force."

"That was wrong of him."

"Maybe. He lost a friend in all of this too. He's just frustrated by the system. The same frustration I felt when I decided I couldn't live in that world. I quit. He didn't. He was inside and couldn't do anything."

"What world can you live in?"

"Is that a rhetorical question?"

Tara was quiet for a time then she nodded and said, "Your world. You can only exist as yourself. You don't answer to anybody for what you do and you don't apologize."

"I shouldn't have to."

"No Jon. That's not the way most people are. Most people, despite what they say, do worry what other people think. They do care what effect their actions and words have on other people."

"I care about you."

"Do you? If you did, would you have risked yourself, risked us, just to avenge Chris?"

"I didn't think I was risking us."

"Jon..."

"No, that's not fair. You left a long time ago. Left me. How much thought did you give to my feelings back then? Jesus, most of the reason I left all those years ago was because of you."

"Jon, don't. I was already gone by the time you left the force."

"Yeah, you were. But not here," I said and tapped my chest once with my sling. Tara smiled a small smile in return. "You left and I didn't know what to be or where to be or who to be. And then the things I thought I could count on, it seemed I couldn't."

"Was I one of those things?"

I didn't speak. I didn't want to answer that one.

"Jon?"

"You did what you needed to. That was where your life was headed. Out west with whatshisface."

This wasn't going in a good direction. I began to realize that the vibe from her that I was feeling was her steeling herself against the disappointment we were heading towards.

With her head down, Tara asked, "What happened that night, Jon?"

"Why is it so important?"

"I need to know."

"Why?"

"So I can know. So I can decide."

"You already have," I whispered. The pressure with which she had been holding my hand eased up and when she looked up at me, her face had saddened. "You've already made up your mind. You just want confirmation that you've made the right decision."

"That's not fair."

"What happened has nothing to with us."

"Of course it does. It has to do with the man you are. Because who you are affects who we are. We don't exist in some kind of vacuum, Jon. We live in the world, or at least I do. And what we do in the world has consequences both in terms of it and us."

"How I feel about you has nothing to do with out there. What matters is here. Right now. That is not this. What matters is how we are. What matters is whether we can be what we are without letting ..."

"The rest of the world in?"

"Yes."

"I can't."

"Why not?"

"Because that's not how I live my life. I like being a part of something larger. I need to think, to teach, to paint, to exist outside of just myself. Of just us. And you don't Jon. You've always been self-contained. You trust yourself and your instincts and your abilities. And when you do things, when you make decisions based on those ideals, then you prove just how little you need anybody else."

"I need you."

"And I need you too. But I can't be with someone who doesn't feel the way I do. I won't."

"So what does that mean for us?"

She sighed and said, "I don't know. I don't want to lose you, but I can't conscience all that's happened. All that you've done. I need some time to think."

I lifted my watch off the dresser with my good hand. "How long do you need? It'll take me two minutes to get dressed; then you decide you love me and then we talk Europe."

She clamped her hand across my mouth and shook her head to shut me up. She took her hand away and leaned down so our foreheads were touching. We stayed that way, with our eyes closed, until she tilted her head and kissed me hard. Then she touched her cheek to mine and walked out without saying another word.

After she left I lay there staring up and slowly and methodically counted all the holes in the ceiling tiles. I made sure to breathe regularly while I did it. When I thought I had counted every one of them, I sat up and swung my legs over the edge of the bed and stood on my own two feet for the first time in almost a week.

Walking gingerly around the room I tried not to jar anything suddenly as I tested myself. Getting my clothes on with one good arm would have been comical to watch but it was annoying to live. Despite Hatcher's warnings, the sling was coming off sooner than two bloody weeks. When I was dressed and had learned to tie my shoes in new and painful ways, I wandered out. The nurse met me outside my door with a wheelchair and insisted that it was hospital policy. I told her she was very sweet and to go the hell away.

Outside I grabbed a cab and when we got stopped at the light at the high hill above the marina I handed him two twenties and got out over his protestations. I walked slowly and deliberately down the big hill. I couldn't see the boat basin because of the winding road. I plodded along painfully, each step jarring my shoulder, my eyes downcast on the road. I was afraid of what I wouldn't see. I wasn't sure what day it actually was but there were a lot of people hustling by — enjoying the noon sunshine, biking and walking. I came out of the shadow of the cliffs into the warmth of the day on my face and the slap of the water on the concrete retaining walls.

Cautiously, I made my way along the water's edge until I stopped staring at my feet on the path and looked up. *The Saracen* gleamed, the sunshine throwing her distorted reflection in the calm, sheltered water. I sighed deeply and had a seat on a wooden bench. Folks walked by me, oblivious, as I sat and stared at my home. Goddamn, she was still floating. Once aboard, I opened all the ports and doors to air her out. The fridge held the last two bottles of Grolsch. The porcelain top made it easy to open with one hand. I eased my arm from out of the sling and tried to let my arm hang at my side. Not bad. Not too much pain. Nothing that drinking for the next couple of weeks wouldn't ease.

"How does this work again? I mean what's the proper protocol?" said a voice from the dock. I went to the back deck and looked down at Mack standing by the boarding stairs.

"You ask for permission to come aboard."

"Permission to come aboard?"

"Permission granted."

After he mounted the stairs, he looked admiringly around *The Saracen*. It suddenly occurred to me that he hadn't seen her yet. He pointed forward with his eyebrows raised and I nodded assent. Mack disappeared below decks and came back a few minutes later with a smile on his face.

"Pretty gorgeous" he said.

"Thanks," I said tonelessly.

"You got another beer?"

"In the galley. Fridge is on the right."

When Mack returned from the galley, I was sitting in one of the rattan chairs on the rear deck. When he sat down across from me he held out his bottle and tentatively clinked the necks together.

"Slainte," he said, betraying our mutual heritage.

"Slainte."

Mack's gaze kept flitting around the boat and the marina, conspicuously avoiding eye contact with me. I let him stay uncomfortable. We hadn't spoken since the night of cards at Jason's. It was his dime.

"I, uh," he started. "How are you feeling?"

"Like I've been shot three times."

Mack made a sympathetic face and took a pull from his beer. He nodded his head and cleared his throat too loudly.

"How did you know I was here?" I asked. I didn't know quite how to feel.

He'd been my friend for so long. I wanted to let him off the hook but it was going to take some explaining before that happened.

"Tara called this morning. Said you'd moved down here temporarily. And the bar's only thirty minutes that way." He pointed back over his shoulder towards the city. "Hey, remember in grade ten? Remember we did that stupid computer-dating thing? We filled out those surveys and they matched us up?" he said.

"Sure, uh, Joanne? Jackie?"

"Jocelyn."

"Jocelyn, that's right. You went to the spring dance with her."

"Yeah, yeah. She was OK. You got matched with Tara."

"Yeah, I did. Even by a goddamned computer."

Mack looked around generally and said, "Where is she anyway?"

"Home."

"She comin' over later?"

"I don't think so."

"How come?"

"Why are you here Mack?"

He played with the flip top a bit and then put the bottle down on the table between us. He rubbed his hands together nervously and said, "I need to apologize about what happened."

"I'll say…"

"The other night at Jason's. I should have told you what to expect."

"Yeah, you should have."

"I didn't know they were gonna pull that. You didn't make it any easier by acting like an asshole."

"Don't even try it. That had nothing to do with me. You set me up."

"No," he said, shaking his head in denial.

"Yes. Yes you did. You and the other two wanted to know what I was doing about your little intrigue so you got me to go."

Mack looked at me pleadingly and said, "No Jon. Their intrigue, not mine."

I felt a wad of nervous anger uncoil.

Mack blew the air from his lungs and stared out across the bay. "Chris, Jason and Paul, what a bunch of pricks. They were always kinda lousy, even when we were kids. Maybe sometime you can't choose your friends. But we were young and dumb. Why did you choose them and me?"

"Cause I didn't have anybody else."

"And the way Tara tells it, you don't need anybody now. Maybe ever. Shit, I'm sorry, that was a cheap shot. She's upset and, anyway, Paul came to me years ago. Said he needed a loan. His practice wasn't going so well and he wanted me to take an equity loan in The Breakers to tide him over. Son of a bitch started crying about he was such a failure. Said things between him and Laura weren't any good anymore. Said he knew how much I cared about her. Even if I couldn't tell her myself. I didn't want to see anything happen to Laura and the girls. So I leveraged what I had in the bar and loaned him fifty K. I found out later what he really needed the money for. It was good faith. It was his entry fee."

"So when he comes to me six months later to repay me like we agreed, he tells me he can make me rich. How I can own The Breakers free and clear. How he's got this perfect deal worked out and it's gonna make us all a barrel-full of money. I tell him no thanks, I just want what he owes me. For Christ's sake Jon, I thought he was in dire straits when I made the loan. I was worried for Laura, man. Anyway, he pays me back in cash. Right then. Hands me an envelope and shakes my hand. Says am I sure I don't want a piece? Says everybody else is in. Told me then how Chris set the whole operation up. I didn't believe him. I, I guess I didn't want to believe that these guys, these guys we were tight with, were part of ... Anyway, I told him and the others to go to hell. By then, though, Laura and I ..." Mack looked at me for a moment and managed to look guilty, proud and unhappy all at the same time.

"I wondered," I said. "There was something at Paul's funeral that..."

"Yeah," he said, "yeah."

"So you had nothing to do with it? Nothing at all?"

"Not a thing, old friend. But Laura's future was tied to his, at least in the short term. She was getting ready to leave him. Then that thing on the Island. We were scared shitless, Jon. We thought maybe the cops would find out about us and maybe think that we had something to do with it. You had just come back and it was great to see you again. I kept wanting to talk to you about it but ... when Jason suggested the poker game I thought...You gotta believe me I had no idea they were gonna ambush you like that. You know they're both out of here? Houses are up for sale."

"Good."

"Don't be surprised if they forget to say thank you."

"I didn't do it for them."

Mack paused momentarily and then asked quietly, "Who'd you do it for?"

I opened my mouth with the fast, angry answer and then stopped.

"It was a debt that I owed."

"To who?"

"When I was still on the force I tried to do the right thing a long time ago and I couldn't. So maybe I did it in the promise of what should have been. Karma debt. A young girl was killed for no reason. So maybe it was just my own promise. Whatever. It needed to be done."

"Yeah, I get it." he sighed. "So what's going on with you and Tara?"

I shook my head. "I don't know. Last night she... this morning we had a long talk. She's having trouble with the idea of being with someone capable of doing what I did. I set them up, Mack. I knew I wasn't going to pull off any agreement with them so I nailed them the only way I could think of. Moral outrage is impotent in the face of reality. Somebody will always run the dark places. Doesn't matter if we agree with it or not. I couldn't see any other way so I ..."

"So you what?"

"I took everything I had to a bunch of hard cases. I figured they'd do whatever was necessary so I ..."

"Fomented a rebellion?"

"Yeah, there needed to be a coup. I couldn't take them out myself. I wasn't willing to, either. Figured they would be ruthless where I wouldn't be. Turns out..." I shrugged.

"That you were actually somewhat without 'ruth' yourself?" he said smiling.

I smiled back. "Looks that way. I didn't have anything else. Besides, who knows what will happen? It's their business now. Maybe they run it, maybe they get taken out. Doesn't matter. It's going to happen anyway."

"That's a good thing, you know? That's a point for your side."

"Maybe. I don't know. I'm responsible for the death of four people. And probably more to come. And I killed three of them. Killed Chris. I pointed the bikers at them as a backup. And in the end, I don't know which I feel worse about."

"Hey, Jon? You did what nobody else would do. What nobody else could do. At some point, old friend, that's going to have to be enough."

"I'm going to lose Tara again, Mack. Over this."

"Maybe. Maybe you will. I doubt it mate. But if you do, it doesn't change the rightness of your actions. You have to believe that, Jon."

I had nothing to say. Memories of the last weeks swirled in front of my eyes. There was too much to process.

"Listen," Mack said. "Are you and I gonna be OK?"

"Sorry?"

"You and me, are we good?"

I looked over at him and smiled. I stuck out my good arm and we bumped fists. "Yeah. Yeah, we're good."

"All right," he said, standing. "I'm out of here. I got a restaurant to run."

"OK. Give my best to Laura," I said, grinning.

"Rather give her mine," he replied. "I'll see you when I see you," and he jumped down onto the dock and walked off. He waved from the end of the slip and then disappeared toward the parking lot.

I went into the salon and grabbed my phone. Joni Mitchell's jazz album seemed like the right choice. I hit shuffle and plugged it into the stereo and poured myself a deep, and hopefully anesthetizing, bourbon.

I pulled myself painfully up onto the fly bridge and lowered myself into the captain's chair. I closed my eyes as Joni's voice poured from the speakers. She sang to me of her disappointments. She told me she'd seen life and love from both sides now. She claimed to know my thoughts and deeds.

And I asked her forgiveness for my sins.

Kinmond Smith is the author of a number of short stories, two plays and now, his debut novel. Armed with a degree in English Literature and Drama from the University of Toronto, he had little choice but to become a teacher. Kinmond is the Program Coordinator for Graphic Design Program at Seneca College.

He makes his home in the Beach, Toronto.

CPSIA information can be obtained
at www.ICGtesting.com
Printed in the USA
LVHW041937150623
749898LV00004B/29